Telling Children's Stories

Frontiers of Narrative

SERIES EDITOR

David Herman
Ohio State University

Telling Children's Stories

Narrative Theory and Children's Literature

EDITED BY MIKE CADDEN

University of Nebraska Press | Lincoln and London

Library of Congress Cataloging-in-Publication Data

Telling children's stories: narrative theory and children's literature / edited by Mike Cadden.
p. cm. — (Frontiers of narrative)
Includes bibliographical references and index.
ISBN 978-0-8032-1568-9 (pbk.: alk. paper)
1. Children's literature—History and criticism.
2. Narration (Rhetoric) 3. Children's literature—Authorship. I. Cadden, Michael.

PN1009.A1T445 2010   809'.89282—dc22
2010018219

Set in Tribute and Minion Pro by Kim Essman.
Designed by A. Shahan.

Contents

Introduction

MIKE CADDEN

To introduce this collection of essays on narrative theory and children's literature, I'd like your indulgence as I discuss one area of narrative theory that takes on different implications when discussed in the context of children's literature: the peritext. It's my way of justifying the intersection of narratology and literature for the young right from the start. The second part of the introduction is more conventional: an explanation of the development of the study of children's literature as an academic field, the development of its literary theory, and the relatively recent embrace of narratology. You'll find particular introductions to the collected essays themselves at the beginning of each part.

The Peritext and Children's Literature

"This is [. . .] the part where the author tells why the book exists and why the reader might want to read it. And you can skip it if you're in a hurry."—Laura Schlitz.

These are the first words of the foreword to the 2008 Newbery Medal–winning book.[1] It seems like a good way to introduce a book about narrative theory and children's literature. An editor's introduction to any book about narrative approaches should begin with some self-consciousness about two separate matters: the role of the peritext and the nature of the implied reader.[2] In fact both matters are discussed in this volume by several essayists.

The peritext is a good example of an aspect of narrative theory of special interest to those who study children's literature exactly *because* it has so much to do with assumptions about the implied reader, itself a central concern in children's literature.

As I was taking my kids to school one day, my then seven-year-old daughter interrupted her reading of Barbie's *Fairytopia* to ask, "Dad, what does "I—n—t—r—o—d—u—"

"It spells 'Introduction.'"

"What's that?"

"Well, that's the part of the book that explains things that you might want to know before you read so you'll understand what you read better."

"Oh . . . I guess I won't read it, then."

"Why not?"

"I don't want to spoil it."

And so she didn't. Harry Shaw points out that for child readers, "being coerced into playing a role [as a reader] is different from being forced into an actual state of belief" (210). And it seems clear that my daughter was neither coerced by the impetus of the peritext nor a believer in its authority. She read about the Barbie-clone fairies of *Fairytopia* without a concern in the world for what the nice person who wrote the introduction might have wanted her to know. Children learn early, whether through experience or the hasty page-turning by tired parents reading to them, the place of the peritext—both literally and figuratively.

A. A. Milne, creator of *Winnie-the-Pooh*, begins his second book of children's poetry with this meta-introduction: "This bit which I am writing now, called Introduction, is really the *er—h'r'm* of the book, and I have put it in, partly so as not to take you by surprise, and partly because, having started, I can't do without it now. There are some very clever writers who say that it is quite easy not to have an *er—h'r'm*, but I don't agree with them. I think it is much easier not to have all the rest of the book." And so it is.

In an age of irony, the peritext also gives us a sense of the implied reader of the book. Do children understand and appreci-ate irony? Is it there for the adults' consumption while the children are meant to get other things? A playful peritext is often the measure of what the author and the publisher in combination believe to be true about the audience(s) of a children's book. Perhaps the most famous jab at the introduction in a children's book is that from Jon Scieszka and Lane Smith's popular picture-book parody of folktales, *The Stinky Cheese Man and Other Fairly Stupid Tales*, which ends with the lines: "In fact, you should definitely go read the stories now, because the rest of this introduction just kind of goes on and on and doesn't really say anything. I stuck it on the end here so it would fill up the page and make it look like I really knew what I was talking about. So stop now. I mean it. Quit reading. Turn the page. If you read this last sentence, it won't tell you anything," and is signed by the character narrator Jack, of "Up the Hill, Fairy Tale Forest." Suspicions about introductions are confirmed for adults and raised for children.

Gérard Genette argues that the introduction is supposed to do a couple of things, after all: get the book read and get it read properly. By whom? Consider implications for children's literature. Who reads the introduction in the bookstore? Parents, librarians, teachers, and other concerned adults. So often in children's literature the introduction is pitched specifically to one or many adult audiences. When this is the use of the children's book introduction, it further mediates the experience for the child. Someone is screening. This is Mom and Dad reading the warning label. "Okay, not too much propyl gallate, potassium bromate, or red dye number three. Enjoy." In the case of the children's book, the implied audience for the introduction is then often different from the implied audience of the text itself. So it sells the book to the parents but not yet to the child. The parent, as an extra layer of mediation, must now sell the book to Junior. In this way the children's book publisher gets to the kids through the parents.

We could argue that the peritext of a children's book is meant for adults (copyright, publication house, introduction, etc.); such an argument implies that children get used to ignoring the packaging information and continue to do so even when they become the adult readers for whom, ostensibly, this material exists. This often is accomplished early on after a child accuses an adult of skipping pages. "Hey, you're skipping!"

"This isn't part of the story."

"Read it!"

"Okay, 'All rights reserved. No part of this book may be reproduced, transmitted, or stored in an information retrieval system in any form or . . .'"

"You can skip it."

Sometimes, children *are* given information in introductions that is necessary in order to understand what's to come. The introduction to Chris Van Allsburg's picture book *The Mysteries of Harris Burdick* tells us that the individual pictures accompanied by a title and an opening line of story (for example, "Archie Smith, Boy Wonder" is followed by "A tiny voice asked, 'Is he the one?'") were left with a publisher by a mysterious man named Harris Burdick who promised to return with the rest of the stories the next day, but he never returned. For a reader to begin with the first picture and page of scant writing only to turn the page to an unrelated picture and written text would likely result in confusion. Here, then, the implied reader of Van Allsburg's book is assumed to be a reader of introductions. *Black and White*, an innovative (and much glossed) picture book by David Macaulay, warns us by way of a note on the title page that we need to consider the relationship between words and pictures—consider that they may or may not fit together as a story. In this way we are given a frame of mind, a challenge, a speculation that help us enter the story. Those who have breezed past this introduction haven't the same advice about "use." And if you don't read the prologue to Sylvia Engdahl's *Enchantress from the Stars*, a science fiction novel marketed to young adults, you won't know that the teenaged character narrator is writing the story from three points of view for her field report as a planetary observer. That book's prologue is now preceded by a foreword from Lois Lowry on the book's importance. This might invite the reader to skip the multiple thresholds leading into the "real" story, leaving her to wonder why everyone sure seems to like this teenager character!

Well, that's because she's the one putting words in their mouths. But who knew?

Note that in some of these cases, we have some narrators or authors addressing the primary implied readership of the text, not just the purchasers (adults). This, we could argue, blurs the lines between what is text and what is peritext as well as those texts that address both children and adults simultaneously, either separately or together. Consider Lemony Snicket's *The Bad Beginning*, the first book of the Series of Unfortunate Events. In this book we have a fiction, a deception, from the title page onward: we are told that the book is authored by "Lemony Snicket" (David Handler employs the name as not only a character narrator but, at first, as an alias). Snicket warns us (who?) in second-person address on the book's first page, "If you are interested in stories with happy endings, you would be better off reading some other book. In this book, not only is there no happy ending, there is no happy beginning, and very few happy things in the middle. [. . .] I'm sorry to tell you this, but that is how the story goes." From the beginning there is a fascinating admission of unhappiness, which is meant to intrigue the implied reader, presumably the middle school child who has had her fill of happy endings and would like a bit of dark humor. The back of the book, another peritextual feature, promises/warns us that this is an "extremely unpleasant" book. So, the opening lines serve as our introduction and both sells with darkness and accurately prepares us for what we're in for. So, too, Avi's *Something Upstairs* contains an introductory "Author's Explanation"—a bit different as a heading, and playing up the idea of providing necessary information. In this "explanation," Avi tells of meeting with young Kenny Huldorf and (after dreading meeting another adoring fan) becomes absolutely fascinated with his story (implication: *you* will be as well). Avi claims only to be the mediary: He says for starters, "This is the strangest story I've ever heard" and finishes with "This is it. His story. My writing. I think it's true." The last line, despite being confusing about what is true—the story or Avi's writing—is one last appeal to our fascination. It's not only fascinating; it's possibly true. It has that well-used appeal to our hope that the story has some connection to reality: "The story you are about to see is true. The names have been changed to protect the innocent." Here, though, Avi (played by himself) is using his own author(ity) to get his young readers to half-believe that he's telling the truth. A famous author wouldn't steer me wrong! And it's stranger than anything this professional storyteller has ever heard. This calls us back to the Van Allsburg ruse: the mystery presumably makes it more interesting than the story or pictures in their own right. Roald Dahl employs a similar move in his fictional introduction to *The Witches*. In the opening "A Note about Witches," our narrator tells us that "in fairy-tales, witches always wear silly black hats and black cloaks, and they ride on broomsticks. But this is not a fairy-tale. This is about REAL WITCHES. [. . .] And if you know about these [survival tips], if you remember them always, then you might just possibly manage to escape from being squelched before you are very much older."

Each of these last three books promises a bit of fascinating darkness, a thrill of the supernatural or horribly natural, the anticipation of truth, and the line between textuality and peritextuality is effectively blurred, especially as young readers almost surely equate the voice of the speaker of the opening lines with that of the author. These are not like those introductions implied to be read by adult screeners of books that go something like "This book has just gobs of educational and morally uplifting information and nothing in the slightest that could lead to your child practicing Satanism, Animal Sacrifice, or Bad Hygiene." These fictional introductions directed to the child, on the other hand, provide an early taste of the subject and, no small matter, of the style or voice of the book, as is the case with *The Mysteries of Harris Burdick* and *Enchantress from the Stars*.

This discussion of something as simple as the strategic use of the introduction in children's books is meant to illustrate just how some aspects of narrative take on greater (or at least different) significance when we consider the special context of children's literature. There are other obvious critical issues particular to children and their literature that, like peritextual elements themselves, append to the text and have been and should continue to be the focus of study, including the use of cover art in the marketing of young adult literature (see Yampbell). This discussion of introductions to children's books in this volume's introduction—offered as a metaperitextual gesture—provides some reasons why we should care about narrative approaches to children's and young adult stories. You are the implied reader of this volume if you care about either narrative approaches or children's stories, though I hope we are successful in implying that the intersection of narrative approaches and children's stories is an important and revealing one.

Children's Literature: History, Genre, and Narratology

This volume, as part of the Frontiers of Narrative series, offers a consideration of the ways in which narrative matters in children's literature—a genre that isn't exactly a new area of study, though from time to time a scholar "discovers" this scholarly area hidden in plain view. It is a "frontier," perhaps, as both a rediscovered reading pleasure for adults and an undiscovered scholarly world to critics who suddenly find themselves with young children. It surprises some that children's and young adult literature has much to offer the world of critical theory. In this arena the canon war is still being waged.

It's important to consider the development of children's literature as an area of study and the development of its narrative theory in particular. Because the development of theory is relatively recent and the development of the literary field unusual, we enjoy right now an explosion of theory in general and of narrative theory in particular (the dates of texts in "Further Reading" point to this phenomenon). There is much ready to be done both in studying narrative theory comparatively across adult and children's literature and considering the poetics of children's literature itself.

Children's literature is a bit unusual as a genre and an academic discipline. Not only is the study often claimed by one of three disciplinary camps in different departments (though it is sometimes practiced by more than one department on more fortunate campuses), it is a bit unusual within the course construction models of most departments of English. Courses tend to be delineated by textuality (genres like poetry, short fiction, the novel), subtextuality (travel literature, monsters, and other themes), or contextuality (the literature of a place or a people—the demographics of race, gender, ethnicity, nation). As a course and genre defined in a contextual way, children's literature is, to quote a favorite "Sesame Street" song, "not like the others." While women's literature, Caribbean literature, and British literature of the nineteenth century are contextually designed, they tend to focus on the producers rather than (or in addition to) the consumers of the texts. Here is where implied audience becomes a necessary consideration to those studying children's literature whether they care about narratology or not. It is the reader alone for whom the genre is defined—a reader almost certainly not present either in children's literature classes or in the ranks of those authors on the syllabus and certainly not among the scholars.

In order to understand the trajectory of theory in the study of children's literature and of children's literature theory itself, we should consider the context of academic discipline. The study of children's literature is a balkanized business. The "English" areas of college composition and women's literature made huge strides in the 1980s, in large part because they didn't remain relegated to departments of English. Composition studies, though somewhat estranged from university departments of communications and rhetoric, became cross-disciplinary as it expanded into programs of writing across the curriculum, writing in the disciplines, and it gained respect among faculty across the university campus through the development of writing-intensive courses. Women's literature became one part of a larger disciplinary movement of women's studies, inviting students and faculty in other disciplines into the literature classroom; women's literature became part of courses in sociology, history, and more. In short, both of these other "English" areas won academic respect and support and strengthened their stake in departments of English by being relevant across campus. The recent movement in childhood or children's studies, begun by Brooklyn College almost twenty years ago, offers some hope here; there are still very few such programs across the country, however. The study of children's literature has been similar to the study of communications divided between English and journalism more than it has been like the successful disciplinary juggernaut of writing across the disciplines. Children's literature is usually relegated to one of three disciplinary houses: education, library science, or English. If its study exists simultaneously in two or three of those departments, it has been coincidental or contentious rather than cooperative; unlike in departments of library science and education, however, scholars of children's literature in English departments have had to justify their business to their departmental colleagues. Rod McGillis explains some implications of the phenomenon:

> Because the texts upon which critics of children's literature write are for children, [. . .] children's literature critics find themselves looked upon with some suspicion by academic critics who work on mainstream literature. From the other end, the teachers, librarians, parents, and children who read children's literature look with some suspicion on those who spend their lives intellectualizing these ostensibly simple books. This double estranging of the children's literature critic puts him or her in an awkward position: wanting to speak to those both within and without the academy and finding, if not hostility, then at least disrespect from both groups. (17)

Children's literature was taught wherever it was established first, and the department that had original ownership rarely saw it pop up in other departments, regardless of the shift in critical emphasis. The idiosyncrasy of this can be even more complicated: at my own undergraduate institution, Virginia Tech, the adolescent literature class is found in the education department, while children's literature is taught in the English department. To add to this problem for the literary study of children's literature, very few doctoral institutions have children's literature courses in their English departments, making graduate study of children's literature from a literary standpoint inconvenient at best. Then, too, those graduating with an emphasis in children's literature have many fewer departments of English available to employ them.

This phenomenon has had an impact on the development of children's literature as an area of literary study. Maria Nikolajeva notes that "the principal difference between research on children's literature and general literary criticism [. . .] is that children's literature has from the very beginning been related to pedagogics" (*Children's Literature Comes of Age* 3), and so much of the early critical work in children's literature was in the context of literacy. Jill May argued in 1991 for a literary approach to children's literature in education departments. Herself an education professor, May bemoaned the attitude that there was "no purpose for the study of literature in the elementary classroom other than as a means to teach other concepts in the curriculum" and having reading instruction identified as the only use for books (275). Maria Nikolajeva, writing in 1996, notes that it has been "only in the past ten years that the literary aspects of children's literature have been noticed and appreciated and subjected to contemporary literary theory and methods" (*Children's Literature Comes of Age* 4), and even then in many fewer American and British universities for the reasons discussed earlier. Nine years later, Nikolajeva still felt the need to comment in the preface to her new textbook, "This book is not about teaching literature to children, but about becoming critical adult readers of children's literature" (*Aesthetic Approaches* v).

As you might imagine, then, apologia has been a healthy strand of critical writing in children's literature. A 1973 *New York Times* article by Children's Literature Association founding member Francelia Butler accuses otherwise broad-minded humanists of being embarrassed by discussing children's books. In 1978 Mary Agnes Taylor pitched a plea in the journal of the Association of

Departments of English to "convince [her] audience that children's literature belongs in college English Departments" (17). In the introduction to a 1985 special issue of *Studies in the Literary Imagination* on narrative approaches to children's literature, editor Hugh Keenan writes that "such a linking of modern critical approaches and children's literature calls for some explanation" (1). Did it? Does it yet? Keenan goes on to say about the journal issue, "As the analyses of these essays show, children's literature is not simple. It is often more sophisticated than we have allowed" (2). Peter Neumeyer argued in 1987 that "children's literature as an academic field is about as childish as pediatrics" (146). A cautious Peter Hunt writes in 1990 that he "would like to think that the cause of children's literature is now won, and that its academic status is secure, but to very many readers it will be a new and questionable discipline, and its critical development needs to be laid out" ("New Directions" 7). The strand is wider and longer than this, but this sampling shows that hand-wringing over children's literature's status as a literature has been, and in some quarters continues to be, a preoccupation with those of us who write about the genre. Added to the dilemma of status is the problem of identity, for all along while arguments are being made about developing courses and even programs in children's literature, critics ask, "Just what *is* children's literature?"

There is the tradition in children's literature circles to ask, "What is children's literature?" and then proceed at great length to avoid answering the question—a phenomenon seen in criticism of other beset genres such as fantasy and science fiction.[3] Sue Gannon considers the task of defining children's literature "likely to be the work of a lifetime" (59) and, paraphrasing Clifford Geertz in a different context, believes the "'progress' toward the answers we seek is [. . .] marked less by a perfection of consensus than by a refinement of the debate" (69). The question is obviously important, perhaps more for the way it leads to decisions about critical approaches to children's literature than for any answer that might be offered. The greatest distinction is that between degree and kind. Those who believe that children's literature is different by various degrees from literature for adults draw more on the work of critics in other fields to point to the marked tendencies of children's literature to do more or less in using different structures or emphasizing different subtexts. Those who see children's literature as different in kind in relationship to literature for adults spend their time arguing about that which makes the genre unique. An important moment in theorizing children's literature—especially through narrative theory—was the fall 1985 issue of *Studies in the Literary Imagination*, edited by Hugh Keenan. The issue's topic was "Narrative Theory and Children's Literature," and the issue featured the field's most influential scholars weighing in on the narrative nature of the genre. The editor notes with enthusiasm that through narrative theory "there promised to be critical ways of answering the perennial question: how is children's literature different from other literatures?" (1). In the same issue Peter Hunt expresses concern that to decontextualize children's books—to treat them just as any book—necessarily means that we ignore what makes children's books unique: "the intended or implied or actual readers" ("Necessary Misreadings" 108). Six years later he argues more forcefully that "what we must look for is a children's-literature-specific theory" (*Criticism, Theory* 192), one that he calls "childist," a sympathetic reading from the perspective of the implied audience parallel to feminist reading. Perry Nodelman, in contrast, muses, "We may conclude that the similarity of good children's books to each other makes children's fiction different from adult fiction—different enough that it requires its own interpretive approach. [. . .] Or we may reach quite a different, and, to my mind, more sensible conclusion—that, in fact, children's fiction is less significantly a special sort of fiction than a serious challenge to conventional ideas about interpretation and distinctiveness" (6). Both scholars were struggling along with the field itself regarding the best literary approaches to an emerging academic discipline.

Of course, there are the critics who suggest that children's literature doesn't exist at all because it includes in its audience—or restricts its audience to—adults. Critics such as Jacqueline Rose and Jack Zipes are influential in debates about children's literature *because* by arguing against the genre's existence, they inspire a great deal of response. Employing psychoanalytical theory, Rose argues that children's literature is an impossible category because the audience is a construct created by adult writers, publishers, and caregivers; a special issue of *Children's Literature Quarterly* devoted to considering the effect of her book *The Case of Peter Pan* twenty-five years after its publication has recently been announced. In chapter 3 of his book *Sticks and Stones*, "Why Children's Literature Does Not Exist," Zipes turns to Marxism to claim that "'children' and 'childhood' are social constructs that have been determined by socioeconomic conditions and have different meanings for different cultures. Thus the concept of children's literature is also imaginary" (40). I'm not sure that people in the textile industry would argue that children's clothing doesn't exist because of the changes over the centuries to fashion that reflect our own adult designs on "childhood" and children. The categories of children's clothes and books are each contested sites driven by both adult and children's own desires and uses. In any case, the critics who deny the existence of children's literature provide an important theoretical position on defining the genre.

It wasn't until the eighties that children's literature achieved this sort of theoretical and critical self-consciousness. In the "Further Reading" section of this volume, you'll note that the texts that could be considered narrative theory published before the mid-1980s are very few in number. Jill May observes that "although children's literature [. . .] always had a theoretical base for study, reading stances that concentrate on literary aspects of children's literature did not evolve until the 1970s" (23), though Peter Hunt notes that "anti-intellectualism has produced much so-called criticism which is simply impressionistic and populist in the worst sense" (*Criticism, Theory* 5). In a 1970 article Paul Heins, long-time editor of the *Horn Book Magazine*, muses whether "the time has come for the criticism of children's literature to be more conscious than ever before of its existence—and better still of its function" (402). It would be a decade or more before such critical and theoretical self-consciousness would become common. Beverly Lyon Clark tells in her award-winning *Kiddie Lit: The Cultural Construction of Children's Literature in America* the story of her own development in the 1970s as a children's literature scholar and notes that she was "not impressed by the scholarship [she] then started to read. Much of it seemed to focus on bibliotherapy, providing lists of books [. . .] . Most of the books seemed to be annotated bibliographies in paragraph form" (xi).

The trajectory of narrative theory in the study of children's literature has been coincidental with the development of theory in the genre, as the question of structure and poetics necessarily follows the self-conscious criticism that Paul Heins asked for in 1970. The years 1984–85 saw the first journal issue devoted to narrative theory in children's literature—a special issue of *Studies in the Literary Imagination*. In the same year, in a *Children's Literature Quarterly* special section devoted to narrative theory and children's literature, Hunt writes what was still possible to write in 1984: "Critical theory may not seem to have much to do with children and books" ("Narrative Theory" 191).[4] As he made the case for narrative theory in the eighties and early nineties, others have provided newer and sophisticated narrative approaches, most notably Barbara Wall, Zohar Shavit, Maria Nikolajeva, Robyn McCallum, Leona Fisher, and Andrea Schwenke Wyile. Deb Thacker, as late as 2000, writes that she is surprised that notable theorists, in an age of intertextuality, haven't seen the value of children's literature to their theories, such as Barthes's notion of *jouissance*, Fish's interpretive communities, Eco's open and closed texts, and more (1). Maria Nikolajeva writes in her 2005 *Aesthetics of Children's Literature* that "other important theories, such as narrative theory and carnival theory, have been used only sporadically" (vi), so influential critics continue to call for more theorizing about children's literature as a genre. And so there is still much work to be done, and we hope that this volume will help spur more work in children's literature using narrative approaches—and of work in narrative theory using children's literature.

There are many opportunities for studying children's and young adult literatures using a narratological approach, as the "Further Reading" section at the end of this book suggests. Beyond the four elements covered in this volume—genre, picture books, narrators and implied readers, and narrative time—there are other important categories of particular interest. Within the larger category of character study, the phenomenon of anthropomorphism is prevalent and important in children's books as it is in no other genre; it is often seen as a subject of identification as well as a distancing strategy. The age of a character narrator is an important consideration in terms of marketing and implied readers. Children's and young adult literature critics note plot patterns that tend to correspond to genre (for example, Odyssean patterns in children's fiction and in young adult literature the "apocalyptic" plot defined by Frank Kermode). While both intertextuality and metafiction have been common features of postmodernism generally, in children's literature they take on new significance when we consider the degree to which we assume children are supposed to recognize aesthetic features or other tales. And the study of ethical narration is an obvious area of interest in children's and young adult literatures as a necessary complement to the subject of censorship. Dorothy Hale observes that "the more deeply [she] looked into new ethical theories of literature, the more [she] came to notice the central role played by one literary genre in particular . . . novels" (189). To my mind the end of that sentence could easily read "children's literature." For as ethically revelatory as the novel has always been, no literary genre has ever taught us more about a culture and its values than the literature published for a society's children. Diachronic studies of the narrative features of series fiction remain to be written, and the relatively new explosion in verse novels (some epistolary, some not) is a great opportunity for research. These verse novels for young readers experiment with polyphony, voice, and focalization in interesting ways. A good deal has been written lately about crossover writing (a book that crosses over readerships in various ways and over time) and writers (like Rudyard Kipling, Gertrude Stein, Maria

Edgeworth, and Ursula K. Le Guin), but the poetics of crossover writing is another field with scholarly potential.

This volume is intended to be of use to a variety of audiences. The essays assembled here offer beginning students access to key developments in the field without making too many assumptions about prior knowledge; thus, technical terms have been kept to a minimum, and where they are used, they are always defined immediately—either in the text or in a footnote. At the same time, the arguments put forward in the essays are nuanced and sophisticated, exploring issues that continue to be relevant for more-advanced students as well as faculty specialists. This collection would be appropriate for students in undergraduate theory classes in which the children's books in question can be read as subjects of study. It would be ideal as a course text in a narrative theory class. It is also intended for those interested in children's literature in a variety of disciplinary realities both in and outside literature departments who have come to think about children's books in a different way.

Although the volume divides the study of narrative in the context of children's and young adult literatures into four parts, the parts speak to one another across those categories. They're hardly mutually exclusive. As matters of genre come into play in the discussion of narrative time, the picture book is considered in terms of narration and focalization—and many issues such as metatextuality, voice, and the implied reader appear over and over again. The collection could be used in such a way that many different juxtapositions of readings could be designed for course use.

It's my hope that this volume can acquaint narratologists with the richness and depth of children's literature and conversely acquaint children's literature scholars and critics with the usefulness of narrative approaches for analyzing this unique genre. The volume will also alert faculty specialists as well as advanced undergraduate and graduate students in each of these areas to the merits of the other.

A. A. Milne ends his introduction to *Winnie-the-Pooh* with the observation that "perhaps the best thing to do is to stop writing Introductions and get on with the book." That sounds like a good idea.

Notes

1. The John Newbery Medal, given by the American Library Association, recognizes the most distinguished contribution to American literature for children of the previous year. It is considered by many to be the most prestigious award in American children's literature.

2. Genette defines the "peritext" as that part of the book "materially appended to the text within the same volume" (344). It includes features such as the title of the book, the author's name, the dedication, the table of contents, prefaces and afterwords, even covers. Genette divides paratext into two classes: the peritext and the epitext. The peritext refers to all kinds of paratext within the book; the epitext refers to paratexts outside the volume, such as reviews and other commentary on the text.

The "implied reader" is the reader for whom a text seems meant. It is the ideal audience for a text as implied by a text's subject matter, linguistic and stylistic choices, and other elements that imply a best recipient.

For more commentary on the peritext in children's literature, see Higonnet, Yampbell, Sipe and McGuire, and Jenkins. Peter Hunt makes interesting claims for the ways children remember a book, including a response to the peritextual element of book-cover color as the means for categorizing or remembering a book (*Criticism, Theory* 67).

3. In the Children's Literature Association's first presidential address, Jon Stott asked, "What is children's literature?" (May 25, 1978). We've been attempting to answer him in the thirty years since.

4. In the first issue of the *Quarterly* devoted to the subject (1990), Hunt—the volume's editor—talks about the important potential of a narrative approach to children's literature, although he laments that, "unfortunately, much narrative theory has tended to the descriptive and classificatory, processes that are not always enlightening" (46). It would be thirteen years until a second narrative-theory special issue of *Children's Literature Association Quarterly* would appear.

Works Cited

Avi. *Something Upstairs: A Tale of Ghosts*. New York: Avon, 1990.

Butler, Francelia. Book review. *New York Times* 6 May 1973.

Clark, Beverly Lyon. *Kiddie Lit: The Cultural Construction of Children's*

Literature in America. Baltimore: Johns Hopkins University Press, 2003.

Dahl, Roald. *The Witches*. New York: Farrar, 1983.

Engdahl, Sylvia. *Enchantress from the Stars*. New York: Atheneum, 1970.

Gannon, Susan. "Perspectives on Children's Literature: An Overview." *Teaching Children's Literature: Issues, Pedagogy, Resources*. Ed. Glenn Sadler. New York: MLA, 1992. 59–71.

Genette, Gérard. *Paratexts: Thresholds of Interpretation*. Trans. Jane E. Lewin. Cambridge: Cambridge University Press, 1997.

Hale, Dorothy J. "Fiction as Restriction: Self-Binding in New Ethical Theories of the Novel." *Narrative* 15.2 (May 2007): 187–206.

Heins, Paul. "Out on a Limb with the Critics." *Children and Literature: Views and Reviews*. Ed. Virginia Haviland. Glenview IL: Scott, 1973. 400–07.

Higonnet, Margaret. "The Playground of the Peritext." *Children's Literature Association Quarterly* 15.2 (Summer 1990): 47–49.

Hunt, Peter. *Criticism, Theory, and Children's Literature*. Cambridge MA: Blackwell, 1991.

———. "Narrative Theory and Children's Literature." *Children's Literature Association Quarterly* 9.4 (1984–85): 191–94.

———. "Necessary Misreadings: Directions in Narrative Theory for Children's Literature." *Studies in the Literary Imagination* 18.2 (Fall 1985): 107–21.

———. "New Directions in Narrative Theory." *Children's Literature Association Quarterly* 15.2 (1990): 46–47.

Jenkins, Elwyn. "Reading outside the Lines: Peritext and Authenticity in South African Children's Books." *The Lion and the Unicorn* 25.1 (Jan. 2001): 115–27.

Keenan, Hugh T. "Editor's Comment." *Studies in the Literary Imagination* 18.2 (Fall 1985): 1–2.

Kermode, Frank. *The Sense of an Ending: Studies in the Theory of Fiction*. Oxford: Oxford University Press, 1966.

Macaulay, David. *Black and White*. New York: Houghton, 1990.

May, Jill P. *Children's Literature and Critical Theory*. New York: Oxford University Press, 1995.

McGillis, Roderick. *The Nimble Reader: Literary Theory and Children's Literature*. New York: Twayne, 1996.

Milne, A. A. *The House at Pooh Corner*. 1928. London: Methuen, 1965.

Neumeyer, Peter. "Children's Literature in the English Department." *Children's Literature Association Quarterly* 12.3 (1987): 146–50.

Nikolajeva, Maria. *Aesthetic Approaches to Children's Literature*. Lanham MD: Scarecrow, 2005.

———. *Children's Literature Comes of Age: Toward a New Aesthetic*. New York: Garland, 1996.

Nodelman, Perry. "Interpretation and the Apparent Sameness of Children's Novels." *Studies in the Literary Imagination* 18.2 (Fall 1985): 5–20.

Rose, Jacqueline. *The Case of Peter Pan: Or the Impossibility of Children's Fiction*. New York: Macmillan, 1984.

Schlitz, Laura Amy. *Good Masters! Sweet Ladies! Voices from a Medieval Village*. Illus. Robert Byrd. Cambridge MA: Candlewick, 2007.

Scieszka, Jon, and Lane Smith. *The Stinky Cheese Man and Other Fairly Stupid Tales*. New York: Viking Penguin, 1992.

Shaw, Harry E. "Making Readers." *Narrative* 15.2 (May 2007): 207–21.

Sipe, Lawrence, and Caroline McGuire. "Picture Book Endpapers: Resources for Literary and Aesthetic Interpretation." *Children's Literature in Education* 37.4 (Dec. 2006): 291–304.

Snicket, Lemony. *The Bad Beginning*. New York: HarperCollins, 1999.

Taylor, Mary Agnes. "Children's Literature and the English Department." *ADE Bulletin* 56 (Feb. 1978): 17–19.

Thacker, Deborah. "Disdain or Ignorance? Literary Theory and the Absence of Children's Literature." *The Lion and the Unicorn* 24.1 (Jan. 2000): 1–17.

Van Allsburg, Chris. *The Mysteries of Harris Burdick*. New York: Houghton, 1984.

Yampbell, Cat. "Judging a Book by Its Cover: Publishing Trends in Young Adult Literature." *The Lion and the Unicorn* 29.3 (Sept. 2005): 348–72.

Zipes, Jack. *Sticks and Stones: The Troublesome Success of Children's Literature from Slovenly Peter to Harry Potter*. New York: Routledge, 2001.

Telling Children's Stories

PART ONE

Genre Templates and Transformations

Part 1 takes on the large matter of genre as a narrative consideration in children's and young adult literature. The opening essay by Elisabeth Rose Gruner examines how the overt and covert fairy-tale structures used in young adult realism and fantasy for girls continue to attempt to offer models of behavior for a young readership. In "Telling Old Tales Newly: Intertextuality in Young Adult Fiction for Girls," Gruner discusses how the structures of fairy tales offer revealing limits for protagonists as well as reader resistance to particular moral positions. Following this essay, Danielle Russell's "Familiarity Breeds a Following: Transcending the Formulaic in the Snicket Series" turns to Lemony Snicket's Series of Unfortunate Events in order to examine the ways that Snicket (Handler) toys with and blends various narrative forms as found in different genres, including the gothic tale, the series tale, and mystery, and ultimately both blends and expands what is possible in children's literature as a moral vehicle for readers. Morality and form—especially fairy tale and the role of the narrator—connect the first two genre studies; Chris McGee's "The Power of Secrets: Backwards Construction and the Children's Detective Story" connects with Danielle Russell's essay as it examines in the genre of children's mystery the role of childhood innocence (as exemplified by character) and plotting, especially the role of the ending.

The three essays in this part, while directly taking on the question of genre, foreground concerns that are common and recurring issues in this collection: the nature of the implied reader of children's and young adult literatures, the use of narrative closure, writerly/readerly texts (or, respectively, texts unformulated by convention and those texts that are clear conventional products for consumption), the assumptions made about intertextuality, and the attendant ethical or moral implications of all these dimensions of the experience of reading literature for children and young adults.

1

Telling Old Tales Newly

Intertextuality in Young Adult Fiction for Girls

ELISABETH ROSE GRUNER

In one of the inaugural articles in feminist literary criticism, "Feminism and Fairy Tales," Karen Rowe followed Simone de Beauvoir's lead in claiming that fairy tales structure the consciousness of girls and women, and in a negative way. As Donald Haase has noted, "In Rowe's view, the fairy tale—perhaps precisely because of its 'awesome imaginative power'—had a role to play in cultivating equality among men and women, but it would have to be a rejuvenated fairy tale fully divested of its idealized romantic fantasies" (5). In the years since Rowe's essay first appeared, however, it has been unclear whether the structuring power of the fairy tale could indeed be reworked for more egalitarian uses, or whether in fact the "replication of an old content and mode of representation [would only] result in the further replication of, for example, old masculinist and antifeminist metanarratives" (Stephens and McCallum 22). Whether they are empowering or disempowering, however, it is clear that fairy tales continue to provide structural and thematic elements for a wide variety of literature for children, especially for girls.

In this essay I examine three novels for young adults—Francesca Lia Block's *Weetzie Bat*, Meg Cabot's *The Princess Diaries*, and Laurie Halse Anderson's *Speak*—in order to consider the ways in which fairy tales surprisingly provide both overt and, especially in the case of *Speak*, covert structures and themes of female empowerment. Refusing the nonplace and nontime of traditional fairy tales, each novel places its heroine in a recognizable landscape, gives her a voice (or at least a position as focalizer, as in *Weetzie Bat*), and refuses the calm certainty of "happily ever after" for a more vexed and less closed movement into the future.[1] (The fact that all three novels have sequels or continuations—though only in the case of *The Princess Diaries* do we have a traditional series—suggests a radical departure from the forced closure of the fairy tale.) Although none of these novels directly retells a single fairy tale, all are so deeply indebted to the genre as to constitute their own conversation with it. This conversation acknowledges both the power of fairy tales and their limits: both protagonist and reader may begin the tales invested in fairy-tale fantasies but are able to revise them significantly by the novels' respective conclusions. All three heroines end their novels uncertain, unsettled, far from the "happily ever after" of fairy-tale romance; this very unsettlement, however, is the result of their refusal to be constrained by others' stories, others' narratives. "Happily ever after" turns out to be a dangerous fantasy; these three heroines reject it for the more realistic option of writing their own futures.

While there are many ways of discussing the ways fairy tales can shape narratives of identity development, this essay focuses on three interrelated elements—place, voice, and closure. I discuss in these novels what John Stephens and Robyn McCallum call "generic intertextuality": rather than retellings or revisions of specific tales, what we find in these works are "no longer folktales but rather original creations which have a general intertextual relationship with folktale schemata, are not indebted to particular tales, and no longer pretend a direct connection with oral tradition" (220). Indeed, we may be seeing what Elizabeth Wanning Harries calls "transliteration": "play[ing] [. . .] on our memory of salient images, often apparently peripheral details, transforming them into new centers of meaning" (135–36). Thus in *Weetzie Bat* we have the motif of the three wishes, familiar from "The Fisherman and His Wife" and many other tales, but without the didactic thrust of such tales; the wishes are fulfilled, but the story goes on. In *The Princess Diaries* (and its various sequels), we have the Cinderella-like transformation of ordinary girl into princess, but with an obsessive focus on the costs and the pain of that transformation. Finally, in *Speak*, we have a heroine who occasionally yearns for a fairy-tale life: "I used to pretend," she tells us—or her journal—"I was a princess who had been adopted when my kingdom was overrun by bad guys. Any day my real parents, Mr. King and Mrs. Queen, would send the royal limo to pick me up" (147). But while most of the fairy-tale references in the novel are negative (the about-to-be-dissected frog, for example, waits "for a prince to come and princessify her with a smooch" [81]), Melinda appropriates one of the most negative ones (Snow White's poisoned apple) with, ultimately, positive results. In all three novels, the "transliteration" of fairy-tale elements helps develop a new "center of meaning" in which passivity is not rewarded, sexuality does not masquerade as death, and the speaking subject can begin to articulate her desires rather than simply appearing as the object of another's.

Place

Most fairy tales begin "once upon a time," and the effacement of both time and place is central to their perceived universality. Jack Zipes notes that "the timelessness of the tale and its lack of geographical specificity endow it with utopian connotations—'utopia' in its original meaning designated 'no place,' a place that no one had ever envisaged" (xiii). Young adult novels, on the other hand, seem to rely on an up-to-the-minute topicality that includes a fairly firm sense of place, and the three novels I discuss here are no exceptions. *Weetzie Bat* takes place in the Los Angeles of the 1980s, *Speak* in mid-'90s Syracuse, New York, and *The Princess Diaries* in turn-of-the millennium New York City (the movie's transplantation to San Francisco notwithstanding). Jan Susina claims that "sense of self and sense of place are intimately connected in *Weetzie Bat*" (191); I'd go further, and suggest that this connection is perhaps especially typical of young adulthood. Place can be central to an adolescent's sense of identity: we are who we are where we are.[2] For Weetzie Bat, Hollywood/Los Angeles teems with significance, and she is distressed at her peers' failure to note it: "They [kids in high school] didn't care that Marilyn's prints were practically in their backyard at Graumann's [...] that the waitresses wore skates at the Jetson-style Tiny Naylor's; that there was a fountain that turned tropical soda-pop colors, and a canyon where Jim Morrison and Houdini used to live" (1–2).

Weetzie's Los Angeles is a fairyland where wishes can come true; her novel is in part an account of her learning—perhaps, after all, like the fisherman's wife—what that means. That is, her coming of age involves not rejecting the fantasy world in which she lives but exploring it ever more deeply.

New York City often appears in contemporary film and television as something of a fantasy world as well, and *The Princess Diaries* series does little to dispel that impression. Although Mia may live in a quasi-realistic downtown loft, her grandmother's perpetual presence at the Plaza (until she decamps to the Ritz-Carlton—and then the Four Seasons—while her suite is converted into a condominium in book 8) has an air of unreality about it. (This may be particularly the case for little girls who have grown up reading *Eloise*.) The fact that the novels (there are now eight, plus three shorter episodes, published between 2000 and 2007) seem not to acknowledge the signal New York event of 2001—the World Trade Center attacks—increases this sense of unreality.[3] But Mia does visit recognizable places and, especially in the earlier volumes, conveys a familiarity with her city that grounds the novels much as the Los Angeles setting grounds *Weetzie Bat*.

Speak's setting is the least fairy-tale-like of the three novels: Syracuse, New York, is hardly a fantasyland. Yet structuring the novel along the school year provides a fairy tale's rhythm to the piece while simultaneously blending with the standard story span of young adult fiction: it begins as the year is dying and ends with the rebirth of spring. One thinks of the movement from winter to spring in "Beauty and the Beast" or "Snow White."

It is the verisimilitude of the settings, rather than their potential connection to fantasy, however, that interests me most. In all three novels the heroines first assert their power, their autonomy, through their familiarity with and mastery of their locations. Weetzie's easy familiarity with Los Angeles marks her as superior to her high school classmates.[4] Mia demonstrates a similar mastery of her environment: "I tried to show my dad how much better suited I am for life in Manhattan than in Genovia by ordering some really excellent food. I got us an insalata caprese, ravioli al funghetto, and a pizza margherita, all for under twenty bucks, but I swear, my dad wasn't a bit impressed!" (84).

Melinda, on the other hand, although she notes her environment, rarely seems to master it. It does move her on occasion to something like poetry, however: "The cement-slab sky hangs inches above our heads. Which direction is east? It has been so long since I've seen the sun, I can't remember. Turtlenecks creep out of bottom drawers. Turtle faces pull back into winter clothes. We won't see some kids until spring" (91). Rather than mastering the Syracuse winter, Melinda takes control of a small "room of her own": the janitor's closet, which becomes her refuge when school becomes unbearable. Furnished with a poster of Maya Angelou (an early hint that Melinda's unspoken problem is, like Angelou's, a rape) and some books from home, the closet is Melinda's domain until the end of the novel.[5]

While fairy-tale heroines are often at the mercy of their environment—Snow White exiled in the forest, Cinderella in the kitchen, Rapunzel imprisoned in the tower—each of these heroines has a place she controls, a place she knows, a place she can be herself. The first indication that these characters will take charge of themselves, then, may be their ability to take charge of their surroundings. And the fully realized details of their surroundings provide another early indication that the novels will reject or at least revise the fantasy of their fairy-tale predecessors; in the intersection of such particularity with the generic constraints of the fairy tale, indeed, we may begin to find an opening for feminist possibility.

Voice

The voice of the fairy tale is detached and dispassionate, an objective narrator who tells what happened but rarely why.[6] There is no interiority in fairy tales, no psychological development of character, rarely even a narrating "I." Young adult novels, by contrast, frequently rely on what is most often called first-person narration and interior monologue: they create the illusion of a speaking subject by representing that subject to us in an unmediated way, with direct address or the illusion of "eavesdropping" on the private diary of the writer.[7]

Of the three novels I discuss, *Weetzie Bat* employs a narrative voice most similar to the fairy-tale narrator.[8] My students frequently complain about the novel's lack of interiority, for example, without (at first) connecting this to the same tendency in the fairy tales they love. Weetzie herself, however, is the most frequent focalizer of the novel—that is, it is most often her perspective that controls our perceptions.[9] That is, although the narrator may seem external and objective, the novel most frequently directs our perceptions through Weetzie's own. As I've already noted, however, this is not the "once upon a time" narrative of most familiar fairy tales. Rather, the similarity to fairy tales is most striking in the narrator's calm acceptance of the fantastic; in much the tone of Perrault's narrator announcing the arrival of the fairy godmother, for example, Block's narrator seems unfazed by the presence of the genie: "Yes, it was more and more solid. Weetzie could see him—it was a man, a little man in a turban, with a jewel in his nose, harem pants, and curly-toed slippers" (26). Weetzie herself expresses astonishment at the sight—"'Lanky lizards!' Weetzie exclaimed"—thus providing the reader with confirmation that, yes, this is like a fairy tale, that is, potentially not real. The ironic (or call it postmodern) play with form continues when Weetzie wishes for world peace.

> "I'm sorry," the genie said. "I can't grant that wish. It's out of my league. Besides, one of your world leaders would screw it up immediately."

"Okay," Weetzie said. "Then I wish for an infinite number of wishes!" As a kid she had vowed to wish for wishes if she ever encountered a genie or a fairy or one of those things. Those people in fairy tales never thought of that.

"People in fairy tales wish for that all the time," the genie said. "They aren't stupid. It just isn't in the records because I can't grant that type of wish." (27)

The genie's matter-of-fact explanation of "the record" simultaneously both increases and decreases the fairy-tale quality of the episode. By suggesting that there is a "record" that does not completely conform to some set of external facts, the genie's words may suggest that other fairy tales are also "true," if limited. More to my point here, however, Weetzie's skepticism suggests that she will not allow a fairy-tale sense of the world to govern her own life. The questioning voice of the adolescent revises the fairy tale in even more striking ways in the two "first-person" narratives under consideration.

I've argued elsewhere that highlighting the figure of the storyteller can be a significant way of revising the Cinderella story, and this is true for other fairy tales as well.[10] Mia's control of her narrative, then, is essential to our reading of it. Though we could see Grandmère as the storyteller—after all, she is the one who breaks the news to Mia and makes her aware of her own history—in fact it is Mia who tells her own story, authoring the tale of her transformation in diaries that also incorporate fragments of her nonprincess life throughout. Math notes, take-out menus, grocery lists, princess homework, and the like are scattered throughout the diary much as we might expect them to be in the diary of a relatively disorganized and busy teenager. The greatest accomplishment of the diaries is not, however, her startling achievement in math (raising an F to a D), but her control of the narrative itself. Although the surface story of Mia Thermopolis is of someone whose life has gone out of control—she can't choose her own clothes, take the subway to school, or even go on a date without media coverage—by writing the diary she has the ultimate shaping control of the storyteller. While Grandmère is remaking Mia, for example, Mia is making us see Grandmère. Mia, in fact, *makes* Grandmère for us. What Mia gives us in Grandmère is not the frightening figure of the evil stepmother or the benevolent fairy godmother (although, in this revision of "Cinderella," she also stands somehow for both) but rather a somewhat ridiculous old woman with tattooed eyeliner, a drinking problem, and a pathetic, rather than frightening, attachment to dictatorial authority. Most tellingly, Grandmère cannot control Mia. She may dress and remake her superficially, and Mia may let us know how distasteful she finds the process, but in the end Mia wins—in the sense that she has laid bare the process that Grandmère would rather conceal. Grandmère's power, like the power of all monarchies, indeed, like the power of gender itself, rests on its appearing natural, foreordained, given. Mia shows it to be arbitrary, unearned, and petty.

In the sequels to *The Princess Diaries*, Cabot becomes even more playful with the narrative technique of the diary, bringing its composition out into the open of the story. In volume 4 (*Princess in Waiting*), for example, Mia's friends frequently comment on her journaling:

> "Do you mean to say you've been in here [the Moscovitzes' bathroom] for the past half hour *writing in your journal?*" Which I'll admit is a little weird, but I couldn't help it. I was so happy, I HAD to write it down, so I would never forget how it felt. (222)

This moment is closely followed by Mia's realization that her "secret talent" (an issue throughout the novel) is writing. Writing then becomes central to the next several volumes, as Mia rewrites scenes from her life in the style of romantic novels, tries to model her own love life on what she finds in the books that she and (especially) Tina Hakim-Baba are reading, does poorly in English (her teacher doesn't appreciate her heavily cliché-ridden style), and, finally, makes friends with another writer.[11] It is this writer,

J.P. (formerly known as the Guy Who Hates It When They Put Corn in the Chili), not Mia, who best articulates the importance of writing, the lesson Mia has implicitly learned as early as volume 1: "I'd rather be a writer than an actor. Because actors, when you think about it, their job is just to interpret stuff somebody else has written. They have no POWER. The real power's in the words they're saying, which someone else has written. That's what I'm interested in. Being the power *behind* the Julia Robertses and Jude Laws of the world" (168).

Melinda, of *Speak*, has no such revelation about her writing—she is characterized far more by her investment in visual rather than verbal arts. And unlike *The Princess Diaries*, *Speak* includes no explanation of exactly what we are reading or why Melinda is writing it. We do learn, early on, that the English teacher (whom Melinda dubs "Hairwoman") "wants [her students] to write in [their] class journals every day, but promises not to read them"—but it is not clear that this is, in fact, the journal we are reading (6). Nonetheless, the journal format—incorporating, as does Mia's, nonjournal materials, including the occasional list, screenplay-style dialogue, and report cards—gives us the illusion of direct access to the teenaged protagonist's thoughts and feelings. In a novel dominated by Melinda's silence, the journal makes sure that "her voice is never internally stilled, even when externally lost" (O'Quinn 55).[12]

The fairy-tale connections to *Speak* are, as I noted at the outset, the least clear of the three novels I'm discussing. But Melinda's voice gives us several clues. In biology class the sight of the frog ready for dissection elicits a memory of "The Frog-King," while her difficult relationship with her parents sparks a recollection of earlier orphan fantasies. One encounter with her rapist in a parking lot becomes a scene out of "Little Red Riding Hood": "He turns his head and sees me. And wolf smiles, showing oh granny what big teeth you have" (97). That is, unlike in the first two novels I've discussed, which have clear references to fairy-tale motifs embedded in their plotlines, *Speak*'s references are more oblique and rest entirely on Melinda's language rather than structural elements in the narratives.

Like Mia, Melinda takes control of her story—in small things, like her refusal to name Andy until she is ready, and in larger, like controlling the entire narrative, including withholding the information about the rape until she has the tools to deal with it.[13] Her most emancipatory acts are acts of writing: first, she writes Andy's name on a bathroom wall under the subject heading "Guys to Stay Away From," and soon thereafter she writes the story of the party in her notebook, in a series of notes passed with Rachel/Rachelle (175, 182–83). Only after writing can Melinda speak, as she does when Andy tries to assault her again in "her" closet. By telling her own story—insisting on her right to her own voice—the fairy-tale heroine becomes an agent rather than a victim.[14]

An Aside

Although this discussion is not, strictly speaking, related to the previous discussion of voice, it's worth developing further the ways in which *Speak* transliterates the fairy tale. Anderson threads throughout the novel two images from "Snow White"—the mirror and the apple—in her subtle revision of that most relevant of tales. While Bacchilega makes the mirror central to her reading of postmodern fairy tales, it seems marginal—almost literally—in *Speak*. In a telling subversion or reinstatement of the mirror's revelatory qualities, Melinda covers the mirror in "her" closet with a poster of Maya Angelou. While she refuses the mirror's image of herself, then, she replaces that image with a potentially emancipatory one of another rape victim silenced by her abuse and then empowered, through writing, to speak. The "magic mirror" reveals, as mirrors always do, an image of herself, though not one she can recognize at first.

It is the apple, however, that most interests me in *Speak*. In "Snow White" the apple is poisonous. A possible echo of the fruit in the Garden of Eden, it simultaneously marks the eater as sexual and punishes her for that sexuality: the stepmother prepares it to tempt the now-beautiful Snow White and to kill her for that beauty. It casts Snow White into a deathlike sleep, but the apple that Melinda eats seems to have quite the opposite effect. It begins as a biology project: each student receives an apple to dissect.

> Applesmell soaks the air. One time when I was little, my parents took me to an orchard. Daddy set me high in an apple tree. It was like falling up into a storybook, yummy and red and leaf and the branch not shaking a bit. Bees bumbled through the air, so stuffed with apple they couldn't be bothered to sting me. The sun warmed my hair, and a wind pushed my mother into my father's arms, and all the apple-picking parents and children smiled for a long, long minute.

> That's how biology class smells.

> I bite my apple. White teeth red apple hard juice deep bite. David [her lab partner] sputters.

> David: "You're not supposed to do that! She'll kill you! You're supposed to cut it! Didn't you even listen? You'll lose points!" (66)

Not only does the biology teacher not "kill" Melinda (as Snow White's apple doesn't really kill her), but she awards her extra credit for discovering the small new growth inside the apple. This apple, then, awakens Melinda—the strong sense-memory that it elicits, the sensual description of the bite ("white teeth red apple hard juice deep bite"), and the growing plant seed all suggest growth, awakening, life, not the death we have learned (somewhat perversely, really) to associate with Snow White's poisoned fruit. Unlike the child Snow White, Melinda is sexually aware, in ways she had no desire to be; the apple reminds her, and us, that she can have other desires, other feelings, and it helps her begin her long process of recovery. Reworking the fairy-tale motifs in this way thus reaffirms Melinda's agency as opposed to Snow White's passivity throughout the traditional tale.

After "once upon a time," "happily ever after" is probably the most characteristic phrase of the fairy tale. Zipes suggests that the two are necessarily linked, and further that they do not imply closure: "The tale begins with 'Once upon a time' or 'Once there was' and never really ends when it ends. The ending is actually the beginning" (xiii).[15] But fairy tales seem more linear: a problem is introduced "once upon a time," and upon its resolution, the tale is over, with the protagonist(s) living (usually) "happily ever after," a closure that belies the possibility that the problem initiating the narrative may—indeed, no doubt will—arise again. The obvious unreality of such a closure has not escaped notice, of course; feminist critics, for example, frequently call into question the "happiness" of the marriage ending.[16] All three of the novels I discuss interrogate the "happiness" of the fairy-tale ending, as well as resisting traditional narrative closure in more subtle ways.

Weetzie Bat takes up the "happily-ever-after" trope the most overtly: after her three wishes are fulfilled, the last one by her encounter with My Secret Agent Lover Man, "Weetzie and My Secret Agent Lover Man and Dirk and Duck and Slinkster Dog and Fifi's canaries lived happily ever after in their silly-sand-topped house in the land of skating hamburgers and flying toupees and Jah-Love blonde Indians" (45). The novel, however, is not even half over at this point, and on the next page (after a chapter break), Weetzie asks Dirk, "What does 'happily ever after' mean anyway . . . ?" (46).[17] The question generates a brief meditation on change, specifically on the changing Los Angeles landscape: the loss of certain beloved landmarks and their replacement by strip malls and vacant lots. The meaning is clear: as Weetzie's fairy-tale landscape is changing, so too is her fairy-tale romance. For starters (like so many fairy-tale mothers), Weetzie wants a baby, one of the most compelling change-agents in human experience. And since her lover doesn't, she turns to others.[18] The traditional fairy-tale closure implicitly recognizes the heroine's sexual maturity as she marries her prince but draws a discreet veil over what, exactly, that might mean.[19] *Weetzie Bat* makes it clear: sexuality brings its own set of experiences, happy and unhappy, and narrative closure is a fiction. By the end of the novel, a chastened Weetzie reflects, "I don't know about happily ever after . . . but I do know about happily" (109). Happiness requires force of will, though, not a magic wand or a genie: My Secret Agent Lover Man's willingness to parent a child he didn't father, Weetzie Bat's similar generosity to his child, Dirk and Duck's reunion after an AIDS-related parting. And indeed "ever after" eventually turns out to encompass four more novels as well, though Weetzie is no longer the protagonist.[20]

The Princess Diaries series similarly refuses closure, though perhaps less self-consciously than *Weetzie Bat*. Although the first novel ends with the acknowledgment that maybe Michael Moscovitz does "like" Mia—and her own acknowledgment that he, not Josh Richter, is indeed the "prince" of her dreams—they are not yet happily-ever-after, nor do they appear to be by the end of volume 8 (as of this writing, the most recent episode). Indeed, Mia has a different boyfriend by the end of volume 2 and spends most of volume 3 trying to break up with him and re-interest Michael. It is clear throughout that Michael is her "prince," for example, when his compliment makes her feel "just like Cinderella all of a sudden" (*Take Two* 211), or when, at the end of volume 3, he finally does kiss her and she writes, "I'm living happily ever after" (*Third Time Lucky* 213). Yet over the next five volumes "happily-ever-after" turns out to include missed communication, anxiety, the potential pressures of sex, and a seeming breakup when Michael goes off to Japan and Mia goes to see *Beauty and the Beast* on Broadway with J.P. Although Mia as a character remains fully invested in romantic closure, the novels' persistent refusal to provide it may (though to a lesser extent than *Weetzie Bat*) undercut her impulse to fairy-tale closure.

Speak begins with the aftermath of a rape, and tells its story both backward and forward, revealing the full extent of the encounter only three-quarters of the way through the novel. If we didn't already know that this was the event she had been trying to repress for over a hundred pages, we might mistake the episode for the love-at-first-sight moment from a fairy tale:

> A step behind me. A senior. And then he was talking to me, flirting with me. This gorgeous cover-model guy. His hair was way better than mine, his every inch a tanned muscle, and he had straight white teeth. Flirting with me! Where was Rachel—she had to see this!

> Greek God: "Where did you come from? You're too beautiful to hide in the dark. Come dance with me." (134)

But the fairy-tale moment quickly turns ugly and violent. Melinda is not Cinderella, not Snow White: the kiss—and then the rape—does not awaken but deadens her, silencing her before she even enters the arena of young adulthood. Reawakened by her apple, her journal, and her art, Melinda is able to confront her attacker when he threatens her toward the end of the novel and finally responds to her art teacher Mr. Freeman's efforts to help her as well. The novel ends not with her final encounter with Andy: "'I said no'" (195)—but with her response to Mr. Freeman: "'Let me tell you about it'" (196).[21]

On occasion I've had students dissatisfied with the ending of *Speak*, which fails to develop the nascent relationship between Melinda and David Petrakis, her lab partner and friend, or to indicate what happens to Andy after the encounter in the closet. Anderson resolutely refuses the potential satisfaction of either the romantic or the judicial closures, ending instead with the invitatory opening line with Mr. Freeman. But in *Catalyst*, Anderson's 2002 novel, Melinda resurfaces. No longer the protagonist, Melinda is a minor character in *Catalyst*'s story of Kate Malone, a senior at Merryweather High who knows Melinda as "Melinda Something." "She's half-famous around here," Kate narrates. "A senior tried to rape her in a janitor's closet last year. She fought him off and pressed charges, which was cool. It made the papers when he was found guilty. He didn't go to jail, of course. White, upper-middle-class criminals go to the state college, not the state penitentiary. Then they join fraternities" (76). Kate's casual cynicism about Andy again reminds us that Melinda is not living in a fairy tale (nor, for that matter, is Kate, a motherless senior whose ambition to attend MIT drives her story). By shifting Melinda from protagonist to minor character in this second novel, Anderson reworks "happily-ever-after" as successfully and as critically as both Block and Cabot.

Fairy tales may indeed still structure our imaginations, especially if we are girls and women.[22] The traces that fairy tales leave in these three novels for young adults, however, indicate that they can be revised, revisited, "transliterated" in unexpected ways. As critics since Bettelheim and historians since Darnton have told us, fairy tales are not all sweetness and light. "Transliterating" them into the sometimes gritty world of young adult fiction restores their more troubling aspects. Like their forebears, Weetzie, Mia, and Melinda face disappointment, danger, threats, and failures—without, however, the consolations of magically derived happy endings. At the same time, the potentially emancipatory plotlines of the novels suggest that despite the power narrative has to shape imagination—perhaps even development—such power is far from determinative. Mia, Weetzie, and Melinda rewrite the tales they seem to be inhabiting, resisting their utopian placement, their silencing, their romantic closures. In so doing they point the way for others to do the same.

Notes

1. Although none of these novels is, strictly speaking, a *Bildungsroman*, all are clearly novels of becoming, as Bakhtin would have it, and these qualities—especially of time and space—are characteristic of such novels (on *Bildungsromane*, *Entwicklungsromane*, and young adult literature, see also Trites 16–19).

2. It would be interesting to explore further in this regard the metaphor of "alienation" with regard to selfhood, a fundamentally spatial metaphor.

3. Although it might seem plausible that the books are simply set prior

to the attacks, it's clear by volume 6 that characters have seen the Disney movie adaptation of the first book (released in August 2001).

4. Patricia J. Campbell writes, "I know of no other writer who has written so accurately about the reality of life in Los Angeles" (57).

5. Elaine J. O'Quinn notes, with reference to the closet, that "a strategic retreat is not a surrender" (56).

6. Harries's analysis of early literary fairy tales suggests that this quality may be related to the "folk orality" invented by Perrault and imitated by the Grimms. The "longer, more complex, and more self-referential model" of tale, most often written by women, may not conform to this narrative style (16; see also 22–23 and 72 for further development of the contrast). See also Bacchilega's comment on the "very simple but powerful narrative strategy that stands as one of the narrative rules for fairy-tale production: an external or impersonal narrator whose straightforward statements carry no explicit mark of human perspective" (34).

7. Mieke Bal, following Gérard Genette, notes that all narrators are grammatically "first person" and develops a layered schema of narrator, focalizer, actor, and character. I use the more familiar "first-person," then, to refer to a situation in which all four elements coincide (also called, by Bal, a "character-bound narrator" [*Narratology* 122; see also *On Story-Telling* 79]). Fairy tales, by contrast, most often employ an external narrator who is neither actor nor character and a shifting focalization.

8. Campbell writes, "The tone is pure fairy-tale" (n.p.).

9. See Bal, *On Story-Telling*, chap. 4, for a more nuanced discussion of focalization. Regarding perspective, we also have occasional access to Dirk—it is, for example, presumably his judgment that terms Weetzie "almost beautiful" early in the novel (2). My Secret Agent Lover Man and Duck are, in this novel at least, more opaque to the reader. Mike Cadden claims that "the voice of the slim novel is singular and irrefutable within the confines of the text" (153).

10. "Cinderella, Marie Antoinette, and Sara" 171. See also Warner.

11. Among the novels that Mia and Tine read, *Jane Eyre* and the fictitious (no) sex-guide for girls, *Your Precious Gift*, feature especially prominently.

12. Cadden's cautions regarding the ethics of adult authors "provid[ing] the young adult reader with an unassailable, seductive, and singular voice in order to sound like that younger readership" are instructive here (153). I would argue, however, that by engaging in dialogue with their fairy-tale predecessors, all three novels may indeed provide the alternative viewpoints Cadden calls for.

13. As Bacchilega notes, "Snow White rarely has a voice of her own" (35).

14. O'Quinn makes a similar argument using different terms.

15. His claim is specifically about the ways in which fairy tales both begin and end in a "utopia," a no-place; thus when the tale is over, it replaces us where another tale can begin.

16. Haase's introduction to *Fairy Tales and Feminism* offers a useful review of some of these arguments, as does Cathy Lynn Preston's essay "Postmodernism and the Fairy Tale," in the same volume.

17. Mike Cadden observes that the popular direct-to-video Disney sequels *Cinderella II* and *Cinderella III* raise similar questions; *Beauty and the Beast: The Enchanted Christmas* sidesteps the problem by creating an episode that takes place within the narrative time frame of the original movie (personal correspondence).

18. Does this episode reflect the odd birth stories of such fairy-tale heroines as Snow White and Rapunzel?

19. This is, of course, not the case in many of the less-well-known versions of heroine tales like "Sleeping Beauty" (who, in the Italian version, bears twins in her sleep) or "Rapunzel," who similarly bears a son and a daughter to her night-visiting prince. The "happily-ever-after" formulation in our most familiar tales, however, usually occurs just at the point of marriage.

20. The Weetzie Bat books, eventually published together as *Dangerous Angels* in 1998, include *Witch Baby* (1991), *Cherokee Bat and the Goat Guys* (1992), *Missing Angel Juan* (1993), and *Baby Be-Bop* (1995). Weetzie appears in most of these, but they are not "her" stories.

21. This ending feels as well like a veiled reference to the opening of that most famous of young adult novels, Salinger's *The Catcher in the Rye*: "If you really want to hear about it [. . .] ." By the end of Melinda's story, we know why we—or anyone else—would want to hear it.

22. As Marina Warner says, "Boys might surrender to the pleasures fairy tales offered before they were taught otherwise, but they soon sternly put them away, like skipping and doll's houses, and would scoff from their superior world of electric trains and airforce yarns" (xvii–xviii). Kay Stone similarly notes that fewer male students seemed to remember fairy tales in later life than females do (398).

Works Cited

Anderson, Laurie Halse. *Catalyst*. 2002. New York: Penguin, 2003.

———. *Speak*. 1999. New York: Penguin, 2001.

Bacchilega, Cristina. *Postmodern Fairy Tales: Gender and Narrative Strategies*. Philadelphia: University of Pennsylvania Press, 1997.

Bakhtin, M. M. "The *Bildungsroman* and Its Significance in the History of Realism (Toward a Historical Typology of the Novel)." *Speech Genres and Other Late Essays*. Trans. Vern W. McGee. Ed. Caryl Emerson and Michael Holquist. Austin: University of Texas Press, 1986. 10–59.

Bal, Mieke. *Narratology: Introduction to the Theory of Narrative.* Trans. Christine van Boheemen. Toronto: University of Toronto Press, 1985.

———. *On Storytelling: Essays in Narratology.* Ed. David Jobling. Sonoma CA: Polebridge, 1991.

Beauvoir, Simone de. *The Second Sex.* 1949. New York: Vintage, 1989.

Block, Francesca Lia. *Dangerous Angels: The Weetzie Bat Books.* New York: HarperCollins, 1998.

———. *Weetzie Bat.* New York: HarperCollins, 1989.

Cabot, Meg. *The Princess Diaries.* New York: Harper Trophy, 2000.

———. *The Princess Diaries, Take Two.* London: Macmillan, 2001.

———. *The Princess Diaries, Third Time Lucky.* London: Macmillan, 2001.

———. *Princess in Waiting.* New York: HarperCollins, 2001.

———. *Princess on the Brink.* New York: HarperCollins, 2007.

Cadden, Mike. "The Irony of Narration in the Young Adult Novel." *Children's Literature Association Quarterly* 25.3 (Fall 2000): 146–54.

Campbell, Patricia J. "People Are Talking about . . . Francesca Lia Block." *Horn Book Magazine* 69.1 (Jan./Feb. 1993): 57–64.

Gruner, Elisabeth Rose. "Cinderella, Marie Antoinette, and Sara: Roles and Role Models in *A Little Princess*." *The Lion and the Unicorn* 22.2 (1998): 163–87.

Haase, Donald, ed. *Fairy Tales and Feminism: New Approaches.* Detroit: Wayne State University Press, 2004.

Harries, Elizabeth Wanning. *Twice upon a Time: Women Writers and the History of the Fairy Tale.* Princeton NJ: Princeton University Press, 2001.

O'Quinn, Elaine J. "Between Voice and Voicelessness: Transacting Silence in Laurie Halse Anderson's *Speak*." *ALAN Review* 29.1 (Fall 2001): 54–58.

Rowe, Karen. "Feminism and Fairy Tales." *Women's Studies: An Interdisciplinary Journal* 6 (1979): 237–57. Rpt. in *Folk and Fairy Tales.* Ed. Martin Hallett and Barbara Karasek. 2nd ed. Peterborough ON: Broadview, 1997. 325–45.

Stephens, John, and Robyn McCallum. *Retelling Stories, Framing Culture: Traditional Story and Metanarratives in Children's Literature.* New York: Garland, 1998.

Stone, Kay F. "The Misuses of Enchantment: Controversies on the Significance of Fairy Tales." *Women's Folklore, Women's Culture.* Ed. Rosan A. Jordan and Susan J. Kalcik. Philadelphia: University of Pennsylvania Press, 1985. Rpt. in *Folk and Fairy Tales.* Ed. Martin Hallett and Barbara Karasek. 3rd ed. Peterborough ON: Broadview, 2002. 391–415.

Susina, Jan. "The Rebirth of the Postmodern Flâneur: Notes on the Postmodern Landscape of Francesca Lia Block's *Weetzie Bat." Marvels & Tales* 16.2 (2002): 188–200.

Trites, Roberta Seelinger. *Disturbing the Universe: Power and Repression in Adolescent Literature.* Iowa City: University of Iowa Press, 2000.

Warner, Marina. *From the Beast to the Blonde: On Fairy Tales and Their Tellers.* New York: Farrar, 1994.

Zipes, Jack. *Spells of Enchantment: The Wondrous Fairy Tales of Western Culture.* New York: Viking, 1991.

2

⁊◉⮕

Familiarity Breeds a Following

*Transcending the Formulaic
in the Snicket Series*

DANIELLE RUSSELL

The fiction series stands out in the realm of children's literature for several reasons. A popular format since its inception in the nineteenth century, series books have always targeted children.[1] Twentieth-century series, Deirdre Johnson asserts, "rest firmly on a nineteenth-century foundation" (147). Content and characters "may reflect twentieth-century perspectives," but the patterns of series books are carryovers from the past (147).[2]

The formulas have been so well established that they are instantly familiar. This fact is incorporated into *The Children's Literature Dictionary* entry for "series": "a group of works centering on a single subject, author, format, or character. Developed in the nineteenth-century . . . based on formulas yielding superficial characters and predictable plots" (Brodie, Latrobe, and White 153). Also carried over from the nineteenth century is a critical response that is often condescending, if not condemning.

The tendency to disparage series fiction has a long history. Both the quality of writing and the sensational content of the books were the target of numerous critics. Peter Soderbergh offers a succinct summary of the protests of the critics: poor prose, a reliance on "exaggeration and sensationalism," and the "assembly-line manner of production" (65). Published in vast numbers at a rapid pace, early series fiction was viewed as less literary because it was mass produced. Nancy Romalov insists that the "campaign against series books" was symptomatic "of the ongoing discourse over 'high' and 'low' culture, of larger debates about literary value and about who gets to do the valuing" (113). It was linked with the public library movement—"larger reform efforts [. . .] that sought to shape public behavior" (113). Literature was viewed, in part at least, as a tool of socialization. The fact that series fiction flourished then and now reveals the futility of the antiseries rhetoric; popular opinion sided (and sides) with the books.[3] But what became of the debate about the literary value of series fiction?

The dire warnings of the nineteenth century have diminished in our time. For the most part the moral tone has disappeared; a lingering suspicion of the incompatibility of literary creation and mass production, however, remains. Soderbergh divides twentieth-century responses to children's series fiction into two camps: classicists ("loath to relinquish the power of choice to the child, genuinely concerned he or she might linger too long on impoverished material") and developmentalists (who deem "debates on literary merit" "unprofitable" and directed parents and teachers to "view reading as a continuum [. . .] and the various reading stages as identifiable elements in the total maturation process") (70–71). The classicists adopt a protective stance, standing between the impressionable child reader and series fiction with its "poor literary quality" (70). In contrast, developmentalists sidestep the issue of literary merit, focusing instead on the need to empower the child. The act of reading, in this context, is key, not the reading material. Series fiction represents one stage in the development of the child reader. The implication is that parents and educators need not be concerned with the books because they are merely a phase (presumably to be outgrown) in the child's literary life. Developmentalists argue in favor of the child reader's autonomy—at least in terms of selecting his or her own books—but do not necessarily differ from the classicists in their assessment of series fiction. As Soderbergh perceptively notes, both approaches avoid why or how series fiction captivates an audience. Neglect has replaced critical bias, proposes Victor Watson; "perfunctory treatment"—focusing critical attention on the first book while summarizing or listing sequels—"implies that to follow a successful novel with a sequel is a loss of writerly seriousness, a decline into repetitive and formulaic spin-offs" (537). Such a dismissive approach is not without risks; critics who rely on generalizations can (and do) get things wrong. The assumption that the formulaic cannot accommodate variety is challenged by the popular Lemony Snicket series. After the first novel each text is instantly familiar; the reading experience is remarkably (or annoyingly) similar. Patterns are quickly established and maintained through most of the series. Difference is found in the content of the narratives rather than the style of the series.[4]

Expanding Territories: Playing with(in) Patterns

"Formulaic?" queries Gregory Maguire of the Snicket books. "Self-consciously, generously, joyously so. The fun derives from watching the formula at work" (30). A Series of Unfortunate Events revels in its predictability and rebels through its pushing at the boundaries of series fiction. Unsuspecting critics who anticipate an allegiance to the initial pattern miss out on the moral dilemmas that the Baudelaire siblings struggle with in the later books. The overarching pattern of the books has the children delivered to an unfamiliar setting and a new guardian. The promise of a new beginning is soon threatened by a disguised Count Olaf. Invariably, the children cannot get an adult to take their concerns seriously. Silenced and seemingly disempowered, Violet, Klaus, and Sunny must take control of their own fates through brain power, books, and their bond of love. A shift, however, occurs from the eighth book onward; the children are alone in the world and have no adult advocate (given the ineffectual adults who have failed them in the preceding seven books, the "loss" is perhaps a mixed blessing!). At this point, the tales become increasingly dark as the line between good and evil blurs, exposure to the negative side of human nature intensifies, and the siblings face increasingly difficult moral decisions.

Although they venture into new territory, familiarity nonetheless characterizes the later books. Snicket does not abandon his formula, he merely modifies it: the cast of characters continuing to draw on prior stories, the ever-present stylistic idiosyncrasies (alliteration, puns, visual jokes, selective vocabulary lessons, disruptions to the narrative, warnings to readers, tantalizing glimpses of the narrator Snicket's "life"), and the pattern through thirteen chapters of the Baudelaires encountering mysteries, villains, and being thwarted in their attempts to uncover the truth. The fact that the stories were conceptualized as a group is readily apparent. Snicket embraces the series format; working within tradition he illustrates how the formulaic can be innovative.[5]

*Visual Echoes of the Past: The Series
and Literary Tradition*

The books themselves offer a unique experience for the contemporary child reader. In a market flooded with paperback novels, the Snicket books stand apart. Evocative of an earlier publishing era, the hardcover books play with the idea of timelessness so often associated with children's literature. Echoes of the past are found in the patterned end papers and the rough edged pages (suggesting that the thick paper pages were cut by the owner in anticipation of reading), and the bookplates at the front suggest a personal library (rather than books owned by consumers in over twenty countries).[6]

The distinctive illustrations by Brett Helquist further enhance the experience of reading a Snicket book. Reminiscent of pen-and-ink and copperplate illustrations found in early children's literature, they mimic an older art form that seems to be worlds away from mass-produced consumer goods. They help to remove the reader from the familiar and mundane. Visually striking, indeed sometimes jarring, the dark quality of the illustrations—literally because they are black and white, figuratively because of the content—helps to establish a gothic sensibility in the physical texts and the stories themselves. The brooding, oppressive atmosphere of the narratives is intimately connected to Helquist's pictorial contributions.

Frequently labeled mock-gothic novels, the Snicket books draw on the conventions of the older literary form. It is not so much a case of ridiculing as it is recuperating; a neglected genre is rejuvenated by adapting it to children's literature.[7] The author identifies the origins of the series as the abandonment of another project: a mock gothic novel for adults (Merkin 164). The Snicket series does not entirely mock the genre nor does it rely on a straightforward use of its conventions. The element of fear, the presence of the uncanny, and the threatening villain remain, but the injection of humor results in a neo-gothic sensibility. John G. Cawelti's assessment of the frequent focus of the gothic novel "upon the attempts of a mysterious and diabolic villain to seduce or murder a confused and bewildered victim" is an apt summary of the interactions of Count Olaf and the Baudelaire siblings (100).

In the series we encounter not a medieval castle but the smoky ruins of the Baudelaire mansion; Count Olaf's medievalesque tower—complete with bats and the ever-present eye in *The Bad Beginning*—creates a visual echo of the gothic. Throughout the narratives subterranean passages and hidden doorways figure into the plots, and the settings are consistently bizarre. Brooding atmospheres are generated through the bleak living conditions, the oppressive presence of Count Olaf, and the relatively (pun intended!) isolated position of the Baudelaire orphans. Count Olaf's threats establish an element of terror; there is mystery surrounding his machinations. He devises melodramatically violent plots and clearly represents an abnormal psychological state. The Snicket series draws on literary conventions associated with adult fiction, thereby expanding the possibilities of children's literature.[8]

Breaking with Tradition:
Complicating Morality

The books further challenge the boundaries of literature written for children by interrogating several of its established forms. The exploration of the aberrant psychological states found in much gothic literature is in opposition to the simple code of the cautionary or moral tale: the good will be rewarded, and the bad will suffer suitable punishments. Cautionary and moral tales teach through examples: warnings against foolish or dangerous behavior are issued; the child character transgresses and is punished. Such narratives are attempts to shape the child into a rational and ethical person; the entertainment is secondary to the instructive quality. Despite the fact that "Violet, Klaus, and Sunny Baudelaire were intelligent [. . .] charming and resourceful [. . .] most everything that happened to them was rife with misfortune, misery, and despair" (*Bad Beginning* 1). Even in the face of adversity and provocation, the Baudelaire children are polite and well behaved. Traditionally these behaviors would ensure a successful outcome for the child characters in children's literature in general and series fiction in particular.[9] In this series, however, good children suffer, and beastly children continue unharmed or corrected.[10]

A sense of injustice pervades the books; the good characters and behaviors of the Baudelaires do not save them. Cautioned by Mr. Poe to "be on [their] best behavior" under the threat of being sent to a boarding school, Violet agrees, "not adding that she and her siblings had always been on their best behavior but that it hadn't done them any good" (*Miserable Mill* 7). Cause and effect is not the pattern of their lives, and the children are painfully aware of it. "Schu!" Sunny observes; a phrase Snicket translates as "It's been a long time since anything in our lives has felt fair" (*Wide Window* 23). The insistence that these are not happy stories and the reliance on dark humor foreground the fact that life is not always fair or pleasant. In this regard the Snicket series breaks from the tradition of series books. Extensive research leads Paul Deane to the bold proclamation: "WITH NO SINGLE EXCEPTION, all series books contain exact demonstrations of justice. Readers are assured that good is rewarded and evil punished. If one acts well, one can expect to benefit" (188, emphasis in original). Such an expectation is obliterated in the Snicket series; the narratives refuse to adopt the model Deane identifies. In fact they seem to go out of their way to avoid any sense of justice. Hardships and disappointments are heaped on the children. The dilemmas they are entangled in obstruct the siblings' efforts to do the "right" thing.

The Baudelaires repeatedly find themselves making difficult moral choices. Each decision diminishes the distance between the children and the villains; in order to survive they must adopt Count Olaf's tactics. "How did you survive me?" taunts Olaf. "You lied to people. You stole. You abandoned people in danger. You set fires. Time after time you've relied on treachery to survive, just like everyone else" (*Penultimate Peril* 211). The siblings prove to be particularly adept at villainous behavior. By the final book the trio fears that in telling "the whole story, they might have looked as villainous as Count Olaf" (*End* 60). Motivation distinguishes them from Olaf and his troupe but, as "Violet and Klaus thought about all of the trouble they were in, [they] wondered if it was all due to simple misfortune, or if some of it was of their own devising" (*Carnivorous Carnival* 275). The collective narrative does not hold the children culpable. It becomes increasingly clear that forces beyond their control have manipulated the trio into "a Hobson's choice [. . .] something that's not a choice at all" (*Grim Grotto* 146). And yet a feeling of complicity complicates the children's sense of identity; eager to do the right thing, they are nonetheless unable to act on that impulse. This ambiguous moral character is a distinct divergence from traditional series fiction. In the "ongoing fight between good and evil," asserts Vicki Anderson, readers and writers may have "had a few moral shortcomings of their own, [but] the heroes and heroines [. . .] never did" (126–27). The ambiguity is compounded by the fact that the Baudelaires have difficulty recognizing what the right thing is; frames of reference from their past do not apply in the Baudelaires' present.

Divisions between "good" and "bad" guys also do not apply in the series. A strict separation of sides is not maintained as the narratives progress. Guilt haunts Violet, Klaus, and Sunny; their actions have been necessary but frequently criminal. Even Count Olaf's villainy is thrown into question: as the orphans try to disarm him, "'What else can I do?' the villain asked, so quietly the children could not be sure they had heard him correctly" (*Penultimate Peril* 230).[11] Doubt swirls around both sides of the battle as they discover that "people aren't either wicked or noble [. . .] . They're like chef's salad with good things and bad things mixed together in a vinaigrette of confusion and conflict" (*Grim Grotto* 222). The end of the twelfth book finds the Baudelaires literally in the same boat as Count Olaf. The next book opens with the quartet's shipwreck on a coastal shelf. Occupying that liminal space is rather fitting; all the characters struggle with the moral and practical ramifications of their choices. In a surprising development a wounded Olaf shares a tender moment with Kit Snicket as she struggles to give birth. The reader's final glimpse of the "arch villain" destabilizes his classification.[12]

Deriding Didacticism: Life
beyond the Fairy Tale

The rejection of the false moral code associated with the series books is evident throughout the experiences of the Baudelaire siblings. Overt and contemptuous references to didactic texts are another tactic employed in the narratives. "When you were very small," Snicket proposes in *The Reptile Room*, "perhaps someone read to you the insipid story—the word 'insipid' here means 'not worth reading to someone'—of the Boy Who Cried Wolf" (141). A countermoral is offered—"Never live somewhere where wolves are running around loose"—with a key divergence from the central message of not lying: "This is an absurd moral, for you and I both know that sometimes not only is it good to lie, it is necessary to lie" (142). The oversimplification of the fable's moral can create an opening for the savvy reader to question not only the original text but Snicket's response to it. An acknowledgment that moral dilemmas are not always clear cut is integrated into the series; interrogating older tales reinforces the complexity of the real world.

Fairy tales in particular are targeted in *The Reptile Room* and *The Ersatz Elevator*—Little Red Riding Hood and Hansel and Gretel are all "dim witted" (143, 101). They prove to be ineffectual role models for Violet, Klaus, and Sunny; nothing in traditional children's literature prepares them for the situations they encounter. "The story of the Baudelaires does not take place in a fictional land where lollipops grow on trees and singing mice do all of the chores," insists Snicket in *The Carnivorous Carnival* (96–97). It "takes place in a very real world [. . .] where children can find themselves all alone in the world, struggling to understand the sinister mystery that surrounds them" (97). The claim to realism stretches the standard definition, but the avoidance of fantasy and constant references to the veracity of the narratives position the series closer to the child reader than the "once upon the time, in a land far away" of fairy tales.

Fairy tales deliberately distance the reader from the story; the Snicket series alternately alienates itself from and allies itself with the reader. The extreme situations that the Baudelaires find themselves in are divorced from the realities experienced by the readers—a point reinforced by the countless reminders that it is a story, albeit a "true" one. A buffer is created by that detachment from the events, but emotional appeals to the audience in turn undermine that detachment. Direct addresses to the reader function as an invitation to sympathize with Violet, Klaus, and Sunny. A memory of their father yelling at them discomforts the siblings: "Everyone yells, of course, from time to time, but the Baudelaire children did not like to think about their parents yelling, particularly now that they were no longer around to apologize or explain themselves. It is often difficult to admit that someone you love is not perfect, or to consider aspects of a person that are less than admirable" (*Grim Grotto* 148). The text foregrounds the fallibility of the parents (possibly), leading the reader into considering her own parents. Identification with the Baudelaires can blur the boundary between the personal experience and the fictional one.

Respecting Psychological Thresholds:
Coping Mechanisms

Although there is a definite shift in tone as the series progresses, the Snicket books recognize that children enjoy being frightened but only to a point—there is a threshold which cannot be crossed. Plot twists and villainous figures have the potential to inspire terror. Creating a buffer zone is an acknowledgment of the special needs of a developing reader without being patronizing.[13] The comfort of the familiar—plotlines, characters, stylistic features—provides a space in which difficult material can be explored. A respect for the abilities of the child reader is embedded in the series. Protection of "innocence" comes not in the form of exclusion or denial but is achieved through a variety of literary techniques.[14] The inclusion of a distinctive setting is one strategy for keeping fear manageable. Snicket refers to "the books [as taking] place in a space that only has to do with other books [. . .] . It distances the visceral horror of the story" (qtd. in Merkin 165). Patterned on real-world locations—cities, villages, country homes, hotels—the settings seem familiar but shift to the bizarre and grotesque. The subsequent distance permits a degree of detachment, a reassuring separation from the disturbing elements of the stories.[15]

Other literary devices that fulfill this requirement are the excessive use of alliteration, verbal and visual humor, and the deliberate signals that it is a story being related after the fact. The play of language, the pure pleasure of punning, takes a reader out of the dark, brooding atmosphere. The selective vocabulary lessons are the product of a wry sense of humor. To some extent they require a degree of sophistication to be appreciated (which need not be equated with an adult audience, just one with a good vocabulary). The comedic effect hinges on recognition: shared knowledge external to the texts. The reader becomes complicit in the joke, a partner in the inconsistency that is over the heads of the uninformed. It separates the knowing from the gullible.[16]

Another feature of the series, which enlists the reader in the process of creation, is the moment of self-consciousness. Pauses in the narratives highlight the construction of the stories.[17] There are multiple asides, tests of the reader's concentration, warnings, cautions—overt breaks in the story—and attempts to mirror a character's actions, which allow the reader to step back from the events. One of the numerous examples is the recreation of Klaus's difficulty reading late at night in *The Bad Beginning*: "Occasionally his eyes would close. He found himself reading the same sentence over and over. He found himself reading the same sentence over and over. He found himself reading the same sentence over and over" (94). It is a visual joke, adding levity to a situation that is intensifying. Although vicariously sharing Klaus's experience— we, too, read the same sentence three times—the reader is positioned beyond the action. Any potentially threatening aspect of the story is depersonalized by the space created by these reminders that it is a story.

Intersecting Stories: Lemony Snicket's Provocative Presence

Much of the continuity of the series stems from the presence of the intrusive and yet reclusive narrator/scribe of the events; the fictional construct of Lemony Snicket is an integral part of the texts. More than a mere narrator, Snicket is what Mieke Bal classifies as a perceptible, character-bound narrator: "Focalization is localized with the character bound narrator who refers to itself and is therefore perceptible in the text" (125). Told from his perspective, the tales are infused with Snicket's distinctive personality—the Baudelaires' story is embedded within that of the Snicket family as both Kit and Jacques Snicket (the narrator's siblings) cross paths with Violet, Klaus, and Sunny at key points. Repeated references to Snicket's location and activities also indicate a life beyond the books. They also help to establish the "veracity" of his account of events as he follows in the footsteps of the Baudelaire children collecting "data."[18]

Despite denials—"the only reason I could possibly have for jotting [the tale of Lemony Snicket] down in the margins of these pages would be to make this book even more unpleasant, unnerving, and unbelievable than it already is"—the Snicket "story" is interwoven, albeit cryptically, with that of the Baudelaires (*Hostile Hospital* 89). His presence is tantalizing, not terrifying; as character narration, Snicket's candid comments and cautions are posited as being protective but function seductively. His paranoid asides and efforts to "shield" the reader from the unhappy tales align Snicket not with moralizing adults but with inquisitive child readers. Maguire's assessment of the tales as "anarchy masked as propriety" is a succinct summary of the technique (30). Snicket's stance suggests a concern for the reader's ability to deal with the unfortunate events he must relate. He seems to be guiding the reader away from the narratives, but the warnings simply whet the reader's appetite. Snicket's asides are more subversive than sincere. They highlight the allure of "forbidden" knowledge and, after the first book (if not during it), fool no one.

A refusal to soften harsh realities characterizes the Snicket books; issues like child labor, physical and mental abuse, violence, and death are incorporated into each text. It is an approach that defies the impulse to protect children from negative material.[19] Indeed, at several points in the series the naive reasoning of the adults behind such protective gestures is exposed. Interrupting the narrative "in order to mollify the publishers—the word 'mollify' here means 'get them to stop tearing their hair out in worry'"—Snicket provides a "piece of advice" to the reader: "If you ever need to get to Curdled Cave in a hurry, do not, under any circumstances, steal a boat and attempt to sail across Lake Lachrymose during a hurricane" (*Wide Window* 145–46). Undercutting the position of the concerned publishers (and their ilk), Snicket "winks" at the child reader over the heads of the adults; it is a shared joke about the gullibility (and therefore vulnerability) of not the child but the adult (in this case, vulnerable to mockery).[20]

Defiant Self-Reliance: Empowered
Child Characters and Readers

Censorship of children's books often occurs as a response to a (real or perceived) threat to the child reader's vulnerability. Independent child characters were an inevitable target of critics of early series fiction. Soderbergh points out that Edward Stratemeyer's characters were considered "worldly, sly, and preternatural" (65). Stepping outside their assigned role—in need of adult or social protection and guidance—the youthful characters were at the center of the action. Johnson links these characters with Jacob Abbott's Jonas character in the Rollo books. It "introduced a type that would later earn series fiction much criticism: the 'adolescent *ubermenschen*,' or ultracapable child wise beyond his years" (149). Violet Baudelaire is identified as a "*wunderkind*," but each of the siblings displays unusual skills and insights (*Wide Window* 174). Natural talents and necessity combine to create a formidable trio in the absence of reliable adults.

Self-reliance is the alternative to victimization for the Baudelaire siblings. The necessity to decipher the mystery of their lives leads the children (and by extension, the child reader) to adopt the role of detective. It is a fairly common role for child characters in children's literature. Difference is found in the adults in this series. Although the powerlessness and vulnerability of childhood is foregrounded in the series, the "powerful" figures are exposed as being equally powerless and vulnerable to exploitation. Adults are almost uniformly incompetent in the books; as a result there is no safety net for the siblings (unlike in traditional series, where a competent adult hovers on the fringes of the action). There is an ever-expanding list of guardians who fail the Baudelaires; through ineptitude, indifference, or malice, grown-ups exacerbate the precarious position of the children.[21] It is the general tendency of adults to dismiss or downplay their concerns that convinces the Baudelaires they must fend for themselves.

Readers of the series are also forced to fend for themselves with the final book. The last installment in the Snicket series, set on an island that fails to be immune "from the treachery of the world," is either the author's greatest act of treachery or a stroke of genius (and quite possibly both) (292). The title seems to be straightforward—*The End*—but, as has been the case throughout the narratives, appearances are not to be trusted. Having invested time in reading twelve increasingly mysterious books, we might reasonably expect an explanation, if not resolution; after all, the hallmark of mystery or detective novels is a revelation of missing information and a tying up of loose ends. *The End* does not provide such an experience. In fact it challenges the very expectation of a closed ending.[22] The neatly packaged series refuses to be contained in a neatly packaged conclusion.

Signals that there will be an unconventional ending surface throughout the narrative. There is the (by now) standard warning by Snicket not to read the book; there is also a cryptic warning that the story cannot be resolved since "the end of this unhappy chronicle is like its bad beginning, as each misfortune only reveals another, and another, and another" (2). Circularity is suggested, but there are inevitable gaps and silences in the story of the Baudelaires. Their story, the book stresses, is intertwined with the stories of countless other characters; the multiple narratives can only be hinted at, not contained, in the final installment. It is a creative tactic that leaves an opening for additions to the series and/or interconnected series.

The conventional definition of "the end" is acknowledged— it "is a phrase which refers to the completion of a story"—but not applied in *The End* (287). It is dismissed as a false or forced formula since "no story really has a beginning, and [. . .] no story really has an end, as all of the world's stories are [. . .] all heaped together" (288–89). The world itself, Snicket theorizes, "is always *in medias res*—a Latin phrase which means 'in the midst of things' or 'in the middle of a narrative'"—thus it is "impossible to solve any mystery, or find the root of any trouble" (289). In this context *The End* is a reflection of the conditions that created it. It is a philosophical approach uncommon in series fiction for children.

The silences in A Series of Unfortunate Events can be viewed as empowering in that they allow the child reader to imagine the outcome. They can also be interpreted as an abdication of responsibility. Genre functions as an implicit contract between the author and the reader—expectations are raised and (to varying degrees) fulfilled. The Snicket series rejects the restrictions of form while relying on the formulaic. Through thirteen books readers anticipate that the children will be in peril, Olaf will be in disguise, and competent adults will be in demand. Less easy to anticipate is the shift the series takes throwing into question good and evil and literary conventions.

Challenges to Critics: The Dangers of Formulaic Criticism

Critical responses to children's series fiction have tended to rest on limited readings rather than detailed consideration of the individual texts and the collective narrative. The assumption that once the formula of the series is deciphered it will be sustained is a dangerous one. It does a disservice to responsible studies of children's literature. Given the longevity and popularity of series fiction, there is a hint of elitism in this practice—a dismissal of the judgment of the child readers who embrace this format. The sheer volume of series fiction (from the nineteenth through the twenty-first centuries) merits attention. Judicious scholars, like the countless nonacademic readers before them, will discover the complex nature of series writing. Contrary to being easily classified, these works resist categorization, insists Watson, "partly because there is an ambiguity of purpose latent in all series fictions: their desire to provide readers with more of the same and simultaneously to tell a new story. While they appear predictable, series fiction [books] are often intrinsically volatile" (535). Balancing the need for continuity (there must be a connection to be a series)with the desire for creativity (fresh material is required to engage the reader)is a deft act. The formulaic may create the framework for the series, but room for maneuvering remains— the volatility Watson identifies.

Experimentation in the Snicket series is achieved, in part, through its formula. It is a paradox built into the genre. Readers of series fiction, Watson asserts, engage in "a paradoxical search for familiarity combined with strangeness" (205). The threats and violence intensify in the Snicket books, but the formula functions as a comfort. Moving toward Uncle Monty's library in *The Reptile Room*, the Baudelaires have the sense that "even though the dark room felt mysterious and strange, it was a comforting mystery and a safe strangeness" (89). The statement could be a commentary on the series itself. Familiarity breeds a following and ultimately permits Snicket to transcend the limitations of the formulaic.

Notes

1. Deane points out that they are "almost the only books that have been consistently produced for the consumption of children themselves" (4). I focus on children's series fiction; developments in series fiction for adults fall outside the parameters of my discussion.

2. Johnson identifies Jacob Abbott's Rollo books (1835, 1837, 1839) as the first series for children; by 1841 "books by Abbott generally bore that notation" and "carried a complete list of titles in the series—a marketing strategy [. . .] that has been employed for promoting series ever since" (148). Soderbergh gives credit to *The Rover Boys at School* (1899) as marking "the modern phase of series book history" (64). For a succinct history of series fiction for children, see Watson's "Series Fiction."

3. Chamberlain questions the extent of the criticism asserting that "series were not universally damned" (188). They also earned "praise" and "balanced criticism" (188). It is a point well taken, but evidence of a vocal and adverse reaction to series fiction exists.

4. Cadden offers an insightful observation on the creative possibility of the formulaic. "Is writing a series of sonnets being 'formulaic,'" he queries (e-mail to the author, 22 Feb. 2007). "We prize the poet who can work in a convention and remain unique," he notes. Formulaic need not equal uninspired.

5. In the interest of simplicity, "Lemony Snicket" (the pseudonymous author/narrator) will be used throughout my discussion rather than "Daniel Handler."

6. One year before the first novel appeared, two before Scholastic's

paperback version, Jean Feiwel of Scholastic identified a new trend in series publishing: a movement into hardcover books with distinctive appearances. Scholastic's Dear America series replicates old-fashioned diaries at an affordable price. Feiwel associates physical quality with literary quality; hardcover books indicate "the high quality of the writing found within" (qtd. in Lodge 32). The implications of the shift from hardcover to paperback in the case of Snicket's books are unclear. Watson, however, points out that in the 1940s and 1950s "the sheer volume of series production and its association with cheap paperbacks" in part led "teachers, librarians and many parents [to perceive series fiction] as formulaic and trivial" (539). The relationship between form and content in this context is provocative but falls outside the scope of my discussion.

7. The gothic novel, popular in the early nineteenth century, incorporated "ghosts, mysterious disappearances, and other sensational and supernatural occurrences" (Abrams 72). Stories set in "a gloomy castle," often with "dungeons, subterranean passages" and hidden doorways, were designed to create a vicarious experience of terror (72). The term has been expanded to incorporate tales with a "brooding atmosphere" and events that are "uncanny or macabre [. . .] often deal[ing] with aberrant psychological states" (72).

8. Although the gothic tradition is not a common presence in previous children's series fiction, its influence can be traced in recent works. Gavin and Routledge theorize that "the current proliferation of series mystery novels such as R. L. Stine's Goosebumps and the Point Horror series [. . .] testify to a contemporary burgeoning of children's mystery literature" (4). The mysteries, they note, "tend to be supernatural in nature" (4). The gothic is incorporated in a muted way; the uncanny is not explained in a rational manner.

9. Rejecting the traditional approach to children's literature that "if you behave well, you'll be rewarded," Snicket draws on a Jewish tradition of "good behavior [as] more or less its own reward" ("Miscellany" 10). He does, however, suggest that children's literature can be entertaining and therapeutic. The Bad Beginning was published two years before the September 11 attacks. Nonetheless, critics have challenged the Snicket series in light of the tragic events. The author counters: "My young readers are not only finding a diversion in the melodrama of the Baudelaires' lives, but they are also finding ways of contemplating our current troubles through stories" (Handler A17). He insists "stories like these aren't cheerful, but they offer a truth—that real trouble cannot be erased, only endured" (A17).

10. Echoes of earlier didactic stories reverberate in Snicket's ironic fear that readers might use "this book as a pillow instead of as an entertaining and instructive tale to benefit young minds" (*Austere Academy* 193).

11. Olaf is labeled "the villain," but the absolute division of villain and hero is challenged by the series, particularly in the final six novels.

12. In book 13, the final volume, Olaf becomes a ridiculous rather than menacing figure—demanding a "shiny new car [. . .] to ram into people" in the middle of the ocean (10). The previously persuasive schemer is stymied by a six-year-old girl who politely but firmly disarms Olaf: "'What about me?' Count Olaf asked. His voice was a little squeaky, and it reminded the Baudelaires of other voices they had heard, from people who were frightened of Olaf himself" (*End* 42). Olaf is now the vulnerable one; he will soon be inconsequential. Olaf is injured in a failed attempt to gain control; his "story came to an end," and the children he had tormented "did not even notice when Count Olaf closed his eyes for the last time" (318). It is an anticlimactic exit for a character who loomed large throughout the series.

13. Audiences of series fiction are presumed to be a committed readership once past the initial book. This built-in progression permits the gradual introduction of more-demanding material—a process evident in the popular Harry Potter series. As the central characters mature, so do the readers (at least in theory). Publication schedules—1997, 1998, 1999, 2000, 2003, 2005, and 2007—have helped to shape Rowling's implied audience. In contrast the Snicket books have been released at a much faster pace: two books in 1999, two in 2000, three in 2002, one each in 2003, 2004, 2005, and 2006. The implied reader is faced with increasingly difficult material over a much shorter period. The pace does, however, slow as more threatening situations and moral ambiguities are introduced from book 8 onward. Of course, once the books are published the pace of reading is up to the individual. Watson astutely observes that reading a completed series is a different experience than reading a series that is in process: "For readers of a current series there is an additional factor: they cannot complete the narrative at their own pace but must wait. This waiting—with its accompaniment of [. . .] anticipation, marketing publicity, literary awards, film adaptations and journalistic speculation—becomes part of the reception process" (535–36). Influences beyond the written text can shape the reader's response.

14. MacLeod proposes that "the apparent purpose of children's books had shifted [from the 1970s onward] from protecting children from untimely knowledge of the dark side of life to acquainting them with the

worst that adult society can do and be" (107). The assertion borders on the melodramatic, and yet MacLeod's sense that concepts of "innocence" and "protection" have altered has merit. The Snicket series moves away from the scenarios she associates with early literature for children: mild and "probable within the realm of middle-class life" with "little that was really bad or deeply frightening" happening and "no fictional child [. . .] vulnerable to a dangerously warped or evil adult" (105).

15. The argument could be made that this tactic actually exposes the illusory nature of safe spaces. Their existence in nonexistent settings calls into question their possibility in the real world. Although this may be true, my focus is on the effect of the fictional setting in the midst of troubling story lines.

16. Moving through the series entails the acquisition of "knowledge"—through sporadic vocabulary lessons, ethical debates, and the (limited) unraveling of mysteries—but the novels also raise numerous questions that are (perversely) left unanswered.

17. McCallum identifies a "broader range of narrative and discursive techniques" used in "metafictive and experimental forms of children's writing" than in traditional works: "overly obtrusive narrators who directly address readers and comment on their own narration; disruptions of the spatio-temporal narrative axis [. . .] ; parodic appropriations of other texts, genres and discourses; typographic experimentation; mixing of genres" (139). Each of these elements is employed in the Snicket series; experimentation occurs in both form and content.

18. The veracity is, however, thrown into question by how the data are presented. Bal theorizes that "if the narrator wants to keep up with the pretence that it relates true facts, it can never represent the thoughts of actors other than itself" (136–37). Snicket moves beyond "verifiable data" in his accounts of the Baudelaire children; the reader is provided with what Snicket claims to be the thoughts and emotions of the central trio and other characters. There is a manipulative quality to Snicket's approach; McCallum's theory that "in experimental fictions narratorial and authorial intrusions often function quite overtly to position readers in relation to a text" (139) is applicable to this series. Snicket's perspective dominates.

19. "Too often," contends Henry Jenkins, "our culture imagines childhood as a utopian space, [. . .] beyond historical change, more just, pure and innocent, [. . .] waiting to be corrupted or protected by adults" (3–4). This concept becomes dangerous to the child when the responsibility is misconstrued as right of ownership—as it does when Count Olaf is granted guardianship and no one questions his parenting techniques. As

Mr. Poe explains, "Now that you are in his care, the Count may raise you using any methods he sees fit" (*Bad Beginnings* 66).

20. Snicket takes the mockery to another level. As Violet begins an invention, the narrative digresses: "We all know, of course, that we should never, ever [. . .] ever fiddle around in any way with electric devices" (153, 155). The ellipses here replace 207 "evers" utilized in the text. The power dynamic seems to shift as the knowledge ascribed to the adult issuing the warning is undermined by the implication that it is ridiculous. Such moments in the series suggest that readers have the ability to separate reality from the fictional events; the failure is on the part of adults who do not give them sufficient credit. In "Frightening News," however, Snicket provides evidence to the contrary. He recounts how after September 11 children wrote asking "if Count Olaf is a terrorist, if the Baudelaires were anywhere near the World Trade Center" (Handler A17). He uses the reference to indicate that children "are struggling with the same issues as the rest of us" (A17). True, but it also reveals that at least some of his readers may (for a variety of reasons) be having difficulty with, or be resistant to, distinguishing fact from fiction.

21. Also ambiguous are their parents: the siblings had "wanted to believe the best about their parents, but as time went on they were less and less sure" (*End* 17). In *The Bad Beginning* Mr. Poe explains that their will "instructs that [the children] be raised in the most convenient way possible [. . .] and this Count Olaf is the only relative who lives within the urban limits" (15). Relationships with subsequent guardians are increasingly unclear: Dr. Montgomery is their "late father's cousin's wife's brother" (*Reptile Room* 6); Aunt Josephine is their "second cousin's sister-in-law" (*Wide Window* 5); "a variety of distant relatives" reject the children, culminating with a "nineteenth cousin," Mr. Fagin! (*Vile Village* 10). "Convenience" and family values—the necessity to be situated within a family—render the children victims.

22. *The End* is further destabilized by the inclusion of "Chapter Fourteen" (labeled "Book the Last"). The thirteen-page addition follows a list of the series titles, a title page, copyright information, and a dedication. It hints at the fates of the Baudelaires and their daughter but remains inconclusive.

Works Cited

Abrams, M. H. *A Glossary of Literary Terms*. 5th ed. New York: Holt, 1998.
Anderson, Vicki. "Series Books." *The Dime Novel in Children's Literature*. Jefferson NC: McFarland, 2005. 126–31.

Bal, Mieke. *Narratology: Introduction to the Theory of Narrative*. Trans. Christine van Boheemen. Toronto: University of Toronto Press, 1985.

Brodie, Carolyn S., Kathy H. Latrobe, and Maureen White. *The Children's Literature Dictionary: Definitions, Resources, and Learning Activities*. New York: Neal-Schuman, 2002.

Cawelti, John G. *Adventure, Mystery, and Romance: Formula Stories as Art and Popular Culture*. Chicago: University of Chicago Press, 1976.

Chamberlain, Kathleen. "'Wise Censorship': Cultural Authority and the Scorning of Juvenile Series Books, 1890–1940." *Scorned Literature: Essays on the History and Criticism of Popular Mass-Produced Fiction in America*. Ed. Lydia Cushman Schurman and Deidre Johnson. Westport CT: Greenwood, 2002. 187–211.

Deane, Paul. *Mirrors of American Culture: Children's Fiction Series in the Twentieth Century*. Metuchen NJ: Scarecrow, 1991.

Gavin, Adrienne E., and Christopher Routledge, eds. *Mystery in Children's Literature: From the Rational to the Supernatural*. New York: Palgrave, 2001.

Handler, Daniel. "Frightening News." *New York Times* 30 Oct. 2001: A17.

Jenkins, Henry. "Childhood Innocence and Other Modern Myths." *The Children's Culture Reader*. New York: New York University Press, 1998. 1–37.

Johnson, Deidre. "From Abbott to Animorphs, from Godly Books to Goosebumps: The Nineteenth-Century Origins of Modern Series." *Scorned Literature: Essays on the History and Criticism of Popular Mass-Produced Fiction in America*. Ed. Lydia Schurman Cushman and Deidre Johnson. Westport CT: Greenwood, 2002. 147–65.

Lodge, Sally. "Breaking Out of Format Formulas." *Publishers Weekly* 9 Nov. 1998: 31–36.

MacLeod, Anne Scott. "An End to Innocence: The Transformation of Childhood in Twentieth Century Literature." *Opening Texts*. Ed. Joseph Smith and William Kerrigan. Maryland: Johns Hopkins University Press, 1985. 100–17.

Maguire, Gregory. "Children's Books." *New York Times* 15 Oct. 2000: BR 30.

McCallum, Robyn. "Very Advanced Texts: Metafictions and Experimental Work." *Understanding Children's Literature*. Ed. Peter Hunt. New York: Routledge, 1999. 138–50.

Merkin, Daphne. "Lemony Snicket Says, 'Don't Read My Books!'" *New York Times* 29 Apr. 2001: SM 162–65.

"Miscellany." *The Writer* 117 (Feb. 2004): 10–12.

Romalov, Nancy Tillman. "Children's Series Books and the Rhetoric of Guidance: A Historical Overview." *Rediscovering Nancy Drew*. Ed. Carolyn Stewart Dyer and Nancy Tillman Romalov. Iowa City: University of Iowa Press, 1995. 113–20.

Snicket, Lemony. *The Austere Academy*. New York: Scholastic, 2001.

———. *The Bad Beginning*. New York: HarperCollins, 1999.

———. *The Carnivorous Carnival*. New York: Scholastic, 2003.

———. *The End*. New York: HarperCollins, 2006.

———. *The Ersatz Elevator*. New York: Scholastic, 2002.

———. *The Grim Grotto*. New York: HarperCollins, 2004.

———. *The Hostile Hospital*. New York: Scholastic, 2002.

———. *The Miserable Mill*. New York: Scholastic, 2001.

———. *The Penultimate Peril*. New York: HarperCollins, 2005.

———. *The Reptile Room*. New York: Scholastic, 2000.

———. *The Slippery Slope*. New York: Scholastic, 2003.

———. *The Vile Village*. New York: Scholastic, 2002.

———. *The Wide Window*. New York: Scholastic, 2001.

Soderbergh, Peter A. "The Stratemeyer Strain: Educators and the Juvenile Series Book, 1900–1980." *Only Connect: Readings on Children's Literature*. Ed. Sheila Egoff, G. T. Stubbs, and L. F. Ashley. 2nd ed. Toronto: Oxford University Press, 1980. 63–73.

Watson, Victor. "Series Fiction." *International Companion Encyclopedia of Children's Literature*. Ed. Peter Hunt. 2nd ed. Vol. 1. New York: Routledge, 2004. 532–41.

3

The Power of Secrets

Backwards Construction and the Children's Detective Story

CHRIS MCGEE

"There are secrets everywhere," Quigley said.
"I think everyone's parents have secrets.
You just have to know where to look for them."
—LEMONY SNICKET, *The Slippery Slope*

As a narrative form, the mystery is structured around the distance between an event, most often a crime, and the revelation of secrets surrounding that event by the end of the story. Mysteries function by suspending knowledge, prolonging the uncertainty for pleasure. The joys of reading a good mystery reside in our drive to discover those secrets on our own, to read actively for the knowledge that has been withheld from us by a clever author, but also to have that knowledge delayed from us for as long as possible and for as long as is pleasurable. In *The Pursuit of Crime: Art and Ideology in Detective Fiction*, Dennis Porter describes this narrative distance as a "logico-temporal gap between a crime and its solution" (31), suggesting that the "crucial narrative principle" of the mystery tale is one of "deliberately impeded form" (30). Answers *are* given to us in a mystery, he argues, but "only after significant delay" since suspense "depends on something not happening too fast" (30). Porter calls this sort of narrative procedure the art of "backwards construction," arguing that "detective novels are constructed backward and are made up of progressive and digressive elements for the purpose of producing suspense" (33). Progressive elements drive us forward in our desire to know; digressive elements keep that knowledge just out of our reach until it is pleasurably revealed. Whether or not mystery writers have their endings in mind when they begin writing, as the old adage goes, endings do determine the structure and the pace of a mystery.

If the mystery form is comprised of hindrances, then one of the central concerns in discussing any particular mystery, particularly children's mysteries, must be what *sort* of hindrances are produced by the mystery writer that keep us from the knowledge we (and the detective) seek. To put it another way, we might ask: How are progressive and digressive elements developed in the narrative to allow secrets to be meaningfully suspended? What plot inventions and framing techniques are employed to delay our acquisition of crucial knowledge, what keeps us from the things we want to know, and to what degree does reader awareness of these tropes add to reader pleasure? Here I explore two children's series that employ hindrances in particularly interesting ways, the popular Harry Potter and Series of Unfortunate events books, mysteries in their own right that utilize long-delayed secrets as a compelling form of backwards construction that allows the authors to stretch an otherwise simple story into a lengthy mystery across many titles. These narrative devices as employed in these books are significant in that they demonstrate the ways in which the delay of secrets connects to much broader and deeper themes in children's detective fiction in general and the ways adult mystery conventions are transformed and altered as they are utilized in fiction for the young. George N. Dove, for example, describes a particularly excellent example of deliberately impeded form found in many adult mysteries in what he describes as "the death warrant": "The death warrant should be recognizable to any experienced reader: a detective in a story, working on an especially difficult case, receives a call from someone who has something vital to the solution of the mystery and is willing to pass it on; they make an appointment for a meeting, which the detective keeps only to find the prospective informant murdered and the important evidence missing" (82–83).

This is an easily predictable mystery element—most readers familiar with mysteries know that when a character announces that he or she knows who did it, that person is going to somehow end up dead. Although it may be predictable, the death warrant is an especially useful narrative technique in that it promises new answers in the form of an outside informant, but it never delivers. As readers we look forward to the answers this informant might give us, but his or her sudden death suspends those answers yet again. Because of their relative simplicity, both in terms of style and plot, children's mysteries are often dismissed as lacking this level of sophistication, in giving away secrets too quickly and too easily. Both Rowling and Snicket's books invoke this particular trope of delay by featuring crucial deaths in the opening scenes, by beginning when sets of parents die unexpectedly and tragically. Although the basic circumstances of their deaths are presented, there is much left unanswered early on, and the mysteries become murkier as the children become targeted by their parents' killers and the circumstances behind their deaths become more complex. Tragic orphans in children's books are of course certainly nothing new, but what marks these texts as *mysteries* in form is that both Harry and the Baudelaire orphans set out over the course of many books, through many tangential adventures, unraveling many secrets, to discover the simple truths behind these initial events: why did their parents have to die and what did their deaths have to do with their children? The opening deaths act as framing devices, plot elements used to bookend and contextualize all intervening plot, and they are nice ones at that. In Dove's terms these parents are informants, the characters who, above all, could give the detectives the information they want to know, yet they are killed before they can relay that information, shockingly early in the narrative. Their deaths provide a progressive drive in that we are compelled to figure out what they knew but sadly could never tell.

Like any good mystery, both of these series are driven forward by the readers' desire to better understand how they started, to circle back to the beginning, while both are held back by hindrances that suspend that knowledge in frustrating and pleasurable ways. The hindrances in these children's texts connect deeply with the nature of secrets, most particularly a desire *not* to know, not to relive such a terrible, unfortunate event. And in that sense these books explore issues very close to the heart of children's literature. As a genre the children's mystery raises concerns all its own, especially when the subject who desires to know is a presumably "innocent" child. Carol Billman cites psychoanalyst Lili Peller, who "has suggested that such stories about the noble uncovering of secrets are 'naturals' with children in the latency years, for whom life is full of secrets adults are guarding" (31). In "The Imaginative Use of Secrecy in Children's Literature," John Daniel Stahl discusses the power that secrets hold for children when those secrets are their own. He writes, "Secrecy is a means for fictional characters to create a meaningful sense of self, frequently in productive, not necessarily hostile, opposition to grown-ups or rivals" (44). All children's mysteries work through this fascination with secrets in one way or another, but unlike common serialized children's mysteries, about errant smugglers or lost objects, Rowling's and Snicket's books cast, as Billman suggests, their mystery elements onto those things that parents don't tell children, those most elusive, frustrating, and commonplace of secrets.

To add to this, as both series progress it becomes increasingly apparent that the parents weren't as innocent as they at first appeared, a key theme in both series. As Quigley Quagmire puts it in *The Slippery Slope*, all parents hide secrets from children, in one way or another, often because of cultural preconceptions that knowledge should be regulated around children. Often children's mysteries are structured around a longing for knowledge, but rarely have two children's mystery series been so dependent on parents who have so much to tell and who are so mysterious themselves. As Porter describes it, the mystery genre is "a genre committed to an act of recovery, moving forwards in order to move back" (29), and a genre that rests on a central paradox, that pleasure results to a large degree from the repeated postponement of a desired end. "The longest kept secrets," he writes, "are the ones we most desire to know" (50). Thematizing growing up as a process of coming to terms with parental deaths by finding out how they died, these two series traffic in long-kept secrets, drawn out over multiple books and published over several years. Although both of these series are progressively driven by their protagonists' desire to know those long-delayed secrets never revealed by the parents, they are also held back by the anxieties that come from learning the consequences of those secrets. So unlike in many simpler, more direct children's mysteries, the child detective in these stories may want to know the answer to an overarching mystery, but it sadly involves learning the answer to other secrets that he or she would just as soon not tamper with.

Harry Potter, Adult Secrets, and Forbidden Knowledge

These two particular series concern themselves with the secret world of adults and are necessarily bound up in questions of power. Christopher Routledge notes, for instance, how the theme of false accusation is rampant in Rowling's books, and thus "much of the detective work undertaken by the trio has to do with establishing the innocence of their friends" ("Harry Potter" 205), which often turn out to be the adult figures and surrogate parents in Harry's life. In one remarkable moment in *The Chamber of Secrets*, Harry sees a young Hagrid protecting a terrible monster and later deduces with his friends that Hagrid has hidden things about his past. Rowling writes, "The three of them fell silent. After a long pause, Hermione voiced the knottiest question of all in a hesitant voice. 'Do you think we should go and *ask* Hagrid about it all?'" (250, emphasis in original). Here Hermione's "knotty" question is an important one when thinking about mysteries:

Do children have a right to become involved in adult problems, and more provocatively, should they confront adults with what they know about them? What inherent boundaries are crossed when children seek out knowledge themselves?

While the Harry Potter books explore the trickiness of adult secrets, the Series of Unfortunate Events books by contrast play with the dangers of knowledge by imbedding warnings into their marketing and advertising themselves as dangerous books, incredibly unpleasant reads, inappropriate for child readers because of the terrible endings. Lemony Snicket exaggerates the conventions of mystery and gothic narratives in order to mock them, the most noticeable example being the dire predicaments in which the orphans often find themselves. Backs of books continually warn readers away, repeatedly reminding them that they'd be better off reading something else, that they are only going to be disappointed if they expect happy endings, that there must be something better to do with their time. The playful but simultaneously dour *Lemony Snicket: The Unauthorized Autobiography* (2002) ups the ante of the subversive potential of reading something that you are not supposed to by being packaged like a questionable item you would receive in the mail, wrapped in nondescript brown paper and packing tape. The inside warns that "the book you are holding in your hands is extremely dangerous" especially if "the wrong people see you with this objectionable material."

In these ways both of the series knowingly play with the nature of secrets and knowledge, and both are driven by the power relationships between adults (and adult authors) who hold that knowledge and the children who seek it out. However, while both of these series work their way through initially similar progressive and digressive elements, the two series are most distinct in regard to the questions of who has knowledge and how it is given to the reader, two key considerations when thinking about how children's mysteries operate. As the Harry Potter books progress, they become increasingly author-driven, singular objects in which knowledge rests more and more in authoritative hands. A perfect corollary of this at the level of plot appears in *Harry*

Potter and the Order of the Phoenix (2003). Early on in the book, Sirius Black (Harry's godfather, adoptive father, and embittered protector) and Mrs. Weasley debate whether Harry should be included in the discussions of the mysterious Order, a group of wizards and witches gathered together to fight the Dark Lord Voldemort and his Death Eaters. Mrs. Weasley, worried about "telling Harry more than he *needs to know*" (88, emphasis in original), urges Sirius to be careful about revealing too much too soon to a boy who already seems overwhelmed. Mrs. Weasley urges Sirius to remember the strict lines between adult and childhood domains of knowledge. There is an age, after all, at which one is entitled to know, and Harry has not yet reached it according to Mrs. Weasley. Sirius, enraged that Harry has to face so many traumas without the knowledge by which he might prepare himself, exclaims, "He's not a child!" to which Mrs. Weasley replies, "He's not an adult either!" (88–89). This turns out to be a common dilemma for Harry.

Routledge writes, "Detective fiction for children often explores the differences and tensions between adulthood and childhood" ("Children's Detective Fiction" 64). During a lengthy confessional toward the end of *The Order of the Phoenix*, we discover that many of Harry's problems come because Dumbledore has struggled with many of the same questions voiced earlier in our discussion: what to tell Harry and when. In stark contrast to this hesitant approach to knowledge, the child characters consistently take it upon themselves to find what they need throughout the series. Conjuring up a Requirement Room, Harry and his friends set out to learn what they need to know to battle forces that the changing institutional powers of Hogwarts have deemed either nonexistent or beyond the concern of children. Still, Dumbledore admits to Harry near the end of the book that he "cared more for [Harry's] happiness than [Harry] knowing the truth" (838), a tricky moral dilemma that seems to suggest mutually exclusive states of blissful ignorance and debilitating awareness. We know, of course, that the binary is not so simple, as Harry faces any number of problems despite not knowing their purpose in his life. For Harry there is no state of blissful ignorance. Much of the weighty plots of Rowling's books concerns the pursuit of the forbidden, often portrayed in the books as a worthwhile, liberating, and sometimes necessary endeavor. The trapdoor in the first book represents just such a dilemma, presented as a forbidden room but one that Harry must enter to protect his friends and solve the mystery.

Yet *The Order of the Phoenix* goes so far as to suggest that these pursuits can sometimes be misguided, especially when Harry's visit to the Department of Mysteries turns disastrous and, in terms of the plot, completely unnecessary, or when Harry discovers repressed memories (not his own) that raise doubts about his own father. Such knowledge, it turns out, makes for a much more complex world. And Sirius's claim that Harry *is* old enough to know reveals something about the underlying ideology of the books. In Sirius's mind, especially as he emphasizes that Harry is no longer a child, the most important thing to consider in all of this is Harry's age. In Jack Cawelti's terms Harry's investigations are in fact more indicative, formulaically, of the hard-boiled era of detective fiction in which the "hard-boiled detective sets out to investigate a crime but invariably finds that he must go beyond the solution to some sort of personal choice or action" (142). Harry does indeed suffer from what he learns; the knowledge Harry gains at the end of the mystery is nearly the opposite of liberating: discovering that his actions have been prophesized, that his life will culminate in either murder or his own death regardless of how he acts. It is a realization matched with all the things Harry has already learned in his mysteries: there is no one he can completely trust, people die, he can never recover the past, and evil comes in many forms.

Lemony Snicket and the Metaphysical Form

In contrast to the type of detection Rowling's series offers, Patricia Merivale and Susan Elizabeth Sweeney describe metaphysical, and by extension what we might call "metafictional," detective stories as being those that "explicitly speculate about the workings of language, the structure of narrative, the limitations of genre, the meanings of prior texts, and the nature of reading" (7). Here the Lemony Snicket series differs noticeably from the Harry Potter titles. One of the predominant preoccupations of the Lemony Snicket books is a feeling of conspiracy, of paranoia, of an avalanche of information hinting at a grand connection that is just out of reach. True, Harry is left alone upon Dumbledore's death and must find the mysterious horcruxes on his own, most of which he has no direct knowledge of, but there are tangible answers to his questions and to ours as readers. This is hardly ever the case in the Lemony Snicket series, which is far more representative of metaphysical detection for children. The series is in fact metaphysical detection of the most childish type, one that transfers the paranoia that characterizes adult noir onto the hegemonic relationship between child and adult, reader and author, and onto the schemata of the institutional insistence that children read only certain sorts of material and that material please and comfort, educate and instruct. The tropes of adult noir fiction—uncanny feelings, inaccessible authority, the defeated sleuth, empty and meaningless daily activity, the vagueness of clues, the "absence, falseness, circularity, or self-defeating nature of any kind of closure to investigation" (Merivale and Sweeney 8)—circulate throughout the books. Merivale and Sweeney write: "In metaphysical detective stories, letters, words, and documents no longer reliably denote the objects that they are meant to represent; instead, these texts become impenetrable objects in their own right. Such a world, made up of such nameless, interchangeable things, cries out for the ordered interpretation that it simultaneously declares to be impossible" (9–10). The sorts of stories Merivale and Sweeney most often refer to are those of postmodern writers such as Thomas Pynchon or Jorge Luis Borges, but Snicket's series is often as experimentally avant-garde as anything in adult fiction, employing a range of self-referential narrative techniques, in fact often paying homage to other avant-garde writers. In a particularly clever nod to Pynchon's novel *V.*, for instance, one of the most important clues throughout the series is the group of letters V.F.D., presumably the name of an organization or group of people that, the Baudelaires are led to believe, had something to do with their parents' death. With each book, the siblings encounter any number of places or situations that have these letters, from the Village of Fowl Devotees to the Volunteers Fighting Disease, all of which seem to have nothing to do with anything remotely related to the mysteries. This running joke picks up speed by the tenth book, so that nearly everything the Baudelaires encounter has, in some way or another, those initials. They encounter the Valley of Four Drafts, Verdant Flammable Devices, and Vertical Flame Diversions. When they eventually encounter Quigley Quagmire, the lost Quagmire triplet, and ask him what he knows about the organization, he replies, "It seems to stand for many things. . . . Nearly everything the organization uses, from the Volunteer Feline Detectives to the Vernacularly Fastened Doors, has the same initials" (166). When, finally, he suggests that the letters probably stand for Volunteer Fire Department, something we have been led to believe all along, Violet is noticeably disappointed, frustrated that answers are not only troublingly elusive and slippery but also rarely satisfying. Such a moment raises questions about whether knowledge is worth seeking if it so disappointing and unhelpful. "I always thought that knowing what the letters stood for would solve the mystery," Violet complains, "but I'm as mystified as ever" (*Slippery Slope* 167).

Readerly and Writerly Tendencies

Porter argues that the mystery, in using progressive and digressive techniques toward pleasurable ends, is a preeminent example of a "readerly" form (82), a term utilized by Roland Barthes. Readerly texts, to use Barthes's meaning, are fully formed texts by the time they reach the reader's hands, texts designed by an author explicitly for consumption by the reader. In the readerly text, experiences, emotions, meanings, and reactions are prepared, nuanced, and manipulated by a trustworthy author for the reader's devouring. Such texts, by their nature, encourage passivity and a rigid contract between knowing author and willing participant. Preferring the term "readable" as opposed to "readerly," Porter writes: "A detective novel is the most readable of texts, first, because we recognize the terms of its intelligibility even before we begin to read, and second, because it prefigures at the outset the form of its denouement by virtue of the highly visible question mark hung over its opening" (86).

Writerly texts, on the other hand, test the limits of intelligibility by insisting on our participation in their creation, and have the characteristics of a pre-text, a preformed experience that needs the reader to create it. Meaning has not been predesigned by the author, and as such the text encourages activity, insisting that the reader become a coauthor and coproducer of the text.

Much evidence suggests that the Harry Potter books encourage active reader participation, encouraging and rewarding analysis. In *Re-Reading Harry Potter*, Suman Gupta describes the books using Umberto Eco's terms of "open texts" and "closed texts." Open texts are those that "can be read (interpreted) at a range of different levels," and thus our "pleasure derives to a large extent in the very act of negotiating between the different and even contrary ways in which sense can be made of them" (30). Yet these lines of authority within the Harry Potter books—who has knowledge, how they reveal it, how it is temporarily suspended for our pleasure—are clearly demarcated, even if they occasionally blur. In almost every way our readerly pleasure resides in seeing what Rowling is going to come up with, what she will allow us to know and when; our pleasure is predicated on the pleasing hegemonic relationship of an author who enticingly keeps us in our comfortable albeit anxious place. Sure, we may wonder who is going to die, but we rarely wonder if our questions will be answered. Although both of these series fluctuate around the progressive and digressive elements integral to the mystery form and participate in various ways in both readerly and writerly tendencies, the Harry Potter books tend more toward the readerly tradition, especially in the ways that Rowling's books operate more traditionally. Look no further than the reborn Dumbledore in Rowling's last book, resurrected to explain nearly every possible answer to Harry, or the comforting epilogue providing readers with even further closure.

The Lemony Snicket books, on the other hand, tend more toward the writerly end of the spectrum in several ways. *The Unauthorized Autobiography*, in particular, encourages active reading practices by coding information (underlined words, poorly glossed illustrations) and providing texts as though we are already supposed to know how to read them, as though there are always deeper levels, even going so far as to suggest that earlier books in the series have a code imbedded in them that can be deciphered whenever we encounter a bell that has chimed. The Snicket books never neglect the physicality of the reading process, always reminding us that we are reading a book, that decisions have to be made, that a text is something created for purposes that have to be deciphered and thought through. David Lewis, in reference to children's picture books, describes a few of these narrative techniques that might be generally called postmodern. He argues that these techniques in children's books emphasize a "refusal to take for granted how stories should be told and thus implicitly comment upon the nature of fiction itself" (260). These techniques include breaks from what we would expect a controlling and capable narrator to do, such as providing too much information, what he calls "narrative gigantism" (261), or giving too little information. In similar ways the Lemony Snicket books play with narrativity and metafictionality much more thoroughly than do the Harry Potter books, which only seem to hint at the possibility. The books concern themselves with the difficulty and slipperiness of knowledge.

The Unauthorized Autobiography is ostensibly a collection of information found in a file in "a box that contained a key which in turn unlocked another box that contained the information that makes up this book" (xv). It is a loose hodgepodge of scraps, blurry photographs, bits of text, scratched out documents, obscure artifacts, and more. The various chapters are titled after our most pressing questions, such as "why is Lemony Snicket on the run?" or "are the Baudelaire parents really dead?" (xviii–xix). Rather than answer these questions, the editor crosses them out, revising seemingly pertinent literal questions to create more abstract metatextual ones of representation. The book is refocused, expanded outward; Snicket (who is the narrator, editor, and executor of this information) tells us in a note, "These are simply not the proper questions" (xviii). Instead of answering the dominant question of chapter 1 (why was Mr. Snicket's death published in the newspaper?), the narrator provides a picture of a small baby and asks in a handwritten note, "Who took this?" (1). Instead of subsequently asking, "Who is this picture of, what does it have to do with the books, why are we looking at it," the question rather highlights and attends to questions of intentionality and subjectivity. The opening pages of *The Unauthorized Autobiography* remind us that "just because you read something printed on a page does not mean that it is true" (xi).

The readers sense that they cannot have access to what they most want to know, not simply because the author won't provide it but often because that information has been destroyed or is known only to certain sources. At different times Snicket often gives us far more than we would want to know, such as a moment of narrative giganticism in *The Slippery Slope* when the narrator repeatedly lists all the ingredients on a shelf in an unnecessarily thorough list. As a mystery concerned with epistemological questions of what knowledge is, who is in charge of it, and what it means to the knower, Lemony Snicket's books are, to use William V. Spanos's term, an "anti-detective story," a series of puzzles and clues that, to use his words, "evoke the impulse to detect . . . in order to violently frustrate it by refusing to solve the crime" (qtd. in Merivale and Sweeney 3). By running with the idea of the inaccessibility of knowledge and its hopeless circularity in multiple discourses, the book seems to have hit upon connections between the theme of childhood and detection and epistemological issues—problems of ideology and identity imbedded in the reading process itself.

Snicket plays with his narrative role in several ways: by overtly exaggerating it, making himself a character who reluctantly tells a story he knows will end badly; by making it seem strangely hazardous, as though he is in constant danger; by emphasizing the flawed nature of his prejudiced perspective, since he is deeply involved and has clearly lost someone close to him; and by toying with the role of an objective mystery genre narrator who is supposed to reveal information in a certain way. In fact it seems clear that the narrator here is one who could reveal information at any point he would like, and he often does in passing slips. This is a narrator who could explain the entire mystery in a few lines if he wanted, so the impediments to his doing so seem to come from the books' sentiments about the nature of knowledge rather than from any half-joking worry that the information is just too horrible for children to know, too difficult for them to handle. The books depict for us an elusive author who seems to be in constant and imminent danger, mediated through both pseudonym and "editor," resisting and mocking our desires to trust the author, to be rewarded for our readerly trust, to be comforted by what we read, a desire to know, a desire for pleasure, a desire to scapegoat villains, and in turn be innocent ourselves. What we get instead is an elusive, slippery, frustrating, confusing set of texts that make readers wonder if they will ever eventually know anything.

Children's Detective Fiction
and the Desire to Know

Billman argues that children's mysteries are especially useful for their readers in developing literacy skills because of the genre's "implicit command to readers to participate in the guessing game of detection" (30). Because mysteries have such an explicit and repeatable form, in which meaning-making processes are closely connected with what she calls the "psychological comfort" of resolutions and the reassurance of identifiable patterns, the genre can "help to solidify for the inexperienced reader the elements and patterns of fictional narrative" (34). "There is very little that is surprising," she argues, once one becomes familiar with the mystery form, especially serialized titles like *Nancy Drew* in which similar events happen in only slightly different contexts from book to book (33). Since readers don't have to attend to complex plots, mysteries foreground metareading processes, which attend to larger patterns and forms that underpin literary structures in general. By reading increasingly complex types of mysteries, she argues, the child reader develops into a sophisticated reader of not only plot but other literary conventions as well. These stories "urge upon their readers [a] constant balancing of the mysterious and the recognized, of the unsettling unknown and the reassuring known" (37).

Both of these series, in their preoccupation with the pleasures to be found in delaying secrets, offer these benefits. The Lemony Snicket books certainly indulge in the pleasure of deferral, but they also explode any notion of stability. They count on their readers' awareness of narrative conventions and the pleasure to be found from confusion, from feelings of conspiracies, and riddles without answers. At the other end of the spectrum, one gets the sense that Rowling has a long story to tell, and it simply takes a while to tell it. But in the end she is the only one who can tell it. It is, in fact, because her answers are so complex and delayed so long that we grow to trust her even more. So in their form and content these two series are similar and also strikingly dissimilar. The Harry Potter books are built around readerly pleasure embedded in the mystery form, with its delayed secrets, its capable narrator, its potent author, its complex world of villains and heroes. True, Harry is deeply troubled by the secrets he finds, particularly as those secrets shatter his comfortable and nostalgic view of his parents, but the Lemony Snicket books are built around openly discouraging the most typical of pleasures by installing and subverting the mystery form, playing with an intrusive and hardly capable narrator, secrets that are slippery and elusive, and a repetitive form that pushes its readers away more than it draws them in. What accumulates in the Lemony Snicket series is in fact a sort of process of defamiliarization in which it is hard to ever look at the mystery form in precisely the same way again. What accumulates in the Harry Potter series is a reinvestment in the mystery form, a delight in its ability to ground a fabulously complex story, to entice our readerly desires, and to reward them, albeit slowly. They are, to use Roger Caillois's phrasing, a part of the pleasure that the mystery form offers in "relation to the mathematical puzzle and the chess problem" (9). The Lemony Snicket books foreground narrative forms in order to seemingly dismantle them, while the Harry Potter books sublimate their narrative tropes in invisible ways so that they seem more capable than ever to convey a good story.

There is of course much to admire in the Harry Potter books. As carefully constructed, well-plotted, broad fantasy pieces, they are far more sophisticated than the Lemony Snicket books and will no doubt have a much more prominent place in the canon of children's literature in the decades to come. As mystery pieces that use magical metaphors to speak of the painful truths of growing up, they are striking examples of the potential of children's mystery stories. Yet, despite their progressive tendencies or occasional narrative playfulness, in comparison to the Lemony Snicket books they far more thoroughly reinvest the adult world with power, for the adults in the books, for the author creating it, and for the children reading them. Our hindrances to knowledge, those digressive elements, arise in the Harry Potter books because of sensitive, caring adults, as well as an all-knowing author and a lengthy story to tell. The Lemony Snicket books are not nearly as sophisticated or developed or even substantially literary, but because they aim at unintelligibility and playfulness and because they thematize their mystery around the inaccessibility of knowledge, this lack of literariness is understandable. They are far more serialized and indebted to overt genre tropes, and they insist on repeatability as a consequence of that. But the hindrances to knowledge they produce come from much different sources and in much different forms, and in many ways prove to be more satisfying in strikingly different ways. Both books begin with the death of parents and take long, circuitous paths to the revelations of secrets behind their deaths. But they arrive in much different places regarding the nature of knowledge, the nature of secrets, and the power (or lack of power) of the storyteller. If anything the questions here say something about the nature of mystery series as they grow, how they build our desires only to stretch them out over time, delaying them for as long as possible and as long as is pleasurable. The Harry Potter books promise that it was all worth the wait by the time we reach the end. The Lemony Snicket books, on the other hand, suggest that we probably would have been better off worrying about something else.

Works Cited

Barthes, Roland. "Style and Its Image." *Literary Style: A Symposium*. Ed. and trans. Seymour Chatman. London: Oxford University Press, 1971. 3–15.

Billman, Carol. "The Child Reader as Sleuth." *Children's Literature and Education* 15.1 (Spring 1984): 30–41.

Caillois, Roger. "The Detective Novel as Game." *The Poetics of Murder*. Ed. Glenn W. Most and William W. Stowe. New York: Harcourt, 1983. 1–12.

Cawelti, John G. *Adventure, Mystery, and Romance: Formula Stories as Art and Popular Culture*. Chicago: University of Chicago Press, 1976.

Dove, George N. *The Reader and the Detective Story*. Bowling Green OH: Bowling Green State University Press, 1997.

Gupta, Suman. *Re-Reading Harry Potter*. New York: Palgrave, 2003.

Lewis, David. "The Constructedness of Texts: Picture Books and the Metafictive." *Signal* 61 (1990): 131–46. Rpt. in *Only Connect: Readings on Children's Literature*. Ed. Sheila Egoff et al. 3rd ed. Oxford: Oxford University Press, 1996. 259–75.

Merivale, Patricia, and Susan Elizabeth Sweeney. "The Game's Afoot: On the Trail of the Metaphysical Detective Story." *Detecting Texts: The Metaphysical Detective Story from Poe to Postmodernism*. Ed. Patricia Merivale and Susan Elizabeth Sweeney. Philadelphia: University of Pennsylvania Press, 1999. 1–24.

Porter, Dennis. *The Pursuit of Crime: Art and Ideology in Detective Fiction*. New Haven CT: Yale University Press, 1981.

Routledge, Christopher. "Children's Detective Fiction and the 'Perfect Crime' of Adulthood." *Mystery in Children's Literature: From the Rational to the Supernatural*. Ed. Adrienne E. Gavin and Christopher Routledge. New York: Palgrave, 2001. 64–81.

———. "Harry Potter and the Mystery of Ordinary Life." *Mystery in*

Children's Literature: From the Rational to the Supernatural. Ed. Adrienne E. Gavin and Christopher Routledge. New York: Palgrave, 2001. 202–09.

Rowling, J. K. *Harry Potter and the Chamber of Secrets.* New York: Scholastic, 1999.

———. *Harry Potter and the Order of the Phoenix.* New York: Scholastic, 2003.

Snicket, Lemony. *Lemony Snicket: The Unauthorized Autobiography.* New York: Harper Collins, 2002.

———. *The Slippery Slope.* New York: Scholastic, 2003.

Stahl, John Daniel. "The Imaginative Uses of Secrecy in Children's Literature." *Only Connect: Readings on Children's Literature.* Ed. Sheila Egoff et al. 3rd ed. Oxford: Oxford University Press, 1996. 39–47.

PART TWO

※

Approaches to the Picture Book

This part moves us from a larger discussion of genre into a more specific look at the structural form that is unique to children's literature. This part is the book's largest in acknowledgment of the picture book's importance as a unique genre within a genre. In fact the picture book in many ways defines the larger genre and points to the unique and special qualities and issues related to studying children's books. When people think of "children's books," they often think of the picture book. The relationship of image to text found in the picture book is weighty with narrative implications. These five essays examine the narrative peculiarities of picture books in a number of different ways.

The section begins with Angela Yannicopoulou's broad discussion of the ideological implications for different focalization strategies found in picture books. "Focalization in Children's Picture Books" shows the complicated tensions and complementarity to be found between visual and verbal texts. Following that essay is Magdalena Sikorska's focused discussion of the strategies of voice (polyphony), space, and narrative time in a particular picture book. "No Consonance, No Consolation: John Burningham's *Time to Get Out of the Bath, Shirley*" demonstrates the possibilities for the genre. Alexandra Lewis's essay, "Telling the Story, Breaking the Boundaries: Metafiction and the Enhancement of Children's Literary Development in *The Bravest Ever Bear* and *The*

Story of the Falling Star," introduces the special nature of metafiction in picture books and considers the matter of irony and the child reader. What are we to think about both the implied audience and the real audience of children when we confront irony, parody, metafiction, shifting narrative view, and other literary features that the common reader doesn't associate with child readers, especially the youngest of readers? From there we read Andrea Schwenke Wyile's consideration of implied readership and the assumptions that we make about children as readers of sophisticated, abstract, and "dark" materials. In "Perceiving *The Red Tree*: Narrative Repair, Writerly Metaphor, and Sensible Anarchy," Wyile asks what it means for children to read picture books that don't simply follow conventional wisdom about safe forms for the child reader. Stories that offer counter narratives can encourage children to truly encounter a text because complicated, highly metaphoric, and unfamiliar text formats require active reading. We end with an essay by Nathalie op de Beeck that further examines the tendency of both critics and noncritics to assume that anything for children is simplistic. "Now Playing: Silent Cinema and Picture-Book Montage" is a study of the relationship between film and picture books that reveals their shared techniques in blending visual and written texts, playing with the paratext, and experimenting with the narrative matters of chronology, space, and time.

4

⁊☙

Focalization in
Children's Picture Books

Who Sees in Words and Pictures?

ANGELA YANNICOPOULOU

In our image-dominated era, it is important to examine who sees, since, as Gunther Kress and Theo van Leeuwen note, "Seeing has, in our culture, become synonymous with understanding. We 'look' at a problem. We 'see' the point. We adopt a 'viewpoint.' We 'focus' on an issue. We 'see things in perspective.' The world 'as we see it' (rather than 'as we know it' and certainly not 'as we hear it' or 'as we feel it') has become the measure for what is 'real' and 'true'" (168). It seems that, either in life or in literature, the consideration of the viewpoint from which certain events are seen has become more and more important.

Thus it is not surprising that the long-standing distinction between "who speaks" and "who sees"—in other words, who relates the story facts and through whose eyes the narrator focalizes them, respectively—has become extremely important with regard to literary works. Gérard Genette coined the abstract term mainly because it solves the problems of "the too specifically visual connotations of the terms *vision, field,* and *point of view*" (*Narrative Discourse* 189).[1] Later Genette himself considered his question "who sees?" too narrow and purely visual and replaced it with "who perceives?" and then with "where is the focus of perception?" (*Narrative Discourse Revisited* 64).

However, since not everyone agrees with Genette on focalization, a post-Genettean argument, based largely, at least at the beginning, on Mieke Bal's critique, is currently taking place.[2] Different narratologists use different terms—for example, Franz Stanzel talks about "first-person," "authorial," and "figural narrative," while Seymour Chatman proposes the terms "slant" and "filter"—in an attempt to describe focalization more adequately.[3] Furthermore, other types of focalization not mentioned by Genette have also been added, such as "collective focalization" (Stanzel, Banfield) through either plural narrators ("we" narrative) or a group of characters ("collective reflectors"), "hypothetical focalization" (Herman, Fludernik) through a hypothetical observer or a virtual spectator who describes events as if they might have been perceived, and "empty center focalization" (Banfield, Fludernik) that is normally observed in scenic descriptions when no character is present and, in spite of deictic words, presented from the point of view of an empty center.

Different Kinds of Focalization
in Picture Books

Although it has been argued that in picture books "we should probably treat the words as *primarily* conveying the narrative voice, and pictures as *primarily* conveying the point of view" (Nikolajeva and Scott, *How Picturebooks Work* 117), it is more accurate to say that picture books require the cooperation of two modalities, verbal and visual, to establish an inherently dialogic relationship leading to the transformation of the textual space into a fertile "arena of conflict between two voices" (Bakhtin 106). Especially in cases where the respective written and illustrated narratives employ different focalization options, the picture book, an inescapably plural genre, results in "irony," as Perry Nodelman uses the term, as an inherent tension between words and pictures.[4] This "irony" that comes from the genre's plurality makes picture books a thought-provoking and rewarding genre for all ages. Different focalization strategies in picture books provide the reader-viewer with different information ranging from a more restrictive to a more encompassing presentation and interpretation of the fictional universe.

In both his *Narrative Discourse* and *Narrative Discourse Revisited*, Genette provides the basis for a systematic taxonomy of modes of perspective, defining three basic kinds of focalization based on the relationship between the narrator and the central fictional hero(es): nonfocalization, internal focalization, and external focalization. It seems that picture books will not avoid demanding types of focalization, allowing, as Margaret Meek asserts, the texts to teach what readers need to know.

Nonfocalization or Zero-Focalization

A narrative that presents a story without points of view of the characters, is a nonfocalized story. The characters remain focal points and are never focalizers. In cases of nonfocalization (or zero-focalization), the narrative presents the story events from a completely unrestricted point of view. This type of focalization has been the one most commonly used in children's literature.

In picture books facts, events, and even thoughts are related in a rather authoritarian and objective manner. The written text describes, in the third person, the words and deeds of others, and the visual narrative delineates the same events while observing them from outside, from a distance.

Both narratives, written and illustrated, obtain access to and acquire a total knowledge of characters—their acts and their deeper thoughts—establishing a somewhat authoritarian and unquestionable text that discourages the reader-viewer from doubting the provided facts. Although narrated words can't completely objectify characters and facts, nor can illustrations reveal them, words and pictures together present the narrated description and the illustrated reality as equally unquestioned and confident.

Internal Focalization

In internal focalization, "vision from within," the narrator is equivalent to the hero(es) regarding perspective; here Genette draws heavily on Boris Uspensky's discussion of an internal character's point of view (88). There is no single term to refer to a focal character, who is also called a "filter" (Chatman), a "figural medium" (Stanzel), a "self" (Banfield), or a "focalizer" (Bal). With regard to picture books, the written and the illustrated narratives seem to agree on the identity of the focalizer(s) and see the story events through her or his (or their) eyes.

Fixed Internal Focalization

Fixed internal focalization occurs when the presentation of events is restricted to the point of view of a single focal character. According to Stanzel's taxonomy, Genettean "fixed internal focalization" can be either a first-person or a figural narrative situation. In cases of relevant or restricted omniscience, the narrator, functioning as a "limited observer," sees in the fictional universe through the eyes of a certain story agent, knows whatever she knows, believes in what she believes, and feels whatever she feels (Rimmon-Kennan 77). Because the narrator, and consequently the reader-viewer, has no direct access to events that the focalizer does not witness in person, this type of focalization is liable to certain limitations, such as restriction from "bilocation" (the ability to be in two places at the same time), the "other minds" problem (no access to the thoughts of other characters), or the restriction from future knowledge. Often fixed focalization presents a restricted or a distorted view of the events.

The focalization process is distinct from the process of narration, however. There are picture books in which the narrator is external, and although the verbal narrative adopts an objective, external tone (third person) and the visual text includes the focalizing character as the main person in every scene (third-person illustration), the fictional world is presented, both verbally and visually, as it is seen through the character's own eyes (e.g., Anthony Browne's *Willy the Wimp*). Thus although the focalized hero is presented in every picture (third-person illustration), she as well as the whole world are depicted as she views it, regardless of whether it is true.

On the other hand, in some other picture books in which the

character narrator relates the story facts in the written text as her personal experiences and perceptions, the illustrations present them externally.[5] The first-person verbal narrator (the "I" who acts, thinks, and talks) is accompanied by a visual narrative that sees not through the eyes of the focal hero but externally. In Anthony Browne's *Into the Forest*, for example, a first-person verbal narrator is accompanied by a visual narrative that includes him in every picture. Thus the reader-viewer of the book does not see with the boy's own eyes but observes him from outside in a filmlike fashion. "As we've seen again and again, the presence of pictures turns first-person narratives into heterodiegetic dramas that establish the extent to which reading a picture book is more like watching a play than reading a novel" (Nodelman, "Eye and the I" 20).

Finally, there are books in which both narratives, written and illustrated, see the story facts through the eyes of a story character and speak with her voice. The narrator prefers to speak in first person, gaining the status of the internal focalizer, and the visual narrative has adopted her aspect of the fictional world presenting it as she sees or perceives it. Anthony Browne's *My Dad* is a splendid example of a book with fixed internal focalization through the narrating character of a loving son who adores his father presented verbally and pictorially in the form that his son has endowed him. Since the narrator-character-focalizer whose perception orients the presentation is the child, and the focalized object (what the focalizer perceives) is his father, the reader-viewer is encouraged to adopt the subjective standpoint of the son and sees the father through the eye and the "I" of the child hero. The internal focalizer is usually the smallest and the least powerful character—a young child, a personified animal, or an animated toy—in order for its own childness to be stressed and the child reader's identification with her encouraged.

Some picture books, however, prefer to watch the world through the eyes of the Other, blocking any possibility of identification by creating for the reader-viewer a sense of unfamiliarity. These are books in which the ordinary becomes extraordinary and familiar is made unfamiliar. In Chris Van Allsburg's *Two Bad Ants*, the world is presented by the outsider's point of view and through unusual angles and perspectives. As the two ants enter the bizarre world of a kitchen and a breakfast table, they find themselves in an eerie landscape where they have to cope with unexpected perils, such as "a giant scoop" (we see a spoon in the illustration) and a "brown, hot lake" (a cup of coffee). A simple, in human terms, walk from the yard to the kitchen is transformed into a life-threatening excursion in the ants' terms. Portrayed in strong pen-and-ink images, the book adopts the ants' view of a huge, dangerous world and becomes an interesting visual puzzle for the reader-viewer, who sees again the old familiar surroundings through the eyes of tiny ants.

Variable Internal Focalization

Variable internal focalization alternates perspective among several focal characters, each of which perceives different focalized objects. Variable focalization is also called "shifting" focalization (Randall), thus placing considerable emphasis where it belongs: on the characters.

A distinct example of variable focalization is found in the twin books *Le loup est revenu!* (The wolf is back!) and *Je suis revenu!* (I am back!), by Geoffroy de Pennart. The same events are presented through two different focalizers. Resembling Durrell's four books of *The Alexandrian Quartet*, Pennart's books succeed in offering a panoramic view of reality through two internal focalizers. In the first book the narrator, in both words and pictures, sees through the eyes of the rabbit and relates, in the third person, the agony and the panic of the wolf's intended victims as they try to protect themselves from their enemy's return. In the second book the wolf, who acts, mainly in the verbal text, as an internal focalizer, delineates the supplementary events concerning his preparations and unsuccessful attempts to catch them. In the first book the innocent creatures are informed about the wolf's return and seek refuge in the rabbit's house; in the second the partially drawn image of the story world is completed when the reader-viewer observes the wolf's failure to obtain his objectives.

If each book is read independently, there is one fixed internal focalizer, either the rabbit or the wolf, who sees those story events that he is able to know. But if they are read in parallel, the readers see the pictorial similarity of protagonists and settings and the nearly identical final pages: the focalization moves from fixed internal to variable. The two books, though each one is limited to the events that each focalizer knows, when read together, result in a complete plot-puzzle and a prismatic vision of one fictional universe. Although each focalizer is able to see some aspects of the reality, the reader-viewer is the only one who, after evaluating the story fragments, manages to get the whole truth.

Multiple Internal Focalization

When identical fictional events are focalized by different focalizers, we have multiple internal focalization. Not everyone accepts multiple as a special kind of focalization but rather considers it a case of variable focalization (Chatman, "Characters and Narrators" 201). However, the difference between variable and multiple focalization is based on the focalized objects; while in variable focalization the various focalizers observe different, complementary story events, in multiple focalization all of them are present for the same event and portray the same event differently. The text presents the event repeatedly, each time seen through the eyes of a different internal focalizer. Either in films (see *Rashomon*, by Akira Kurosawa), or especially in electronic literature, where using the "switch point of view" link re-presents the whole story from another focalizer's viewpoint. The same incidents presented through different perspectives create an intricate web of human perception and understanding that endows the reader-viewer with a prismatic view of reality.

In Anthony Browne's *Voices in the Park*, a brief journey to a city park is recounted by four different persons: a bossy mother, her lonely son, an unemployed father, and his cheerful daughter. In four short first-person narratives, each character narrator provides four unique aspects of his or her encounter with the others and their dogs. At a different emotional level, their perspectives are reflected in the shifting landscapes and seasons; annoyance for the woman in the fall, boredom at first and later hope for the boy in the spring, depression for the man in winter, joy for the girl in the summer. Four different voices and visions mirrored in four different fonts recount the same facts, which seem different because they are seen through different eyes.

Moreover, in the picture-book domain, Catherine Heller's *The Untold Story of Snow White* renarrates the same familiar events of the traditional tale twice: from the hero's and the villain's standpoints, respectively. Along with Snow White's well-known version of the fictional events, her stepmother explains the difficulties of raising a stubborn stepdaughter, offering plausible excuses for every event concerning the old fairy tale. The book's reproach to the dominance of a single perspective is reflected in its striking flip-around format that encourages the reader-viewer to turn the book upside down and back to front in order to get, along with the traditional story related by the hero, the reverse version of it offered by the long silent antihero. The device is brilliant for it manages to parallel the physical action of the reader with the metafictional technique of reversing the truth of the tale.

External Focalization

In narratives with external focalization, characters know more than the readers, and a riddlelike picture book is constructed; a twist at the end of the narrative normally occurs. Since a series of purposely misleading elements, both verbal and visual, escapes the attention of the reader-viewer, she becomes unable to evaluate them correctly and judge their full implications. In books with external focalization, the reading route takes the form of a round trip; as soon as the reader-viewer reaches the last page and discovers its surprising end, she feels compelled to turn again to the beginning, searching for clues revealing or concealing the main character's secret, which had remained unnoticed until the end. The reader-viewer attempts repeated scannings of both text and illustrations and, scrutinizing and reevaluating the story elements, reconstructs a new fictional universe.[6] In similar innovative picture books, it is obvious that neither the text nor the pictures lie. The clues, mainly visual, were always there, but the reader-viewer neither understood them sufficiently nor deciphered them correctly.

In Ruth Brown's *One Little Angel*, the surprising ending changes the story, showing that things are never quite as they appear. A magical twist at the end relocates the story in a different time and space—from the sky to the earth and from Jesus's birth to the present day. As the reader-viewer's previous certainties regarding the story theme are dismantled, it is revealed that the narrative is about not Jesus's birth but a school's Nativity play. At text level the reader is trapped in a series of misunderstandings by words with double meanings, such as "Gabriel," a name ironically shared by the biblical angel and the school principal. At a pictorial level the viewer is "deceived" first by the warm watercolor-and-acrylic illustrations that provide a golden warm glow and render a divine cast of characters vulnerable and lovable; the reader is also "deceived" by the blank stage backdrop into thinking that the characters are in heaven. The third "deception" comes either from the distant "scene-shots" or the "close-ups," which successfully conceal the difference not only between a real angel and a tousle-haired child in an angel costume but also between a spiritual halo and its wired imitation. In picture books with external focalization, both the written and the illustrated narratives establish a tone of uncertainty as they violate the conventional hierarchy, which wants the narrator and the reader-viewer to know more than the story agents. In stories in which things are never as they appear, nobody can be sure about the truth.

*Discrepant Modes of Focalization in
the Verbal and Visual Tracks*

Since in some picture books the two narratives, written and illustrated, make different choices regarding voice (*voix*), tense (*temps*), or mood (*mode*), a fascinating interplay between words and images is established. In cases where the focalizing options happen to be different in the two narratives, there is established a highly ironic tone—as Nodelman defines "irony." As the picture books "prise open the gap between the words and the pictures, pushing them apart," the reader-viewer is forced "to work hard to forge the relationship between them" (Lewis, "Constructedness of Texts" 141).

The most common case of different choices regarding focalization occurs when the written narrator sticks to a fixed internal focalization, while the illustrations view the situation externally and present events that even the main hero or verbal focalizer is unconscious of. Ellen Raskin's *Nothing Ever Happens on My Block* is one of the most outstanding examples. The first-person character narrator, positioned in the foreground facing the reader, constantly complains about the monotony of his life, while in the background a panorama of exciting events take place. In a striking example of dramatic irony, the six-year-old Chester Filbert is unaware of events that the viewer of the book knows due to the illustrations that present the story from outside and above. As different modalities stick to different focalizers and pictures constantly undermine the hero's words, the relationship between them becomes highly ironical (Nodelman, *Words about Pictures* 193–222).

The different options regarding focalization between the written and the illustrated narratives also create books that relate the same events from two different perspectives; the written text constantly echoes the view of one fictional hero, while the illustrations delineate the same events as perceived through the eyes of another story agent. As the reader shares one aspect of fictional reality communicated to her by the verbal internal focalizer, and the viewer shares a contrasting one while observing the scenes through the eyes of a visual focalizer, the reader-viewer simultaneously shares the two contradictory versions of the story. Once again the written text constantly disagrees with the illustrations and vice versa, establishing an ironic relationship between words and pictures (Nodelman, *Words about Pictures* 193–222). Similar books recall David Lewis, who considers that a picture book "always has a double aspect, an ability to look in two directions at once and to play off the two perspectives against each other" so that a picture book "is not just a form of text, it is also a *process*, a way of making things happen to words and to pictures" ("Going Along with Mr Gumpy" 109–10).

In the well-known book by Satoshi Kitamura, *Lily Takes a Walk*, the straightforward written text adopts young Lily's perspective of her stroll through the town, while the simple, child-like pictures present her dog's view of it.[7] The smiling child's confident walk as narrated by the written text is complemented by illustrations of the imagined monsters (e.g., a snake, a mailbox with teeth, the Loch Ness monster) as seen through the eyes of her anxious-looking dog, Nicky. Thus an interesting interplay between the real and the imaginary, the focalizer of the written and the illustrated narrative, the words and pictures, is created. The device remains constant throughout the book, even after their return home, when Lily recounts to her parents her experiences (written text), whereas Nicky reviews his terrifying encounters in image balloons. In the so-called perspectival counterpoint, a dynamic relationship develops "where words and images collaborate to communicate meanings beyond the scope of either one alone" (Nikolajeva and Scott, "Dynamics of Picturebook Communication" 226). As the inherent, ironical interconnection between words and pictures is once again reinforced, the difference between two focalizers, one of the written and the other of the illustrated narrative, builds an absorbing story and creates a rewarding reading experience. When reality is presented through the eyes of two focal characters, certainties seem rather impossible.

Ideological Implications

Ideology is interwoven, either explicitly or implicitly, into every text in the sense that events are seen in terms of a certain value system (Shavit 112–13; Stephens 8). As Aidan Chambers observes, "Every story, every poem, every piece of literary writing carries a message, even if the writer doesn't know it's there. All works of literature are moral systems: they will, without exception and however slightly, deal in the stuff of life and the nature of being"

(12). Either as an affirmation of the dominant ideology or as a total questioning of it, reading literature "is a social transaction" (Inglis 67), and it seems that the moral imperative is present in all picture books; the extent to which this is explicit varies (Marriot 1–24).

Although, according to Shlomith Rimmon-Kenan, focalization is in itself nonverbal ("seeing") as opposed to narration ("speaking"), in the verbal texts focalization can be expressed only through language (82), a factor replete with ideological implications.[8] On the other hand, visual images are also a vehicle for conveying ideological issues, especially as they evoke affective responses from the viewers.

Different types of focalization bear various ideological implications. In zero focalization, where a godlike narrator reports the facts without the apparent subjective intervention of an internal focalizer, the story, and consequently its prevailing ideology, gains the status of an undeniable authority and the authenticity of an objective presentation. Since the omniscient narrator, possessing an unrestricted knowledge about the represented world, seems neutral or uninvolved, the cultural norms are usually taken as authoritative and become transparent and invisible, especially when the fictional facts are confirmed by the visual narrative, which acquires more objectivity than it might already naturally have. In picture books with zero focalization, things are presented as "they are" and nobody has the right to doubt.

On the other hand, the privileged position that the focalizing hero occupies within the character constellation of a narrative text (internal focalization) elevates the status of her beliefs compared to those of the other heroes. As Mieke Bal states, "If the focalizer coincides with a character, that character will have a technical advantage over the other characters. The reader watches with the character's eyes and will, in principle, be inclined to accept the vision presented by that character" (*Narratology* 104). Because the story facts are presented both verbally and visually through a single dominant perspective, all the other ideologies exposed in the text are evaluated from this enhanced angle.

Consider this in contrast to a godlike narrator who offers the reader a somewhat detached viewpoint. When the story facts are presented almost entirely through the consciousness of a single character, the audience will be more likely to sympathize with her, even to accept her beliefs. Although internal focalization does not present the world with infallible authority and provides the readers the right to disagree with the focalizer, readers seem apt to accept the focalizer's version of reality.

The immediacy imposed on the reader by a fixed, single viewpoint can be reinforced by unframed illustrations that call the viewer to step into the fictional universe (Moebius 150); this facilitates the identification of the reader-viewer with the focalizer, a process that may encourage the acceptance of the focal hero's ideological commitments. It seems that the more a character is "subjectified—made into a subject" and "given an active human consciousness"—the more a reader will identify with that agent, especially if the character-bound narrative is communicated by a first-person presentation (Lanser 206).

On the other hand, narratives with focalization through the Other provide an interesting example of the ideological implications of fixed internal focalization. In children's books where the world is presented through the eyes of the Other (e.g., an alien, an insect), the reader-viewer is forced to see the everyday world from a fresh, new standpoint where the familiar becomes strange, the natural unusual, the unquestionable debatable, and the transparent visible. In books where the focal character is a cultural outsider (see, for example, Jeanne Willis's *Dr Xargle's Book of Earthlets*, where a zany, extraterrestrial pedant describes the Earth's more bizarre species, babies, and the baby-parent relationship), "the 'automatic' view of culture and history becomes decentered, its hegemonic perspective called into question and ultimately undermined and substantially altered" (Fisher 164). Focalizing through the "different hero" results in defamiliarization and the reexamination and reevaluation of dominant cultural values.

The internal focalizer does not simply impose her ideological beliefs on the reader-viewer, however. The text's focalizer is undermined when the panoramic illustrations are in counterpoint; this allows the reader-viewer to know more than the verbally focalizing hero, and therefore the focalizer's ideological assumptions are proved extremely unreliable. It seems that when dramatic irony is established, the reader-viewer is invited to question written narrative's ideological configurations. When the reader-viewer constantly affirms her intellectual superiority over the written text's focalizer, the textually expressed ideological assumptions are not likely to make serious claims for validity and authority. While words ask readers to empathize with the story protagonist—she is a child or childlike—pictures invite viewers to be detached and remain outside observers. Because pictures show more than what the protagonists see, they result in pushing the reader-viewers away from identification with a verbal text's focalized protagonist. Thus, although visual text is considered childlike, it actually operates as a second focalization revealing the limitations of the innocent perceptions of children, both intratextual characters as well as extratextual readers. Thus these books assume "not only that child-readers can change but they must, since the ability and inevitability of change is part of what defines them as children. Childhood is a time when people change" (Nodelman, *Hidden Adult* 31).

In other cases internal focalization is selected in order to accommodate those disputed ethical and social assumptions with which the author herself prefers not to be connected. Internal focalization, especially in the first-person narratives, is purposely chosen by the author, who is conventionally connected to a third-person, external narrator, in order to express controversial beliefs without their being credited to her. The beliefs of the traditional antihero-focalizer—the wolf in John Scieszka and Lane Smith's *The True Story of the Three Little Pigs*—are presented in a highly individualized tone, while the irony that constantly hides behind his words weakens his argument.

Furthermore, picture books like *The True Story of the Three Little Pigs* show that although fixed internal focalization bears an inherent tendency toward monological and single-stranded speculations, an alternative standpoint (to that of the famous traditional tale "The Three Little Pigs"—not included but presumably familiar to the reader) provides a constant dialogue between the focalizer of the new text and the omniscient narrator of a well-known pre-text. Thus the restrictions concerning the single point of view, which consequently limit the possible ideological assumptions available to reader-viewers, are replaced by ideological alternatives that provide polyphony. Intertextual connections invite the reader-viewer to consider the traditional story in a more critical way, including its ideological implications.[9] Reading the multiple versions of the same story events seems to evoke literary insights that would have been missed had the events been presented singly.

Moreover, contemporary picture books for young children dare even variable and multiple focalizations. Multi-viewpoint stories present, through a pluralistic narrative, different and even contradictory aspects of the same events by denying a dominant standpoint of a single focalizer. Different viewpoints construct polyprismatic facts and establish a celebration of ambiguities and uncertainties. As subjectivity is stressed in literature, a pervasive insecurity about reality is inevitably implied.

The same sense of subjectivity is also communicated by picture books with external focalization. In books that have an unexpected twist of their plotlines toward the end of the narrative, the main ideological implications seem to be that things are not always as they appear. As the reader-viewer realizes that both she and the narrator know less than the story agents, who constantly lead them into a series of misunderstandings, rigid certainties are washed away, solid beliefs fade, and an inconsistency between how events seem and what they really are is gradually established. Since in picture books with external focalization the narrator, and consequently the reader-viewer, become those who are last to learn, the normal hierarchy is challenged, the conventional authoritative relationships are reexamined, and the ideological superiority of anyone is no longer credited a priori.

Although children's picture books have been considered simple or even simplistic, in fact they have been proved a particularly interesting and ambitious genre that lends itself readily to serious critical analysis. Regarding focalization even picture books for young children are not limited only to easily comprehensible types but offer their reader-viewers more demanding ones, educating them to become more competent. As Nodelman argues, "In treating children like children, we may well doom them to a conviction in and inability to transcend their inadequacy" ("Other" 32), and our assumptions about children tend to create self-fulfilling prophecies. The more acquainted children are with multilayered picture books, the deeper and richer are their responses (see Arizpe and Styles). Since an important criterion for selecting a picture book is not to make it "easy for you to find things: but to make us think more" (Kiefer 280), children learn to read critically by reading widely, and thus they grasp sophisticated theoretical models and become aware of how discourse acts upon them.

Children's books inevitably convey, explicitly or implicitly, certain ideological assumptions, even through the options of focalization. A current trend toward polyphonic narratives in picture books reveals an intention to encourage children to become competent readers and critical of their own reading process. As Peter Hollindale states, "Our priority in the world of children's books should not be to promote ideology, but understand it, and find ways of helping others to understand it, including the children themselves" (10). It seems that, along with focalizing options that challenge monological approaches, picture books, based on two modalities, by their very nature do not lend themselves to single presentations. The double narrative of every picture book, written and illustrated, inherently results in the multiple depiction of a polyprismatic reality that symbolically implies the passing from one Truth to many personal truths.

Notes

1. Gradually the term gained predominance over others, like "perspective," since it can be easily rendered as a verb or a noun. Also, as a techni-

cal term derived from photography, it fits well in the technical character of narratology (Bal, "Narrating and Focalizing").

2. Bal emphasizes focalizing subjects and focalized objects and the restrictions of the perceptible and imperceptible objects. She disagrees with Genette on the issue of external focalization, a type that, as she asserts, is based on confusion between the subject (who sees) and the object of focalization (what is seen). In contrast she talks about external focalization (outside the narrative) and internal focalization (participates as a character). For an adequate and comprehensible review of focalization, see Jahn, *Narratology* N3; and Jahn, "Focalization." On post-Genettean focalization theory in English, see Bal, *Narratology*; Herman; Jahn, "Windows of Focalization"; O'Neill; Rimmon-Kenan; Ronen; Toolan.

3. Stanzel places great emphasis on *mediacy*, which describes the degree of revelation or disclosure of the voice of the narrator to her readers, and proposes a typology of a threefold distinction between (a) first-person narrative situation, where the narrative "I" (the narrator) is also an experiencing "I" (a character); (b) figural narrative situation, which is heterodiegetic-overt with the story presented as seen through the eyes of a character; and (c) authorial narrative situation, which is heterodiegetic, and the story is presented by an authorial narrator who knows everything. Chatman argues that the phrase "point of view" has multiple meanings, such as "perspective," "stance," and "interest." He proposes that the narratorial point of view be called "slant," that is, "the psychological, sociological and ideological ramifications of the narrator's attitudes, which may range from neutral to highly charged" (*Coming to Terms* 143).

4. "Because they communicate different kinds of information and because they work together by limiting each other's meanings, words and pictures necessarily have a combative relationship; their complementarity is a matter of opposites completing each other by virtue of their differences. As a result, the relationships between pictures and texts in picture books tend to be ironic: each speaks about matters on which the other is silent" (Nodelman, *Words about Pictures* 221). For more about "irony," see Nodelman, *Words about Pictures* 193–222.

5. See the spectrum of homodiegetic narrators in Lanser 160.

6. The most striking example of external focalization is *The Murder of Roger Ackroyd*, by Agatha Christie.

7. For a discussion of the book, see Doonan; Nikolajeva and Scott, *How Picture Books Work*; and Arizpe and Styles.

8. Both Stephens (*Language and Ideology*), who analyzed narrative techniques from an ideological point of view, and Knowles and Malm-

kjaer (*Language and Control*), who carried out a linguistic analysis of ideology of children's books, affirm that children's literary texts inevitably communicate ideological beliefs.

9. See Beckett's *Recycling Red Riding Hood* for a discussion of how retellings reveal ideology. See also Crew.

Works Cited

Arizpe, Evelyn, and Morag Styles. *Children Reading Pictures: Interpreting Visual Texts.* London: Routledge, 2003.

Bakhtin, M. M. *Problems of Dostoevsky's Poetics.* Trans. R. William Rotsel. Ann Arbor MI: Ardis, 1973.

Bal, Mieke. "The Narrating and the Focalizing: A Theory of the Agents in Narrative." Trans. Jane E. Lewin. *Style* 17.2 (1983): 234–69.

———. *Narratology: An Introduction to the Theory of Narrative.* Trans. Christine van Boheemen. Toronto: University of Toronto Press, 1985.

Banfield, Ann. *Unspeakable Sentences: Narration and Representation in the Language of Fiction.* London: Routledge, 1982.

Beckett, Sandra. *Recycling Red Riding Hood.* London: Routledge, 2002.

Brown, Ruth. *One Little Angel.* London: Andersen, 1994.

Browne, Anthony. *Into the Forest.* London: Walker, 2005.

———. *My Dad.* London: Picture Corgi, 2001.

———. *Voices in the Park.* New York: DK, 1998.

———. *Willy the Wimp.* London: Julia MacRae, 1984.

Chambers, Aidan. "The Difference of Literature: Writing Now for the Future of Young Readers." *Children's Literature in Education* 24.1 (1993): 1–18.

Chatman, Seymour. "Characters and Narrators: Filter, Center, Slant, and Interest-Focus." *Poetics Today* 7 (1986): 189–204.

———. *Coming to Terms: The Rhetoric of Narrative in Fiction and Film.* Ithaca NY: Cornell University Press, 1990.

Christie, Agatha. *The Murder of Roger Ackroyd.* Pocket, 1939.

Crew, Hilary. "Spinning New Tales from Traditional Texts: Donna Jo Napoli and Rewriting of Fairy Tale." *Children's Literature in Education* 33.2 (2002): 77–95.

Doonan, Jane. *Looking at Pictures in Picture Books.* Essex: Thimble, 1993.

Durrell, Lawrence. *Balthazar.* 1958. Harmondsworth, England: Penguin, 1991.

———. *Clea.* 1960. Harmondsworth, England: Penguin, 1991.

———. *Justine.* 1957. Harmondsworth, England: Penguin, 1991.

————. *Mountolive.* 1958. Harmondsworth, England: Penguin, 1991.

Fisher, Leona W. "Focalizing the Unfamiliar: Laurence Yep's Child in a Strange Land." *MELUS* 27.2 (2002): 157–77.

Fludernik, Monica. *Towards a "Natural" Narratology.* London: Routledge, 1996.

Genette, Gérard. *Narrative Discourse: An Essay in Method.* Trans. Jane E. Lewin. Ithaca NY: Cornell University Press, 1980.

————. *Narrative Discourse Revisited.* Trans. Jane E. Lewin. Ithaca NY: Cornell University Press, 1988.

Heller, Catherine. *The Untold Story of Snow White.* Illus. Karen Stolper. Secaucus NJ: Carol, 1995.

Herman, David. "Hypothetical Focalization." *Narrative* 2.3 (1994): 230–53.

Hollindale, Peter. "Ideology and the Children's Book." *Signal* 55 (1988): 3–22.

Inglis, Fred. "Reading Children's Novels: Notes on the Politics of Literature." *Children's Literature in Education* 2.2 (1971): 60–75.

Jahn, Manfred. "Focalization." *The Cambridge Companion to Narrative.* Ed. David Herman. Cambridge: Cambridge University Press, 2007. 94–108.

————. *Narratology: A Guide to the Theory of Narrative.* 26 May 2009. http://www.uni-koeln.de/~ame02/pppn.htm.

————. "Windows of Focalization: Deconstructing and Reconstructing a Narratological Concept." *Style* 30.2 (1996): 241–67.

Kiefer, Barbara Z. "Children's Responses to Illustration: A Developmental Perspective." *Journeying: Children Responding to Literature.* Ed. Kathleen E. Holland, Rachel A. Hungerford, and Shirley B. Ernst. Portsmouth NH: Heinemann, 1993. 267–83.

Kitamura, Satoshi. *Lily Takes a Walk.* New York: Dutton, 1987.

Knowles, Murray, and Kristen Malmkjaer. *Language and Control in Children's Literature.* London: Routledge, 1996.

Kress, Gunther, and Theo van Leeuwen. *Reading Images: The Grammar of Visual Design.* London: Routledge, 1996.

Lanser, Susan. *The Narrative Act: Point of View in Prose Fiction.* Princeton NJ: Princeton University Press, 1981.

Lewis, David. "The Constructedness of Texts: Picture Books and the Metafictive." *Signal* 61 (1990): 131–46. Rpt. in *Only Connect: Readings on Children's Literature.* Ed. Sheila Egoff, et. al. 3rd ed. Oxford: Oxford University Press, 1996. 259–75.

————. "Going along with Mr Gumpy: Polystemy and Play in the Modern Picture Book." *Signal* 80 (1996): 105–19.

Marriot, Stuart. "Picture Books and the Moral Imperative." *What's in the Picture? Responding to Illustrations in Picture Books*. Ed. Janet Evans. London: Paul Chapman, 1998. 1–24.

Meek, Margaret. *How Texts Teach What Readers Learn*. Woodchester, England: Thimble, 1988.

Moebius, William. "Introduction to Picturebook Codes." *Word & Image* 2.2 (1986): 141–58.

Nikolajeva, Maria, and Carole Scott. "The Dynamics of Picturebook Communication." *Children's Literature in Education* 31.4 (2000): 225–39.

———. *How Picturebooks Work*. New York: Garland, 2001.

Nodelman, Perry. "The Eye and the I: Identification and First Person Narratives in Picture Books." *Children's Literature* 19 (1991): 1–30.

———. *The Hidden Adult: Defining Children's Literature*. Baltimore: Johns Hopkins University Press, 2008.

———. "The Other: Orientalism, Colonialism, and Children's Literature." *Children's Literature Association Quarterly* 17.1 (1992): 29–35.

———. *Words about Pictures: The Narrative Art of Children's Picture Books*. Athens: University of Georgia Press, 1988.

O'Neill, Patrick. *Fictions of Discourse: Reading Narrative Theory*. Toronto: University of Toronto, 1994.

Pennart, Geoffroy de. *Je suis revenu!* Paris: L'Ecole des Loisirs, 2001.

———. *Le loup est revenu!* Paris: L'Ecole des Loisirs, 2004.

Randall, Neil. "Shifting Focalization and the Strategy of Delay: The Narrative Weaving of 'The Fionavar Tapestry.'" *Canadian Literature* 129 (1991): 40–54.

Raskin, Ellen. *Nothing Ever Happens on My Block*. New York: Atheneum, 1978.

Rimmon-Kenan, Shlomith. *Narrative Fiction: Contemporary Poetics*. London: Methuen, 1983.

Ronen, Ruth. *Possible Worlds in Literary Theory*. Cambridge: Cambridge University Press, 1994.

Scieszka, Jon, and Lane Smith. *The True Story of the Three Little Pigs*. New York: Viking, 1989.

Shavit, Zohar. *Poetics of Children's Literature*. Athens: University of Georgia Press, 1986.

Stanzel, Franz, K. *A Theory of Narrative*. Cambridge: Cambridge University Press, 1986.

Stephens, John. *Language and Ideology in Children's Fiction*. London: Longman, 1992.

Toolan, Michael. *Narrative: A Critical Linguistic Introduction*. London: Routledge, 1988.

Uspensky, Boris. *A Poetics of Composition*. Trans. Valentina Zavarin and Susan Wittiq. Berkeley: University of California Press, 1973.

Van Allsburg, Chris. *Two Bad Ants*. Boston: Houghton, 1988.

Willis, Jeanne. *Dr Xargle's Book of Earthlets*. Illus. Tony Ross. London: Andersen, 1988.

5

No Consonance, No Consolation

John Burningham's Time to Get Out of the Bath, Shirley

MAGDALENA SIKORSKA

The interpretation of childhood and children's literature seems to be immune to change, at least a radical change, and traditions and stereotypes appear to dwell longer than in other social and cultural areas.[1] This is most probably why much of the subversiveness embedded in childhood and its folklore, culture, and literature passes unnoticed, frequently labeled safely as either "humor" or "fantasy." John Burningham's *Time to Get Out of the Bath, Shirley* is subversive, very serious, and although it employs numerous fantastic elements, the conclusions and meaning are painfully realistic. The book undermines several pivotal assumptions associated with children's literature, picture books in particular, and penetrates the dark side of the world of childhood by deconstructing the taboos of emotional rejection and isolation within a family environment.

Design and Plot

To reach the full meaning-making potential of Burningham's picture book and the mechanism behind its polyphony or multivocality, we should start with clarifying the design and plot intricacies. Not only is *Shirley* a multistranded narrative that incorpo-

Are you listening to me now, Shirley?

rates one written and two distinct pictorial story lines; it is also a rare example of a picture book whose particular stories, with a few exceptions, do not overlap except in time.[2] To a great extent the book's polyphonic canvas resembles Witold Lutosławski's counterpunctual technique called "controlled aleatorism."

Shirley features the eponymous young girl and her mother at bath time. While physically Shirley is taking the bath in the family's bathroom, metaphorically she sets off on a fantastic journey, accompanied first by her rubber duck, then by a knight on a horse, and finally, before "coming back home," she is entertained by a royal couple.

The picture book is built on a curious temporal and spatial frame: the beginning and the ending of a child's bath. Only the book's points of departure "from" and return to the frame show more than one narrative story line; the first page reveals the coexistence of the verbal and one of the visual layers and two elements of foreshadowing toward the other pictorial story, a rubber duck and a towel (see fig. 1), while the concluding page includes elements of both pictorial stories but lacks the verbal one. All other pages of the book split into three ostensibly independent stories elaborately composed within the aforementioned frames.

Two of the three story lines, one verbal and the other pictorial, are interconnected through Shirley's mother; they are organized within one picture frame, and with the exception of the opening of the picture book, they appear on the left-hand page. Conversely, Shirley's image-only story occupies the right-hand position in the book, juxtaposed radically with the mother's stories. To signal a further plot complication, there is hardly any thematic correspondence between the mother's story lines and Shirley's visual narrative.

Even more interestingly the mother's pictorial and verbal narratives do not tell exactly the same story and often depart from each other. The written text consists of short sentences, either affirmative or interrogative, whose main objective is to confirm the stereotype of a dissatisfied and tired mother who is ready only to complain about her daughter's absent-mindedness, carelessness, or misbehavior. Clichés such as "You really ought to have a bath more often, Shirley," or "I have better things to do than run around tidying up after you" address the stereotype most forcefully. While the verbal line of the mother's story is mainly concerned with complaints and often alludes to the fact that the mother perceives herself as a victim of the household routine, at the same time several scenes of the mother's visual story show her as a woman preoccupied with watching her figure or relaxingly combing her hair.

The verbal and the visual of the left-hand side (or the mother's) story are juxtaposed in a noticeably ironic manner. Analyzing the verbal text of the mother's story and its dissonant relation to the visual line, one has an impression that the mother is not fully in control of what she is actually saying aloud, and her monologue sounds dangerously automatic and perhaps ironically unself-conscious. Being physically present in the bathroom where her daughter is taking a bath, she seems to inhabit a world of her own, as if unaware of the daughter's presence.

Curiously enough, Shirley's presence is even more problematic; the girl, who is the only addressee of her mother's remarks and complaints, seems to inhabit a completely different world.

I have better things to do than run around tidying up after you

Already in the second illustration (the right-hand story is transmitted solely through pictures with no accompanying words), she is depicted escaping through the water pipes, riding her rubber duck, and heading toward a fantastic world. In the latter part of her story, she travels through a world inhabited by knights, a king, and a queen set in an unspecified historical past. The girl concludes her imaginary journey conquering the queen and the king in an amusing water battle. The last image shows her back in the bathroom, where her mother is silently waiting for her with a towel.

Problematic Causality

Burningham's picture book is innovative in its challenge to conventional causality. Traditional picture books addressing younger readers frequently exhibit high fidelity toward the cause-effect structure of the story, which can be checked using a simple test of jumbling the sentences or pictures in a given picture book and then restoring the previous order. The task usually proves to be an easy one, as many clues are present to help the attentive reader-viewer recapture the book's original story and layout. *Time to Get Out of the Bath, Shirley* does not allow the reader to enjoy similar comfort.

Shirley's visual narrative is mostly organized according to the chronology of the girl's fantastic journey, with only a few illustrations clearly revealing their position within the book. The mother's double story (visual and verbal) would allow complete freedom on the reader's part were it not for the fact that the book is bound in a given order and the reading chronology is thus technically imposed. Jumbling the mother's story lines (with the exception of the first and the last illustrations) would demonstrate how her narratives challenge the traditional concepts of chronology and causality. Some points in the mother's and Shirley's stories are very loosely interlinked in a way that can be compared to the cinematic technique of a "match cut," a sequence of two shots of totally different scenes where two objects in both scenes "are 'matched,' so that they occupy the same place in the shot's frame" (Felluga), becoming for a moment one of the focal points of the scenes. To illustrate this point, it is worth considering Burningham's use of the word and image of "soap" as the focal point at the beginning of the book.

On the second page of the picture book, the mother says to her daughter, "You haven't left the soap in the bath again, have you?" and the left-hand picture, which is part of Shirley's story, shows a bar of soap left in the bath and the girl escaping through a water pipe. The match cut employed allows the reader-viewer to perceive the images in both stories as interrelated, though clearly not in a traditional, logical, or chronological way. Developing the cinematic allusion a bit further, we should note the picture book's striking unsuitability for traditional animation; the perceived unsuitability is a direct result of the book's problematic causality.

Multivocality, Dissonance, and
Controlled Aleatorism

In Burningham's picture book, the design and the metaphor go hand in hand, revealing a highly specialized form of artistic harmony, which, quite paradoxically, is rooted in contradiction and dissonance. The form, showing the complexities of a polyphonic or multivocal technique of controlled aleatorism, opens the book toward a figurative reading of its multiple-meaning potential.

The concepts of polyphony or dialogism in literature originated in Mikhail Bakhtin's writings, and it should be stressed that the terms refer more to a characteristic type of thinking, a philosophy of creation, than to an artistic technique. The central aspect of literary polyphony is a plurality of voices and perspectives within a single work of art; what is more, the plurality is not an interpretative option, as "everything in the novel is structured to make dialogic opposition inescapable" (Bakhtin 18). Although Bakhtin developed his theory analyzing the novels of Fyodor Dostoevsky, his concepts are to a great extent universal, and children's picture books display a variety of possibilities for application of these ideas.[3]

In *Time to Get Out of the Bath, Shirley*, Burningham, through a highly specialized form of polyphony, a type of counterpunctual technique called "controlled aleatorism," makes the reader-viewer forget about the possibility of a classical consonance between the (multi)visual and the verbal. The adoption of the technique allows the author to compose a multilayered story in which the relationship between particular narrative lines is uniquely complex.

The aleatory technique appeared in music only in the twentieth century, and "controlled aleatorism" was mostly developed by Witold Lutosławski. It was also described as one of the controlled chance techniques, on the one hand, giving particular voices a significant independence and high individuality and, on the other, retaining authorial control over pivotal points in a given composition. Aleatorism is built on a paradox where the work's polyphony is achieved through the layering of independent, individual strands. Controlled aleatorism also entails the use of sophisticated parallelisms, both rhythmical and concerning the work's pace.[4]

Controlled aleatorism is in many aspects a twin artistic solution to Bakhtin's dialogism. Both are rooted in the juxtaposition of individual, musical, or in the case of Burningham's picture book, narrative lines; both depend not on traditional causality but rather on the coexistence of highly independent elements arranged around a few pivotal points such as the opening and the close of the artistic work (in Burningham's *Shirley* the opening and the closing illustrations incorporate at least two of three story lines) and the rhythm of the consecutive pages. Characteristically, in both aleatorism and dialogism the more evident or dominant effect is that of a dissonance and lack of coherence between particular lines, which stimulates the listener or the reader-viewer to seek the work's meaning.

The rhythm of Burningham's *Shirley* is patterned according to a truly aleatoric method. There are just a few points where it has been coordinated: for instance, there is coordination at the opening and the closing of the book and at moments when Shirley's and the mother's stories have been interlinked through the match cut. Otherwise, particular story lines realize individual rhythmical patterns, which in effect are divergent. While Shirley's story seems to be the more dynamic one, with many events happening and long distances covered, the mother's both visual and verbal narratives are very static; the pace is slow, and the character's movements very limited, for the mother uses mainly her hands and arms (combing her hair, folding the daughter's clothes).

Graphic Dissonance

The significantly incoherent story lines of the mother and the daughter reveal the physical and metaphorical gap between the characters. The communication distance between the pair is not only strengthened by separating their stories into left- or right-hand sides, but it is also visually supported by the existence of rough black frames drawn only around the mother's story lines. No contact seems possible; no consonance, only the segregating dissonance, everything and everybody different placed within a single time framework.

The depiction of the (generation?) gap is successfully executed by Burningham's use of color. The dullness of the mother's auto-

You really ought to
have a bath more
often, Shirley

matic monologue is harmonized with her stories' visual background; the wall and floor tiles in the bathroom are arranged
with an uneventful regularity in a checked pattern, while in some
other illustrations the mother's comments are synchronized with
the whiteness of the background to suggest the emotional void
behind them (Shirley's backgrounds are colorful). Generally, the
mother's pictorial story line shows few elements and minimal
detail, with blue (the mother's clothes), gray, and pale yellow
being the dominant colors. It is undoubtedly significant that the
mother is wearing different shades of blue, the color of emotional
distance and detached calmness.

Conversely, Shirley's visual story is transmitted with the use of
a very vivid, lively color palette. It can be noticed that the further
from the bathroom she travels, even though only metaphorically,
the more colorful Shirley's world becomes. To the orange, yellow, and brown of the initial pages of the girl's story, there are
bright pink or deep green hues added in the last pictures. The
girl is never shown against an empty background, and although
her voice seems to have been muted (judging from the context
and the illustrations, she is old enough to be able to speak), she

metaphorically speaks out with the vividness and colorful power of her imagination.

This discussion of the structure of Burningham's picture book highlights the crucial elements of the author's artistic techniques, the authorial control over the pivotal moments, and the deliberate appearance of randomness—verbal, rhythmical, and graphic—of the remaining elements. Employing such a complex system must be purposeful, and the discussion that follows will reveal the equally complex meaning-making potential of the book.

Essence

"It is not only the heroes who quarrel in Dostoevsky, but separate elements in the development of the plot seem to contradict one another: facts are decoded in different ways, the psychology of the characters is self-contradictory; the form is a result of the essence" (Shklovsky, qtd. in Bakhtin 40). In this passage Victor Shklovsky, a Russian literary theorist, was commenting on Dostoevsky's novelistic structure. Similar to Dostoevsky's work, in Burningham's book the essence stimulated or enforced the polyphony of the form; the communication gap between the characters and the resulting isolation of the girl and perhaps the mother as well have been translated by Burningham into the language of the book's structure.

Joseph Zornado in his insightful book *Inventing the Child: Culture, Ideology, and the Story of Childhood* takes a critical look at the dominant culture, which defines picture books, for instance, "as 'innocent' and for the child" (xv), but which, overtly or covertly, reinforces the hierarchical dependence of the child on the adult. The culturally shaped self-contradiction concerning children's stories alluded to by Zornado is powerfully exemplified by Burningham's picture book. "Hierarchies of superiority and inferiority are implicit between the adult and the child, and the dominant ideology offers unconscious justifications that then justify the conscious use of subtle and chronic displays of power and violence often coded as the adult's love for the child" (Zornado xv). Apparently a simple, unaggressive family story depicting the routines of taking a bath by a child accompanied by her mother becomes a bold statement of a depressing impossibility of mutual understanding and potential isolation in Burningham's version. Offering a counterpunctual vision of the traditional perception of the adult-child relationship, which sees love, security, and understanding as the pivotal points, Zornado shows power and violence as inherent components of the relationship between children and adults, and Burningham's picture book confirms Zornado's hypothesis about the use of power. In *Shirley* the mother's power is signaled through her power to speak out, the power of the word. Paradoxically, the verbal story that results is not an individual and truly personal story; rather it is the voice of the dominant culture and the stereotype of the tired, unfulfilled life of a woman that speaks through her.

Unfortunately, there is also violence between the mother and the daughter, though not of a physical nature, but rather more subtle and hence more difficult to name and disarm. It lies in the implicitly understood pressure for unconditional obedience and submission on the part of the child. There is not even a hint of possible understanding; it is as if in her monologue the mother is attacking her daughter with a sequence of rhetorical questions that address the problem of a child's adaptation to the unquestioned rules of the world, the adult world, obviously, and the resulting detachment if the child does not comply to the rules: "I wish you would learn to fold up your clothes nicely," or the already quoted, almost aggressive statement, "I have better things to do than run around tidying up after you." In writing about adult culture widely practicing detachment, Zornado observes that "blaming the child for adult detachment is a central element of this tradition" (5). Thus if the child does not obey the cultural rules and does not submit, she deserves punishment, emotional detachment, rejection, and isolation.

Burningham's Time to Get Out of the Bath, Shirley as Antipastoral

"The antipastoral constructs a landscape of fear, but unlike the dark pastoral, it is a rejection of the possibility of pastoral [. . .] . It is about the dislocation of childhood, children severed from the world of adults, or the child part of the adult from a more acceptable adult self. It is an imaginative disconnection, a landscape of isolation" (Natov 159). Where in *Shirley*, a picture book delicately painted in watercolor and seemingly innocent, is there a place for fear? A close examination of Shirley's visual story line reveals various elements that might constitute fear. The third consecutive image after the girl escapes from her bath shows a night scene set in the dark woods. The full moon presides over the strange landscape; the trees are big and bare, and on one of the branches an owl has roosted. The tree trunks offer a hiding place for at least three unidentified and unnamed characters who might be wizards (if we notice their black pointed hats and long overcoats or cloaks) or spies (when we accentuate their suspicious behavior). In the picture Shirley sits on a horse behind a knight; they seem not to talk at all, but judging from her body language (her head turned back toward them), the girl is fully aware of the strange characters' presence in the woods. The color scheme designed for this particular illustration with the dominance of black, gray, and dark green visually supports the fear interpretation.

Fear might be the answer, although it is perhaps a slightly less supportable possibility for why the girl does not speak in the book. Caught in the flow of her mother's automatic speech, Shirley is afraid to break it. At the same time, the mother, as if hiding behind the formulaic artificiality of her monologue, is afraid to speak in her own voice and lets the voice of the dominant adult culture speak through her. The eventual respect the mother would wish to stimulate would be built on both the power of the adult over the child whom Zornado describes and Shirley's fear, not her love and admiration for her mother.

The dislocation of childhood that Natov mentions is in *Shirley* both actually and metaphorically. The girl must travel far to become a subject, not an object in the dominant culture. In the fantastic world she is a heroine able to act independently, worthy of fighting (and winning!) a water battle with the queen and king of the land. Back in the ordinary world she is muted and mildly but repetitively abused. She has no right to be a subject; Shirley serves as an object of her mother's complaints. The paradoxical message hidden in the picture book is that, contrary to expectations, the adult introducing the propaganda and imposing a given power relationship on the child is never the winner. More or less consciously, the mother, being the victimizer, also becomes the victim of the adult propaganda, for it is not the individual voice of the adult that decides but the uniform voice of the dominant ideology.

No Consonance, No Consolation

A review excerpted on the book's cover advises: "This book will be enjoyed by busy mums and their escapist children" (*Practical Parenting*), and one can certainly wonder whether this really might be the case. The profoundly incoherent story lines reveal the gap between the mother and the daughter; the "busy mums" alluded to in the recommendation may not enjoy the bitter realism: the lack of constructive family bonds (almost explicit if the mother's monologue and Shirley's reaction, an escape, are set side by side) and emotional indifference on both sides. Escapist children do not become so without reason; they always escape from something or somebody. This book is highly original and thought provoking, but is it enjoyable?

These interpretative suggestions lead to the conclusion that Burningham's *Time to Get Out of the Bath, Shirley* is implicitly an adult book. Surely the problems it raises are traditionally perceived as adult, yet the book is of much interest to a younger audience as well. That audience may not find the psychological or ideological implications of the dissonant polyphonic structure readily accessible, but the book's situational realism and the fantastic journey Shirley undertakes do not pass unnoticed by children.[5] Nonetheless, it seems to be one of the most complex contemporary children's picture books, both for its structural sophistication and its interpretative suggestiveness. Burningham makes use of a curious mixture of textual and emotional dissonance, which in effect produces a true gap, both literal and metaphorical. The discovering of the gap is, undoubtedly, one of the bitter pleasures of reading this subversive book.

Notes

1. Childhood and children's literature critics have been using research tools widely available to culture and literary scholars for only about twenty-five years. Earlier the research in children's literature was limited to historical, biographical, or pedagogical perspectives and generally ignored the changes that culture and literary theory underwent at that time.

2. Further possibilities and detailed analyses of the ways picture-book narratives involve the reader can be found in David Lewis's *Reading Contemporary Picturebooks*, Maria Nikolajeva and Carole Scott's *How Picturebooks Work*, and Perry Nodelman's *Words about Pictures*.

3. "Polyphony" or "dialogism" means an active participation of all the individual voices within a given artistic work where the voices are in equal dialogue so that none becomes more prominent ideologically.

4. A specialist in Witold Lutosławski's music, Charles Bodman Rae writes about Lutosławski's mature works: "[His] compositions did not follow the more general principles of indeterminacy. Lutosławski's aleatory technique involves no improvisation, nor any opportunity for players to choose what or when to play during the performance [. . .] . Pitch material is fully specified as is the rhythmic material of each individual part.

Only the rhythmic coordination of parts within the ensemble is subject to an element of chance" (Rae 385–86). Rae goes on to introduce a modified, more precise term for Lutosławski's technique, namely, "aleatory counterpoint." However, as the term has not yet been popularized, I have decided to retain the more general and more easily searched "controlled aleatorism."

5. Burningham's *Shirley* is a genuine double-address book. It addresses both groups of implied readers, adults and children, on different interpretative levels. Both groups can participate in the reading experience of this challenging book on their own terms, reaching their own conclusions. An interesting discussion of the questions of address and audience in children's literature can be found in Barbara Wall's *The Narrator's Voice: The Dilemma of Children's Fiction*.

Works Cited

Bakhtin, M. M. *Problems of Dostoevsky's Poetics*. Trans. R. William Rotsel. Ann Arbor MI: Ardis, 1973.

Burningham, John. *Time to Get Out of the Bath, Shirley*. London: Random House, 1978.

Felluga, Dino. "Introduction to Narratology. Terms and Concepts." *Introductory Guide to Critical Theory*. Last updated 28 Nov. 2003. Purdue University. 10 June 2007. http://www.cla.purdue.edu/academic/engl/theory/narratology/terms/.

Lewis, David. *Reading Contemporary Picturebooks: Picturing Text*. London: Routledge, 2001.

Lutosławski, Witold. "Controlled Aleatorism." BBC. 12 Apr. 2006. http://www.bbc.co.uk/music/profiles/lutoslawski.shtml.

Natov, Roni. *The Poetics of Childhood*. New York: Routledge, 2003.

Nikolajeva, Maria, and Carole Scott. *How Picturebooks Work*. New York: Garland, 2001.

Nodelman, Perry. *Words about Pictures: The Narrative Art of Children's Picture Books*. Athens: University of Georgia Press, 1988.

Rae, Charles Bodham. "Witold Lutosławski." *The New Grove Dictionary of Music and Musicians*. Ed. Stanley Sadie. 2nd ed. Vol. 15. New York: Grove, 2001. 381–89.

Wall, Barbara. *The Narrator's Voice: The Dilemma of Children's Fiction*. New York: St. Martin's, 1991.

Zornado, Joseph L. *Inventing the Child: Culture, Ideology and the Story of Childhood*. New York: Routledge, 2006.

Magdalena Sikorska ❦ *99*

6

Telling the Story,
Breaking the Boundaries

*Metafiction and the Enhancement
of Children's Literary Development in*
The Bravest Ever Bear *and* The
Story of the Falling Star

ALEXANDRA LEWIS

Recent cultural interest in metafiction—fiction about fiction—has found a strong voice in children's literature.[1] *The Bravest Ever Bear* (text by Allan Ahlberg and illustrations by Paul Howard, 1999) simultaneously pays attention to this interest and to the needs and understanding of its primary audience of young readers with great success, in such a way that the metafictive devices employed (both language and image features) do not operate at cross-purposes to but rather function to enhance the possibilities for children's literary development. As the bravest ever bear journeys through traditional story forms, which are unsatisfactory and unsuited to his purpose, the conventions of fictive writing in general and the fairy-tale genre specifically are parodied through both text and illustration, including a meeting of the traditional and the modern (Goldilocks on roller skates) and a suggestion of the possibilities for a feminist revisioning (the desires and actions of the princess). In addition to these features, the shifting narrative viewpoint and visible jostling for control of the text by characters within the text; the pictorial representation of the process of and opportunities for authorship; the problems of narrative closure and compartmentalization; and the further excess and boundary breaking involved in the interpellation and direct questioning of the reader firmly establish the work of Ahlberg and Howard as "writing which self-consciously and systematically draws attention to its status as an artefact in order to pose questions about the relationship between fiction and reality" (Waugh 2).

Ahlberg and Howard engage their readers in the creative and intellectual dimensions of literary composition, encouraging recognition of the inherent constructedness of fictive texts through their overt manipulation of such elements as character, plot, theme, voice, and temporal organization. This recognition or process of discovery not only endows the child reader with a transportable framework of understanding to apply to other texts encountered throughout life but may also, by analogy, facilitate a broader personal development. Each reader's metafictive explorations may bring to light "the possible fictionality of the world outside the literary fictional text" (Waugh 2) and the need to challenge seemingly immutable boundaries and versions of authority found in both realms. Metafictive texts provide opportunities for the realization of the functionality or use of writing and language. In challenging and stimulating their child audience, these texts extend the invitation not only actively to engage and interact with literature as readers but also, in breaking down the barriers between the apparently definitive authority or "truth" of what is written and the myriad ways in which it may be told or interpreted, to become authors as well, with the courage and desire to tell their own stories.

The Story of the Falling Star (told by Elsie Jones, a collaborative effort in terms of photography, reenactment of journey, maps, and illustration, 1989), as a metafictive work that is most successful in paying attention to—and indeed actively constructing—its primary audience, incorporates many innovative language and image features specifically for the benefit of Australian Aboriginal children. *The Story of the Falling Star* possesses a heightened sense of purpose, seeking to use metafictive devices to begin to overcome a history in which notions of white, male "author-ity" have suppressed or made difficult the telling of indigenous, orally based, communally owned tales by elder women. In doing so the text might play a part in redressing the tangible disparities between the literary (and literacy) development of indigenous and nonindigenous children created by a history of literary marginalization and underrepresentation (which has occurred alongside wider social, cultural, political, and economic injustices).

The notion that texts for children such as *The Bravest Ever Bear* might *not* be successful, or may achieve only limited success, in simultaneously paying attention to their primary audience and to recent cultural interest in metafiction is interesting insofar as it exposes the common misconception that there is necessarily something childish or simplistic about the construction, purpose, or effect of children's literature. Such an approach inevitably limits works for children to the status of, at best, "good old favourites" but never "the sophisticated avant-garde" (Lewis, "Constructedness of Texts" 259). As David Lewis has commented, "Our familiar ways of thinking and talking and writing about picture books" tend to limit the depth and scope of our perceptions when, in fact, "by its nature, the picture book tends towards openness, the playful, the parodic-fertile ground in which the metafictive can flourish" ("Constructedness of Texts" 260, 273).

The specific deployment of numerous metafictive devices in *The Bravest Ever Bear* and *The Story of the Falling Star* extends and exploits the natural openness of the form in a manner that is clearly for the benefit of child readers. There is no struggle here to find a balance between two different areas or reading groups to which attention must be paid (simple childish enjoyment and complex adult metafictive or postmodern academic pleasure), for such a clear division does not exist. Although it is certainly a valid argument that, in general, "metafictional levels in books for young readers exist within two separate semiotic systems or groups of artistic codes: that of the adult and that of the child," so that some of the metafictional structures may be "hidden and addressed only to the adult co-reader" (Nikolajeva 192), this does not appear to be the case in either Ahlberg and Howard's or Jones's work. Rather, in recognizing that "metafiction always involves a game with the reader which is based on previous experience" (which Maria Nikolajeva cites as the main reason why some metafictive devices may be apparent only to the adult coreader of children's texts [192]), it appears to be the intention of the authors and illustrators of both books to situate their metafictive tools and strategies within the bounds of experience accessible to their primary audience. The narrative voices of both works employ neither the single address (narrator bypasses either the child or the adult audience in favor of the other) nor the double address to which Nikolajeva refers (with both audiences being addressed, but on different levels—this was common in the Victorian era, when often a moralizing narrative voice "exhibited strong consciousness of the presence of adult readers" [Wall 9]). Rather, they use what Barbara Wall has termed the "dual address" (9), appealing to the child and the adult simultaneously and with the same techniques, invoking the same recognitions. The implied adult audience—as coreaders, coquestioners, and fundamentally primary purchasers of these texts—is, it seems, present but certainly not prioritized in the metafictive narrator-narratee relationship at work. Ahlberg and Howard, for example, draw on material from familiar childhood fairy tales and nursery rhymes, and in Jones's work metafictive questions and interruptions of the central narrative are uttered by child characters or participants in ways and with concerns appropriate to child (as well as adult) readers.

The works are clearly positioned not merely to dazzle clever adult purchasers who have an interest in metafiction but above all to translate the wealth of that theory and practice into an accessible artifact that children will use, and will want to use, thus facilitating a greater understanding of the interrelationship between fiction, reality, and the literary. The fundamental importance of the young reader's enjoyment and development is at all times retained as the central focus. Indeed, the success of *The Bravest Ever Bear* and *The Story of the Falling Star* may be attributed to their presentation of an age-appropriate metafiction. Challenging yet ultimately accessible with practice, revisiting, and coreading, the works may be viewed as sites for interaction within what Lev Vygotsky termed the zone of proximal development (84).[2]

Both *The Bravest Ever Bear* and *The Story of the Falling Star* engage in the practice of boundary breaking (or frame breaking), a metafictive device that holds much positive significance for children's literary development. The breaking of boundaries draws the young reader's attention not only to the existence and operation of conventions in language and literature but also to the freedom and pleasure to be gained from experimenting with and subverting them. In both texts "characters within a story are allowed by their author to wander beyond the narrative level to which they properly belong" (Lewis, *Reading Contemporary Picturebooks* 94), upending or rearranging familiar and expected structures. The bear's movement in illustration across, above, and behind the pages of the story; his continual commentary on its progression; and his direct appeal to the reader for assistance and interaction ("What's going on?") and advice or opinion regarding the writing process ("What shall I do?") make explicit to primary audience members their situation, in this and all texts, as implied or anticipated reader, along with the interpretative privileges and responsibilities such a role might entail. Similarly, Elsie Jones actually appears in a text that is described not as written but as spoken or "told by" her. She alternates between location *within* the illustrated action (pictured in photographed community dialogue as she relates the embedded "story within a story," raising the question whether it should be more appropriately viewed as a "reality within a reality") and involvement in more conventional, yet still transparent, narration (visible in corners and bottoms of pages below the figures and past events she describes). Jones's appearance in each of these layers of "telling" explodes the distinction between author and narrator: she is even pictured on the back cover of the book, providing a summary and appraisal of the tale she has carefully unfolded within its pages.

The Story of the Falling Star evolves not in spite of but because of the prompting, questioning, and spontaneous reactions of a "real" audience of Aboriginal children, also made present in the book through vivid photographs and collage. This mode of narrative development makes clear the strong equation between readership and coauthorship, promoting a reading style involving interactive participation and interpretation in the search for meaning. Although the narrative voice of the first few pages of *The Bravest Ever Bear* is distant, strange, unidentified, and therefore, by default, authoritative, the subscription to a closed, unmediated, and definitive view of text that such a voice or style might encourage is quickly challenged by the bear. His brave antics reveal to the young reader that, in all fiction, language, and even daily communication, "it takes two to say a thing. [. . .] An author creates a relationship with a reader in order to discover the meaning of the text" (Chambers 35–36).

Both the bear and the Aboriginal children are positioned as characters with whom the reader might easily identify or form a sympathetic relation, so that their responses to text and textual practices become, or at least guide, our own. The young bear's commonality with the reader is established as he sleeps, bathes, and dresses before the stories officially begin (demonstrating familiar shared routines and suggesting the existence of a life and identity beyond the fictional work), his excited appearance below the table of contents subtly endorsing an eager reading and exploring attitude.[3] Just as the open space of the bear's white body in Anthony Browne's *Bear Hunt* (1979) provides an entry point for the reader into the story and an interpretative space to occupy, the friendly, accessible Ahlberg-Howard bear extends a similar invitation through his direct eye contact and gesture, and through the vocalized immediacy of his comments, endowed typographically with prominence over the rest of the text (the "proper" story) with a bold and distinctive font. The later positioning of the bear side-on and facing forward at the typewriter further encourages the reader to identify with or be otherwise inspired by the strength of his ambition to write his own story.[4]

The interpellating gaze of the children in Jones's work fixes the reader as an extension of that visible listening community, enhancing the reading audience's sense of immediacy and participation in the journey regardless of the temporal and spatial divides between themselves and the inscription of the story. This poses an interesting challenge to nonindigenous readers, who are required to assume the reading position and cultural knowledge of an Aboriginal child, in a kind of assimilation in reverse.[5] The bravest ever bear's triumphant exclamation that the story is both for and about him ("That's me!") works to implicate the reader in the center of the action, demonstrating the manner in which individual experience is brought to, and informs our reading of, the texts we encounter as we find aspects of ourselves or our imaginative lives mirrored in story. This is shown to operate even where the life-fiction intertextuality is not so immediately apparent as the link between written "Bear" and narrating/writing bear (who become, in the space of the short story that takes the book's title, one and the same).

Conventional fictional constructs are further broken, and the illusion of the authority of the printed word revealed, through the dialogic qualities of both works. The struggle for control of the text within *The Bravest Ever Bear* in particular, first between bear and unseen author, then between several characters, draws the reader's attention to the fact that writing, interpretation, and criticism are "not about error, not about being right or wrong. [. . .] There never can be a definitive reading, but only additional readings" (Chambers 127). The bear seeks to interrupt or delay "the [premature] end" of the second stilted piece, more description than story, by standing in between the printed words on the page and demands a work that is "fun" and will interest him. His initial reactions to the developing plot(s) encourage children to have the confidence to ask questions of and about the text even as they navigate their way through its unfamiliar territory.

Certainly, in a sense, the first stories are "ridiculous," with "The

Three Bears" providing a parody of the planning of a story or elements of plot in its "shopping list" approach. Humor arises from the speed with which the familiar fairy-tale elements are evoked, as well as the unconventional yet entirely logical modernized ending complete with courtroom scene. Reliance on the "once upon a time [. . .] the end" formula is clearly shown, through parodic repetition, to be insufficient to conceal a void of meaningful content or satisfactory development in "The Bear," "The Other Bear," "The Penguin," and "The Sausage," which merely introduce each character before hastily concluding. The nonsensical "Four and Twenty Black Bears," almost as abrupt as the stories that surround it, is nevertheless entertaining. Its explicit and easily recognizable intertextuality plays with the subversive "freeing"—through illustration and notable omission from the written text—of the black birds from the bounds of their role (or stifling pie!) in traditional rhyme. The bear, a demanding reader-critic, is yet unhappy with this state of literary affairs. His resolve to amend the situation by climbing down off the page "to write the next one" is laudably adventurous, resulting in the production of increasingly complex and interesting pictures and text by his creative imagination. His intervention demonstrates that satisfaction with storytelling and the use of language to communicate and express arises through realization of its richness and numerous inherent possibilities: a functional approach to conveying and comprehending the reasons and uses for reading and writing.[6]

Despite his heroic efforts, the bear himself is by no means transformed into an omniscient narrator. Instead, the work, with its sustained multiplicity of interrupting voices, repeatedly emphasizes the manner in which, ideally, different perspectives will enliven and enhance one another. More dialogic still is *The Story of the Falling Star*, where the benefits of a communal approach to story sharing are evident in both plot and actual method of production. Jones acknowledges that "without the contribution of this very large number of people"—over 150 involved in funding, advice, contribution of maps and illustrations, compilation of glossary, and appearance in the story—"it would have remained a dream," and her inclusive style of presentation itself calls to mind the vital process of coreading that occurs between adult and young child at home and at school (Slaughter 4). Paving a different readerly path to a similar realization, *The Bravest Ever Bear* demonstrates that the printed word is not the "truth" but one writer's version of it by revealing (almost in contrast to Jones's unwavering celebration of collaboration) the often self-serving motivations for writing and the impact of personality and ideology on the end product. The bear's ego is obviously highly involved in his dissatisfaction with stories from which he is excluded as well as the "*perfect*" world he creates as a substitute, having grasped the transformative power of language and the literate self ("When he grew up he did . . . hm . . . lots and lots of very brave things"). Similarly, the irony of the imperfect grammar of the "Perfectest Ever" Princess reinforces her self-centered bias in describing a character she imagines to be synonymous with her actual self as "the fairest in the land—*of course*."

The absolute "truth" is, indeed, either nonexistent or incomprehensible, but it may be most closely approximated or approached by the processes of open communication between and cooperation of many perspectives, symbolized by the communal feast and the mutually "happy" existence it makes possible in the final pages of *The Bravest Ever Bear*. The corroboree in *The Story of the Falling Star* has much the same function, operating within the text to enable a compromise between modern pressures and realities and a respect for and sense of connection with ancestors and the dreamtime. The Paakantji children possess differing levels of traditional knowledge and, as hinted at in the metafictive dedication page for characters whose images appear in the story but who died before it was finished, live in constant danger of obliteration by various social pressures. Jones's emphasis on cooperation and the link between past and present will have important repercussions outside the text. The valuing of the contributions made by the children of Wilcannia to the text, and their recognition of the role they might play in preserving and transmitting that knowledge, is likely to have a positive impact on their own further literary development. It might also inspire other young Aboriginal readers who are displaced from the setting, and encouragement, of a wider Aboriginal community. By extrapolation the text may influence the literary development of nonindigenous children in such a way that they are made aware at an early age of such concepts as acceptance and celebration of difference, which would have positive implications for the ongoing process of reconciliation.

In this way both works enable not only literary development but also the realization of important life lessons, pursuing through the metafictive process of "formal self-exploration" such broad questions as "how human beings reflect, construct and mediate their experience of the world," by drawing on "the traditional metaphor of the world as book" (Waugh 2–3). To this end both works are inherently optimistic, disclosing a "strong humanistic belief in the innate goodness of human nature and in the capacity for all human beings to outgrow childish solipsism" (Stephens 64). This will be vital for the development of young readers, whose lively imaginations are nurtured "by the stories they are told and the images provided them by their culture" (Kohl 62).

Notably, the metafictive works of Ahlberg and Howard and Jones overcome two very real concerns expressed by commentators on the direction of children's literature. In *Sticks and Stones* Jack Zipes explores the notion that, in line with Theodor Adorno's connection between the culture industry and the demise of critical thinking, children's literature, culture, and lives are becoming increasingly standardized (preface). Similarly, in *Should We Burn Babar?* Herbert Kohl discusses the fear that an increasingly economically rationalist society has resulted in the production of children's stories so obsessed with individual success that thought about solidarity and group struggle is "relegated to minority status" (63). Not only do the metafictive works discussed explicitly encourage critical thinking and interaction, undermining the "unreflective and naïve reading of stories" (Lewis, *Reading Contemporary Picturebooks* 94); they also present a viewpoint where the individual and group concerns, so often portrayed as oppositional, are involved in a complex interrelationship in which each may inform, rather than eclipse, the other, in both fictive constructs and, by analogy, lived experience.

The politics of identity indeed figure prominently in metafictive books for children (Morgado 254), with the process of self-discovery often the central focus (Moss 79). For the bear and company, selfhood is found through self-expression, highlighting the importance of language as a powerful tool and enabling the child reader's recognition of the construction of subjectivity. In *The Bravest Ever Bear* the interweaving of characters from popular fairy tales has the instructive benefit of making clear the operation of intertextuality, in turn encouraging an acknowledgment that reading is a highly contextualized process, both informed by and transformative of the life experience and prior literary contact of each individual in a highly personalized way (Meek 22). The inclusion of these intertextual figures also provides a springboard for the recognition of the multivariate possibilities for selfhood and the importance of avoiding the constraints of prescribed social roles and stereotypes.

Typical of the largesse and excess of metafiction, a whole cast of known and familiar characters is included in *The Bravest Ever Bear*, many of whom are not even mentioned in the text but appear in illustration in guises that belie expectation—Goldilocks on roller skates, for example, and a reappearing Gingerbread Man who is secure in his safety, walking rather than running through the pages. Several traditional elements are maintained (note the [literally] little pigs climbing up a spire, attempting to escape, and trapped on a wolf's sandwich in "The Perfectest Ever Princess"), but these may be seen to supply the control or stability "against which the experimental strategies can foreground themselves" without confusing the primary audience (Waugh 18). As Patricia Waugh points out, metafiction lays bare the structures and conventions of realism but does not abandon them completely (18). The metafictional language and image devices that further literary development by engaging children's attention and fostering an interactive approach to readership are in no danger of causing confusion, for the same reason that Kornei Chukovsky presents in his compelling argument for the sense of nonsense verse (102). Metafictional works simultaneously strengthen each reader's sense of the everyday world (how things are) while "problematizing" that "sense of reality from a conceptual or philosophical point of view" (Waugh 34), giving rise to a consideration of how things might otherwise (plausibly) be.

The familiar characters are not constrained by the language of the texts from which they originated, revealing to the reader the hidden potentialities of self, and the empowering notion that language is not a passive mirror for the world but creates and inscribes its own meaning upon it, forming part of the very thing it seeks to describe. The perfectest ever princess chooses to refute imposed patriarchal ideals of feminine weakness and marriage to the strongest suitor (rejecting the bravest ever bear, who quite insightfully attributes his loss of control to a problem of genre: "I thought this was a bear book"). She is depicted not as a passive Rapunzel in her tower but as a resourceful woman seeking to disengage from meddlesome males: "Push off, Prince!" A related metafictive element here is the subverted temporal organization, not only in terms of the rapid and parodic development of plot (she moved out, "started a career [. . .] and went shopping") but also in the meeting of traditional and modern. The construction cranes, supermarket, and busy parking lot faintly visible in the background, not to mention the highly individualized black belt bears, suggest the enduring power of literature through the ages. As such they provide a form of encouragement, perhaps even on a subconscious level, for children to persevere with their literary development in order to possess the necessary skills and knowledge for effective social and cultural participation.

A focus on the complex interplay between fiction and reality is at all times maintained, with the page curling upward, or burnt by the dragon's flame, or cut along the dotted line to reveal the writer's desk and typewriter shared by a variety of characters. When the troll and other stereotypically frightening or malevolent creatures (which is indeed how they are viewed by the bear and the princess) take over the storytelling, the manner in which both the practice of scapegoating and the idea of the "normal" will differ for every author and reader is made clear. In this antifolklore of loyal and happy wolves, the act of "eating little pigs (three at a time), little girls, [. . .] grandmas and so on" is not the fearful climax of a story but the placid beginning, and the bear "with a *fire engine!*" or savior in a previous story is, from this perspective, the infamous villain. Traditional heroic discourse ("All for one and one for all!") appears to be parodied, with its meaning subverted when uttered by these characters, yet subtle parallels and commonalities between these conventional villains and the more admirable characters are drawn through a shared interest in food and feasting. The wolf's final resounding "BURP!" (which is metafictively enacted, interrupting the narrative rather than being reported in it) prefigures the gorged bear's endearing "put me to bed but don't bend me," their shared "bulging" replicated in the curving typesetting and bubble of text and ultimately shown to be universal. In just one example of the fine illustrative detail, even the delicate Tinkerbell appears to be holding her stomach and covering a large burp. While the monstrous remains menacing, conventional juxtapositions and oppositions (for instance between good and evil) are shown to be simplistic, and naturalized meanings are successfully interrogated and often frustrated.

The disruption of the expectations associated with "easily recognised stories, incidents [and] motifs from the classic texts of childhood" (Stephens 66) finds particular strength in the problematization of narrative closure in both *The Bravest Ever Bear* and *The Story of the Falling Star*. Despite the apparent attempt to present each story as distinct and provide them with a specific "end," the subjectivity of selecting an appropriate moment of finality is highlighted in the princess's indignant comment in *The Bravest Ever Bear*: "It's not the end [. . .] . It's not even the beginning." As a participant in the story, she canvasses the self-reflexive and confounding notion that it might be the "*wrong* story," raising the possibility that it is either untrue, or undesirable, or to be told at another time. But what is the "right" story? And how should it unfold? Complete compartmentalization of stories, tangents, digressions and multivariate viewpoints is shown to be unachievable, even mythical. In *The Bravest Ever Bear* stories are multiple, interrelated, and self-generating ("speaking of sausages . . . Once upon a time there was a sausage"). Significantly, neither work has numbered pages, and *The Bravest Ever Bear* seeks to make the page-turning action fluid (rather than a noticeable false break dictated by the size of the paper), often providing a mental connection with the use of ellipses leading from one page to the next ("No, no, you forgot one thing . . ."; "Now, let's see . . ."). Linear cohesion is shown to be a "falsification of experience" (Hollindale 63) and is thus repudiated through parody of the "folktale incremental narrative structure" (Stephens 65).

The moment of closure, it appears, is "always arbitrary" (Stephens 72) and is likely to be determined by the perceived desires of the majority of its implied readers, that is, by its marketability ("The End? I doubt it"), although not all readers will "like" the book and its progression on these terms. Furthermore, an "ending" can never really be permanent, with a symbolic blank page indicative of future inscription by the penguin and the sense that the bear will inevitably wake from his welcome sleep, refreshed and ready to tackle new adventures in language. In *The Story of the Falling Star* even temporary closure is resisted, with the final question, or challenge, as to the nature of the falling star remaining unanswered ("we don't know") and set within the context not of a book whose cover can be closed upon itself but of a living history that is ongoing. Even the princess's escape from past literary obligations and conventions is one of characteristic metafictive indeterminacy, leaving "relationships and outcomes obscure" (Lewis, *Reading Contemporary Picturebooks* 96). Her happy departure, suitcase in hand, opens up a realm of possibilities outside the bounds of the very text that has granted her freedom.

One of the distinct advantages of a metafictive text in terms of the literary development of child readers is its potential to play a pivotal "role in training" them to "deal later on with still more complex texts" (Stephens 71). Just as the princess gains a suitcase that, as evidenced by the many stickers with which it is adorned, will be of use on many and varied travels, the reader, through interaction with the text, gains knowledge and a framework for literary interpretation that is transportable. Fundamentally, *The Bravest Ever Bear* and *The Story of the Falling Star* are highly successful in this regard, for both demonstrate an awareness of the centrality of the "pleasures of the text" (Touponce 175). Children's literary development (in terms of language, literacy, intellectual, personality, social, moral, aesthetic, and creative development) will no doubt be heightened if they are eager to become not merely children "who can read" but children who "do read" (Rolton vi). The natural process of learning by engaging in play through and with the literary (Beecher and Arthur 23) is accelerated when the texts of play are metafictive. Here language and image devices enable a greater sense of understanding and subsequent interpretative confidence as the explicit and implicit commentary being made about the book, within the book, is explored. In a sense the "thought aloud" comments of the bear and other characters provide a parallel for the language voiced spontaneously in play at around three to four years of age. Although this may already have become the language of inner speech for the primary audience, the metafictive bear, in appealing to or simulating this voice, demonstrates to child readers how they may react when encountering a book in which the narrator has been naturalized and there is no such prominent figure to guide them.

Metafictive books such as these might also, in a very practical sense, play a role in overcoming, or at least reducing, "the complex problem of variation in literate practices in different social locations" (Williams 19). In the context of differential access to childhood texts (a problem dramatized by the geographical isolation and economic constraints experienced by children in the Wilcannia community, in which *The Story of the Falling Star* was produced) as well as the possible range of approaches to coreadership at school and at home, metafiction empowers the child reader. Adult engagement may occur along a vast spectrum, from the notion that children should be encouraged to participate in an interactive process of textual and self-discovery, to storytelling as a closed, didactic, one-way system that, while entertaining, keeps audience members "in their place" (Chambers 40) and thus threatens to slow the rate of learning. Explicit invitations to question and interact decrease the reliance of the young learner on the prompting of the adult coreader, both "creating a place [. . .] to enter the text" (Trites 123) and affirming the impulse to do so.[7] With their "polyphony" (Otten and Schmidt 3) of voices, the illustrated metafictive texts become a conversation or dialogue into which the reader is drawn, rather than a monologue to which he or she must listen and observe without interruption.

The Bravest Ever Bear and *The Story of the Falling Star* pay simultaneous attention to their primary audience of children and to recent cultural interest in metafiction with great success, using a range of metafictive language and image features to further the literary development of young readers. The entertaining and engaging nature of the text and illustration, and the boundary breaking, excess, indeterminacy, intertextuality, and parodic elements of both works ensure that the benefits for the reader extend beyond a facilitation of learning in the realm of literacy and language to encompass an understanding of the conventions of plot, theme, temporal organization, and narrative voice in fictive writing, as well as of the possibilities for freedom that arise when these are exposed and subverted. This literary development will ideally equate with a wider personal development, as metafictive explorations bring to light the possible "fictionality" of the world beyond the realm of the literary text.

Such a process of literary and personal development is available to all readers, even the humble penguin ("Yes—what's wrong with penguins?"), who takes up the baton of (self)authorship when the satisfied bear goes to sleep. The crossing (and blurring) of conventional boundaries between the roles of author, narrator, reader, and subject by several characters in *The Bravest*

Ever Bear, who persevere in the increasingly familiar world of textual practices despite the crumpled "false starts" that litter the floor beneath their shared writing desk, provides a model for the development of similar courage and inspiration in members of the primary audience. Just as the initial resonant image of the typewriter in *The Bravest Ever Bear* symbolizes the metafictive process of "laying bare" the conventions and constructs of fictive writing in which both works engage (seeking to make them as familiar, unthreatening, and accessible as the cup of tea and half-eaten cookie), the final blank page extends an invitation to young readers to apply that knowledge and widened scope of perceived possibility in their future engagement with all forms of textual practice and, by analogy, in the creation of their own life narrative.

Notes

1. For a comprehensive introduction to metafiction, see Ommundsen; Waugh.

2. As Vygotsky explains, childhood learning occurs when interaction with peers and adults stimulates a variety of internal developmental processes. The zone of proximal development is the space between "*the actual developmental level as determined by independent problem solving and the level of potential development*" when working under the guidance of or in collaboration with "*more capable*" others (86, emphasis in original).

3. The bear's activities here not only establish points of commonality with the young reader but also, on another level, mirror the function of the title page and table of contents on which he appears (as an introduction to or preparation for the story). His initial actions thus facilitate literary development regarding knowledge of the parts of the book, while simultaneously parodying its construction (much as *The Stinky Cheese Man* [Scieszka and Smith] ironically and self-reflexively proclaims its "Title Page"). The bear's pre-textual or extratextual activities and preparations also call attention to the sense in which a range of external factors might influence the way we choose, approach, and read a text, gesturing to Gérard Genette's notion of the paratext—the potential impact of our prior knowledge of a text; its packaging, adornments, and accompaniments (the peritext); and our resultant expectations, upon readerly

assumptions and interpretations. The bear does not read reviews of the text in which he is to appear (though he will certainly voice criticism as it unfolds!) and does not approach the work armed with specific external cues in that regard, but the depiction of his process of preparation to read certainly highlights the operation of a relation to books and fiction extending before and beyond the mere reading of the story as given.

4. As Nodelman and Reimer note in their discussion of picture books in *The Pleasures of Children's Literature*, left-to-right movement and orientation (such as that exhibited by the bear as he writes his own story) make readers feel comfortable, generally causing them to assume that the motion is natural and not difficult (293).

5. A glossary or guide to Paakantji "sounds, spellings and meanings" is provided at the end of *The Story of the Falling Star*, offering a bridge to greater understanding for those unfamiliar with the language. Note that the sense of what might constitute "cultural knowledge" is particularly complex in the Australian Aboriginal context, a reality made clear by the metafictive image features. If the experience of reading Jones's work may be viewed as a kind of assimilation in reverse for non-Aboriginal readers, it is an undoubtedly positive one, posing a challenge to any sense of the perceived superiority of the English language and associated customs without requiring that readers relinquish their own cultural heritage—fostering interest and personal development rather than a narrowing loss.

6. A recognition of the functionality of writing (that is, its practical as well as purely creative applications) is vital to the process of children's literacy and literary development.

7. In an interactive rather than didactic approach to reading aloud, interruptions to and questioning of the text being read, as well as exclamation over links discovered with other texts and with real life, will be encouraged and expanded upon. The possibilities for children's literary development are enhanced by questions from and dialogue between the child and adult coreaders.

Works Cited

Ahlberg, Allan, and Paul Howard. *The Bravest Ever Bear*. 1999. London: Walker, 2001.

Beecher, Bronwyn, and Leonie Arthur. *Play and Literacy in Children's Worlds*. Newtown: Primary English Teaching Assn. (Australia), 2001.

Browne, Anthony. *Bear Hunt*. London: Hamish Hamilton, 1979.

Chambers, Aidan. *Booktalk: Occasional Writing on Literature and Children*. London: Bodley Head, 1985.

Chukovsky, Kornei. "The Sense of Nonsense Verse." *From Two to Five*. Ed. and trans. Miriam Morton. Rev. ed. Berkeley: University of California Press, 1968. 89–113.

Genette, Gérard. *Paratexts: Thresholds of Interpretation*. Trans. Jane E. Lewin. Cambridge: Cambridge University Press, 1997.

Hollindale, Peter. *Signs of Childness in Children's Books*. Woodchester, England: Thimble, 1997.

Jones, Elsie. *The Story of the Falling Star*. With drawings by Doug Jones and collages by Karin Donaldson. Canberra: Aboriginal Studies, 1989.

Kohl, Herbert. *Should We Burn Babar? Essays on Children's Literature and the Power of Stories*. New York: New Press, 1995.

Lewis, David. "The Constructedness of Texts: Picture Books and the Metafictive." *Signal* 61 (1990): 131–46. Rpt. in *Only Connect: Readings on Children's Literature*. Ed. Sheila Egoff, G. T. Stubbs, and L. F. Ashley. 3rd ed. Oxford: Oxford University Press, 1996. 259–75.

———. *Reading Contemporary Picturebooks: Picturing Text*. London: Routledge, 2001.

Meek, Margaret. *How Texts Teach What Readers Learn*. Woodchester, England: Thimble, 1988.

Morgado, Margarida. "A Loss beyond Imagining: Child Disappearance in Fiction." *The Yearbook of English Studies* 32 (2002): 244–59.

Moss, Anita. "Varieties of Children's Metafiction." *Studies in the Literary Imagination* 18.2 (1985): 79–92.

Nikolajeva, Maria. *Children's Literature Comes of Age: Towards a New Aesthetic*. New York: Garland, 1996.

Nodelman, Perry, and Mavis Reimer. *The Pleasures of Children's Literature*. 3rd ed. Boston: Pearson, 2003.

Ommundsen, Wenche. *Metafictions? Reflexivity in Contemporary Texts*. Melbourne: Melbourne University Press, 1993.

Otten, Charlotte F., and Gary D. Schmidt, eds. *The Voice of the Narrator in Children's Literature: Insights from Writers and Critics*. New York: Greenwood, 1989.

Rolton, Gloria. *Read to Me: A Practical Guide to Sharing Books with Your Child in the Vital Preschool Years*. Melbourne: Australian Council for Educational Research, 2001.

Scieszka, Jon, and Lane Smith. *The Stinky Cheese Man and Other Fairly Stupid Tales*. New York: Viking Penguin, 1992.

Slaughter, Judith Pollard. *Beyond Storybooks: Young Children and the*

Shared Book Experience. Newark DE: International Reading Assn., 1993.

Stephens, John. "'Did I tell you about the time I pushed the Brothers Grimm off Humpty Dumpty's wall?': Metafictional Strategies for Constituting the Audience as Agent in the Narratives of Janet and Allan Ahlberg." *Children's Literature and Contemporary Theory.* Ed. Michael Stone. Wollongong NSW, Australia: University of Wollongong, 1991. 63–75.

Touponce, William F. "Children's Literature and the Pleasures of the Text." *Children's Literature Association Quarterly* 20.4 (1995–96): 175–82.

Trites, Roberta Seelinger. *Waking Sleeping Beauty: Feminist Voices in Children's Novels.* Iowa City: University of Iowa Press, 1997.

Vygotsky, Lev S. "Interaction between Learning and Development." *Mind in Society: The Development of Higher Psychological Processes.* Ed. Michael Cole et al. Cambridge MA: Harvard University Press, 1978. 79–91.

Wall, Barbara. *The Narrator's Voice: The Dilemma of Children's Fiction.* Basingstoke, England: Macmillan, 1991.

Waugh, Patricia. *Metafiction: The Theory and Practice of Self-Conscious Fiction.* London: Methuen, 1984.

Williams, Geoff. "Children Entering Literate Worlds: Perspectives from the Study of Textual Practices." *Literacy and Schooling.* Ed. Frances Christie and Ray Misson. London: Routledge, 1998. 18–46.

Zipes, Jack. *Sticks and Stones: The Troublesome Success of Children's Literature from Slovenly Peter to Harry Potter.* New York: Routledge, 2001.

7

Perceiving *The Red Tree*

Narrative Repair, Writerly Metaphor, and Sensible Anarchy

ANDREA SCHWENKE WYILE

Skillfull perception is the practice of intentionally sensing
with our eyes, pores, and hearts wide open. It requires
receptivity and the participation of our whole selves, despite
the potential pain. It means fully witnessing both the
magnificence and the destruction of our Earth. It is allowing
one's identity and boundaries to be permeable and flexible.
I refer to this way of perceiving as *ecological perception*.
—LAURA SEWALL, "The Skill of Ecological Perception"

As [the novel] cannot be read at one sitting, it deprives
itself, of course, of the immense force derivable
from *totality*. [. . .] In the brief tale, however, the author
is enabled to carry out the fullness of his intention,
be it what it may. During the hour of perusal the soul
of the reader is at the writer's control.
—E. A. POE

"Sometimes the day begins with nothing to look forward to /
things go from bad to worse / darkness overcomes you": *The Red
Tree* is a picture book that dismantles dichotomies and hierarchies

of certainty and invokes the muses of perception. Readers must open themselves to the unusual. Shaun Tan's allegorical narrative and profoundly affecting page openings, which convey a series of moments in the day of the nameless redheaded protagonist, lead us to reconsider familiar notions like "common sense" and "I'm having a bad day" and also basics like how to read and what narrative becomes when verbal and visual elements combine. The protagonist's day is introduced with the iterative marker "sometimes," which suggests that the nature of this day is not an isolated event and also that the day itself is a metaphor for a relative period of time. These moments are minimally narrated in the second person, thereby implicating readers to some degree and "requiring receptivity and the participation of our whole selves, despite the potential pain" (Sewall, "Skill" 204). The totality of *The Red Tree*'s immense force results from readers' interactions with the many meaningful and meaningless aspects of the protagonist's overwhelming world and the lacunae of every page turn that forms the story's narrative links. The book is eminently readable because the force derived from the writerly metaphors on all the page openings (which are all effectively double spreads) invite what Laura Sewall calls "ecological perception" ("Skill" 204)—if we're willing to give our whole selves over to reading and rereading, this soul-affecting brief tale may dramatically alter our views of children's books and of narrative.

The familiar adage of "a method to the madness" reminds us that careful study and contemplation can lead us to "see" differently. This seeing is what governs the narrative by implicating readers/narratees. *The Red Tree* is a book that has as much to offer narratologists as it does picture-book scholars; members of both fields will need to stretch themselves in order to achieve the necessary initial flexibility, but from there new perceptions will propagate with increasing ease and wonder. To truly perceive what Hilde Lindemann Nelson terms "the oppressive identity" (150) of the redheaded protagonist, we must feel our way to knowledge by tasting the grayness and hearing the red and yellow rumbles of rush and rage and touching the pencil of time and seeing the pain underneath the unwieldy scuba mask and smelling the *sol-i*-tude, *i-sol*-ation, and *lone*-l-*i*-ness of *you*, the *uni*-que addressee. Be *you* single or plural, my hyphenation of these singular words indicates how they play out the central theme of *The Red Tree*'s writerly metaphors, drawing attention to components and wholes. The synchronous relationship of Sewall's notion of ecological perception; Lindeman Nelson's discussion of oppressive identities, counterstories, and narrative repair; and Roland Barthes's formulation of the writerly inform what I've come to call the sensible anarchy of collaborative reading. The totality of these combined theories enables readers to perceive *The Red Tree* with greater intention and flexibility.

Sewall's stance on perception informs the experience of reading and discussing *The Red Tree*. For Sewall "perception is a participatory act" (*Sight and Sensibility* 16) and "vision is a power" (15), "the ultimate power of vision being the ability to co-create the world we see and act upon. Our actions upon the world further our co-creative influence" (15–16). Applied to *The Red Tree*, the participatory act of perceptive reading becomes a form of synesthesia and a writerly act. In "Style and Its Image," Roland Barthes describes the writerly text as open ended and plural, a series of narrative segments that need to be brought together, or made sense of, by the reader, who thereby becomes a producer of the text. Each of *The Red Tree*'s nineteen page openings is a narrative segment. The coherence of such a book is not immediately evident—it is something one has to work on perceiving, and the usual "single-vision," be this of eyesight or of singular interpretation, doesn't get one very far. The writerly text requires the careful consideration of its layers. While there is no secret narrative kernel from which the text's meaning will sprout, the complex heart of the matter beats on every page opening, and its force circulates through each layer of the story body created by the text and its readers. Writerly metaphors depend on writerly readers, which in this context means readers attuned to the skill of ecological perception. As one goes deeper into the cumulative reading and sense-making process, juxtapositions begin to make sense in new ways—the writerly metaphors are the gateway to perceptive plurality. To achieve the level of participation that ecological perception requires, we need to reconsider what seeing, or this type of re-vision, entails.

Oppressive Identity, Counterstories, Narrative Repair

One way of achieving such receptivity is by actively creating counterstories to the master narratives of our culture, which have placed great emphasis on "normality" and aggressive conventionality as Hilde Lindemann Nelson argues: "Identities pick out certain people as candidates for certain treatments [many of which] are morally indefensible. If you belong to a group that bears one of the required identities [. . .] you may think that you should always put others' interests ahead of your own, live in the conviction that there is something seriously wrong with you, or take pride in being the person others perceive you to be. In short, you are too much an object of others' actions, not fully enough a moral agent in your own right" (150). The redheaded protagonist of *The Red Tree* clearly has such an "oppressive identity" (150). Over several readings, readers glean that s/he is effectively a social alien. The protagonist's gender is not definitive; s/he is nameless, voiceless, aimless; s/he is imperiled, mocked, and othered; s/he cannot function in the state that s/he is in. The protagonist's identity is oppressed by a social master narrative to the point that s/he doesn't know what s/he should do, who s/he is, and where s/he is. As readers we potentially belong to the oppressor group that judges the redhead and her/his moral worth, but in the process we must also judge our own status. We can join in the oppression, or we can choose to resist the master narratives, "the stories found lying about in our culture that serve as summaries of socially shared understandings" (Nelson 6), by creating counterstories and making "the damaged identity [. . .] whole. Through their function of narrative repair, counterstories thus open up the possibility that the person could attain, regain, or extend her freedom of moral agency" (150). In its representation of the redhead's aggressive experience, Tan's book simultaneously encourages the kind of recognition that opens the door to counterstories and is therefore potentially a story of repair.

The master narratives of our culture have placed great emphasis on "normality" and aggressive conventionality. Depression was long popularly conceived of as an abnormal condition particularly reserved for poor or artistic adults; however, this view has gradually changed in the popular consciousness. The metaphorical representations of the child protagonist's experiences suggest a strong counterstory of childhood depression. *The Red Tree* is fablelike in its treatment of the topic. Depression is not named nor are its causes or results. We're given a character's position in a series of events, be they real or imagined, over the course of a day and are left to connect the dots we're given. Nelson explains the process of how counterstories come about: "Many counterstories are told in two steps. The first is to identify the fragments of master narratives that have gone into the construction of an oppressive identity, noting how these fragments misrepresent persons [. . .] and situations" (7). The production of counterstories can come about through writerly readings of conventional narratives, but this sort of reading against the grain is of quite a different order than reading a writerly text that only consists of metaphorical fragments placed within a vague semblance of a hero's journey. The moments or scenes in *The Red Tree* are these fragments. The child's oppressive identity is the result of alienation from her/his environment. We aren't given the history—that is something we're left to fill in ourselves. This lack of specificity is one of the strengths of the narrative, for it leaves the construction of the story up to readers. Perhaps the situation is that the protagonist is an orphan, an immigrant, a social outcast, or has some other personal or social disadvantage, be it physical, emotional, or mental, or some combination of the possibilities. Such details would narrow the scope of the story, allowing for more specific critiques and established patterns to govern readings.

The second step Nelson identifies is to "retell the story" so that suppressed details become visible. "Since a powerful group's mis-perception of an oppressed group results in disrespectful treatment that can impede group members in carrying out their responsibilities, the counterstory also opens up the possibility that group members can enjoy greater freedom to do what they ought" (7). Here the strength of Tan's book is that the narrator only provides basic process statements ("sometimes you wait and wait and wait") and the pictorialization leads readers to contemplate the protagonist's feelings. We don't know the nature or kind of "troubles" that "come all at once" nor of the "inevitable" terrible fates (see fig. 1). Because the morally relevant details are made visible metaphorically within an open-ended and loosely connected fable, and because the pictorial focus is on the redheaded protagonist, s/he and the story are revealed as respect-worthy moral agents. Because we are freed from the prejudices of specific master narratives concerning topics such as childhood and depression, readers are to some degree themselves freed from their own oppression regarding such topics and can engage their perceptive abilities in new ways; thereby the aim of counterstories to alter oppressors' perception (Nelson 7) is achieved. The writerly nature of Tan's book presents the impetus for such a shift. Through discussion with others, readers then begin to create their own counterstories regarding related concerns. As Nelson states, "Counterstories don't just offer a different but equally viable way of representing you. To one degree or another, they resist a representation" (154). Because Tan does not provide closure, readers are left wanting to make connections and propose conclusions. This desire for something more than single vision coupled with the plural possibilities of Tan's metaphors lures us toward ecological perception and thereby encourages a more ambivalent view of children's literature in the positive sense espoused by Perry Nodelman in *The Hidden Adult: Defining Children's Literature.*

The Red Tree itself resists the representation of picture books as dealing with happy, fun, pastel childhoods. Nelson also notes that "the proper target of a counterstory is a master narrative that has been generated by an abusive power system to impose on a particular group an identity the system requires" (154). In this

context we might ask whether our current social system requires a master narrative of happy childhood stories to mask all the unhappy ones much as we find ways to mask environmental degradation through persistent consumer propaganda. These two topics are clearly interconnected in the deaf, senseless world of the protagonist. The perception of such details can counter the master narrative.

Ecological Perception

Tan's graphic expression calls on readers to employ ecological perception from the outset though they're unlikely to realize this until later in the rereadings phase. The cover of *The Red Tree* (see fig. 2) really does cover the whole of the narrative in one metonymic illustration; it provides insight and a sort of summary, which works as a starting point and could also represent a moment along the protagonist's journey into darkness and through trials, the stages of which are simply listed by the unknown narrator. In effect the journey is as much ours as the

redhead's. Because of the second-person narration, s/he could be telling us about ourselves, or we or some external source could be telling the redhead's story to her/him or to an unknown audience—"darkness overcomes you." While the pictures present us with a protagonist, there is a surprising intimacy and ambiguity in the narrating "you" that complements the graphic expression of both the verbal and the visual texts, which are in a synergetic relation.

Although many page openings do convey meaning on their own, so that one can dip in and out of the narrative at will, a picture book is a sequential cumulative narrative. Even though reading *The Red Tree* entails flipping back and forth, its force derives from its totality. The progression of images makes sense if we accept the gaps, but there is no evident logic to the order of the fragments. Nevertheless, although this fact frees us somewhat from the usual tyranny of ordered sequence, it also leaves readers in the lurch as they strive to make sense of the red tree and the redhead's imagination.

Since what could be considered the story proper begins with the narration ("sometimes the day begins with nothing to look forward to") and the pictorialization of the protagonist waking

to a new day, the preceding cover, gray end pages, and the megaphone and clock pages (see fig. 3) could be understood as dream images that serve to illuminate the protagonist's subconscious. (Interestingly, on his Web site Shaun Tan refers to several of the images as the result of the protagonist's imagination or as dreamlike situations.) The sky's coloring fits with early morning and dawn (megaphone page), and what I think of as the "red leaf time" clock page could signify the wake-up call to the day with nothing to look forward to.

The red leaf clock may foreshadow the idea that for every seven black leaf hours there is one red leaf hour, thus encapsulating the ratio of troubled to trial free narrative moments. The leaf on the front cover and on the clock is of the same bright red as those on the tree at the end, but the protagonist does not see these. The single red leaf on other pages is more muted and remote. The leaf represents an idea and functions as a synecdoche; once one has read the book through, it becomes clear that the part (leaf) represents an expectation or possibility of the whole (tree) and that somehow the protagonist's journey enables the transformation from leaf to tree, from one idea to another. Things begin by going from bad to worse. Prior to the end, which looks as dire as the beginning, the protagonist has lost all sense of purpose, self, and place. S/he is clearly at risk. The tree represents a moment of inspiration and confidence, but does not or cannot banish the ills of the external world. However, the fact that the redhead sees and acknowledges the tree suggests that alterations in her/his life are possible. As readers we are left to imagine what these might be. The tree is not a hallucination; it is an imaginative manifestation of the redhead's spirit or life force. The final end pages are a pulsing web of textured red—a close-up of a red leaf? of a heart? The throbbing vitality of the closing end pages contrasts sharply with the washed-out, drab grays of the opening end pages.

Sensible Anarchy

Because of its parallels to ecological perception and the writerly, the theory of anarchy offers another excellent means of making sense of *The Red Tree*. The less commonly known dictionary meaning of anarchy is the "cooperative and voluntary association of individuals and groups as the principle mode of organized society," though for my purposes, "of organized society" is better replaced with "for reading and discussing picture books." While the allegorical narrative reveals a strong sense of confusion, chaos, and a seeming lack of individual control in society, the order of the narrative whole itself is carefully sequenced and empowering. Although the ultimate connections are left open to readers, each page is a proverbial dot presented in a particular sequence with varying magnitudes of page-turn gaps. Each dot is worth contemplating in its own right, and myriad connections can be made between noncontiguous pages.

My appropriation of "anarchy" here refers to a way of reading wherein the association of individuals and groups are writers, publishers, and readers who come together through books and the ideas they represent in order to broaden their perceptions. In effect all critical reader response is such a form of anarchy— its voluntary and cooperative purpose is to make sense of literary art. When this is done in a group setting, be it a book club or a classroom, the organization of the participants and the communication among them will determine how genuine the exchange can be. For the practice of reader-response anarchy to make sense, participants must all adhere to the principles of ecological perception toward the book in question and toward each other as a community of readers. To rephrase the Sewall epigraph, "it means fully witnessing both the magnificence and the destruction of our" ideas about the book and the world and about others' ideas. "It is allowing one's identity and boundaries to be permeable and flexible," to embrace plurality of vision, sense, and feeling, "despite the potential pain."

In conjunction with Barthes's concept of the writerly, an anarchist approach to picture-book discussion, the teaching or public discussion of a book such as Tan's *The Red Tree* shines a light on the master narratives of age appropriateness. This book is one of the most important I have encountered because it addresses the very common but still taboo notion that despair is a palpable and ferocious force in our world in a way that is accessible to anyone who knows the basics of how books work. Even though this book is undeniably sophisticated, it is not beyond those with limited literacy skills, particularly if such readers have access to an open and mindful listener willing to cooperate in their sense making. Although not necessary, it is certainly advantageous for children and less experienced picture-book readers to benefit from the sensible anarchy of collaborative reading. Likewise, narratologists benefit from the intersection of theory and practice that such a book lays open in terms of telling, showing, and the ambiguities of such terms in the face of picture-book form.

Writerly Metaphor

The Red Tree is important precisely because it does not gloss over existential dread or uncertainty. Unlike so much else in our world that encourages materialism and unecological perception or unconsciousness, Shaun Tan's work is arresting. The pause it gives us might nudge open the taps of awareness; to achieve ecological perception, we can use the sensible anarchy of collaborative reading to help the waters to flow past the drains and dams of the group's internal and social censors—our own included.

The experience of discussing *The Red Tree* with students in three classes and many other people corroborates for me its force and importance as a cocreative and collaborative text; I thank these students for our discussions and their papers. In the first fantasy class, where we used the Lothian paperback, someone proposed that the gender of the protagonist is ambiguous. The second class wanted to contest this notion based on the use of the pronoun "she" on the Simply Read Books dust jacket, highlighting the power of the peritext (which includes parts of the book such as covers, dust jackets, introductions, indexes, tables of contents, and other features sometimes considered "extraneous" to the main text). Those students would no doubt be pleased that Shaun Tan also refers to the protagonist as a girl on his Web site—authorial intention does hold sway. Nevertheless, he also made the deliberate choice to use second-person narration, leaving the protagonist nameless and avoiding gendered pronouns. The physical representation of the redhead is surely also deliberate: s/he is dressed in a shapeless tunic, has a basic blunt hairdo, and a cartoon-style face. Scott McCloud argues, "When you look at a photo or realistic drawing of a face—you see it as the face of *another*. But when you enter the world of the *cartoon—you see yourself*" (36). Although *The Red Tree* is not a comic, the principle of the face and the representation of the protagonist applies. McCloud maintains that "the cartoon is a *vacuum* into which our *identity and awareness* are pulled . . . an empty shell that we inhabit which enables us to travel in another realm. We don't just *observe* the cartoon, we *become* it" (36). Ultimately, the protagonist is "just a little piece of you" (37), a fact reinforced by the second person narration. In this instance the "you" may be more powerful than the more familiar "I" because of the uncertainty of who "you" is, perhaps because readers may wonder whether they somehow cause the redhead's journey by narrating it. The redhead's silence is part of this power and of the implication of readers. Although one could argue that her/his age is also ambiguous and that the figure could represent either a child or an adult, it is the thought that s/he is a child that causes the strong reactions that many readers of all ages have to this book.

In my experience readers initially respond to the force of the book's graphic expression with awed recognition of its soul-affecting power and/or by questioning its intended audience. *The Red Tree* is radical because at its root is the possibility that it expresses not just a recognizably bad day in the life but a much more drastic existential dread with the way things are or could soon be and because it makes this possibility accessible to all, from the very young (I place my bets on age three as a starting place) to the very old. A typical first question after people have leafed through *The Red Tree* is "who is this book FOR?" The possibility that it might be a book for children is enough to throw many readers for a loop, partly because of the content and partly due to its open narrative structure. Once readers move past the blocks of content and structure expectations and spend some time contemplating what they *perceive*—which activates readers' involvement and investment—it doesn't take too much for even reluctant adult readers to admit that whatever emotional hair triggers they're trying to avoid, *The Red Tree* is a work of art that provokes an exploration of many truths regarding alienation, despair, environmental degradation, existential crisis, loss, perception, power, vision, and voicelessness, to name a few. Nevertheless, much endorsed as plurality may be, it is a pedagogical challenge because one cannot predict clear outcomes, and one must be mindful not to intervene in ways that hinder discoveries or communication. Students may be reticent and/or resistant because writerly texts and anarchic order are unfamiliar and initially appear senseless, and also because students may be unschooled in the writerly enterprise of collaborative reading that I call sensible anarchy. This resistance has two main sources. First, such reading involves the personal risk of saying what you really feel and think, a risk that should be mitigated by the fact that there are no wrong answers and by a respectful and cooperative discussion environment. Second, children's literature has long been under the restraint that the subject matter of *The Red Tree* is not for children, although the natural order of human life suggests otherwise, much as we deny tragedy and irony as modal approaches in children's literature generally, despite their presence in children's lives. The emotions of fear, anxiety, loss, uncertainty, determination, and quiet watchfulness provide common ground among all children, and these are the feelings that *The Red Tree* allows us to perceive to the best of our abilities.

While the majority of the ninety or so readers I've heard from favor the red leaf motif as representing the hope of life, some read it as the hope of suicide and death. Is one party wrong? Or does it mean that the metaphor of the leaf is writerly, open ended and plural, leaving readers to make sense of it as they see fit in the context of the series of narrative segments presented? If so, then the writerly text, which has been considered an impossibility, can exist in a meaningful and accessible way, and it can be a children's book, too.

Individuals and society would be better served by seeing from several perspectives. The openness of *The Red Tree* helps to dismantle hierarchies of certainty and encourages us to perceive on new levels. Shaun Tan's Web site commentary on the book corroborates this view:

> Any apparent meaning is always laced with uncertainty. The red tree may bloom, but it will also die, so nothing is absolute or definite; there needs to be an accurate reflection of real life, as something that is continuously in search of resolution [. . .] . The ideas of the original book are very broad and I think point more to a method of expression—of "emotional worlds"—rather than any very specific content, so it not only endures variable interpretations, it almost demands them. This seems appropriate, as everyone's experience of "suffering" or "hope" is unique and personal.

Tan's intention is to invite contemplation rather than to expound on a topic. Similarly, Sewall maintains that "to see" includes listening and hearing, touching and feeling, sniffing, licking, and tasting. These are the ways we sense our world. *To see* is visceral, symbolic, a path to enlightenment, a choice. Unfortunately, those of us conditioned by Western values tend to bring little awareness to the exchange between ourselves and our surroundings (Sewall, *Sight and Sensibility* 58). Robert Scholes made a related argument in 1978 in his "most important and controversial" suggestion: "It seems to me self-evident that *the semantic field for many verbal signs is not exclusively verbal*"; that is, "our interpretive equipment" and "part of language itself" constitutes "an enormous amount of information that is not normally considered linguistic" (203). Picture books are self-evident examples of both Sewall's and Scholes's points. The contemplation of Tan's illustrations and words are likely to be a visceral experience. If we take our cues from Colin Thompson's *Looking for Atlantis* and *Falling Angels*, two other picture books, and see with our hearts—which is another way of expressing the notion of ecological perception— then looking is no longer enough: understanding is a process that deepens with time and is fed by many streams and rivulets and altered by the tides. Rereading and discussion are a crucial part of such a process. Having engaged in this process over the last few years, I've come to a few conclusions.

The writerly metaphors on each page opening coupled with the fragmentary story combine to yield a recognizable yet open narrative, which is meaningful and accessible to a wide range of readers, with or without damaged identities. Each page of the book presents us with a central metaphor, and the longer one actively peruses the text, the more intricate the web of metaphors becomes. Toward the beginning of the story, the protagonist risks suffocation in a shower and a rising tide of black leaves. This feeling is then represented through other related images throughout the book, among them the fish of darkness, the bottle of solitude, the crowd of isolation, the culture—or cityscape—of alienation, the snail of eternity, the ships of calamity, unattainable marvels, monstrous mechanisms, performance anxiety, and being lost to oneself. As readers of any age are bound to recognize from their own experiences, the outside world can be intimidating (see Tan's

Web site for more images). This notion is most clearly depicted in the deaf machine and without sense or reason pages and the troubles and terrible fates pages. A linear reading seems to favor some version of a hope/discovery/happy ending narrative. Yet even a linear reading must account for the many cycle motifs and various other circles and connections. Many readers don't become aware of the red leaf until after they've read through the book at least once (unless they've read the Simply Read Books dust jacket), and there's arguably an implicit link between the red tree of the ending and the black leaves at the beginning.

The central image motif is of the leaf or leaves, which links directly to the writerly metaphor of the red tree. I would argue that the story is predominantly about black leaf experiences. If the red leaf symbolizes hope, as the popular consensus seems to have it (based on the Simply Read Books dust jacket and various World Wide Web commentaries such as those on http://www.quaker.org), the dark leaves must therefore symbolize gloom or despair. The red leaves will inevitably fall and turn dark. I am unsatisfied with the notion that the red leaf or the red tree symbolizes hope, of whatever kind, and would like to propose that the red leaf is a synecdoche for the tree and that both the leaf and the tree are metaphors for the redhead's spirit. The leaf parallels the redhead's journey, and both achieve a point of transcendence in the final moment. The book could be read as a commentary on the ills of a depersonalized and dehumanized existence in an industrialized and unsustainable society where the days are marked by suffocating, relentless repetition of meaningless actions, all of which are cruel on some level because they deny meaningful relations with a community. The protagonist is fully isolated even when others are present.

The redhead's heart seems locked away until the final pages, when it finds full expression in the tree and a smile—the only facial expression in the whole book. I've come to the conclusion that this is very much a book about learning to see and varying levels of perception and vision. One can read it as a sort of vision quest for both the protagonist and the reader: The hero goes out into the world. S/he encounters a great many challenges and questions and has no evident guides or helpers (though there are friendly birds). After experiencing a sort of "dark night of the soul," however, the hero returns home to her/his intuition ("just as you imagined it would be") and finds "it": the vision of the red tree, which symbolizes a profound sense of realization and of self, of spiritual awareness and a compassionate heart, a form of repair. The reader's quest, meanwhile, is more literally the endeavor to re-vision, to perceive more broadly and fully. The suddenness of the leaf seedling's transformation into a tree (despite the page turn, not much clock time seems to have passed, though the clock on the night table has notably vanished) befits the momentousness of the vision. While such a description makes the vision sound temporary, this too is fitting, for the repetition of the word "sometimes," which also began the narration, suggests that this is likely not a once-in-a-lifetime crisis that has been overcome, thereby supporting the cyclical nature of lives and living.

The single red leaf and the protagonist maintain the filament or flame of soul and heart needed to make it through a figurative black leaf day. By the end of the journey, nearly having lost a sense of self, the protagonist has a vision of change: the red tree, which represents awakening, being, and wholeness. While the leaf stands in for the tree throughout the narrative, it is detached and blown about by the vagaries of fate and numbing routine. The leaf, forlorn as the protagonist throughout, is a sign of her/his spirit. A leaf is more readily visible than a seed; the leaf nevertheless seems to represent the metaphorical seed of an idea that is actualized at the end of the day. This moment of illumination is a kind of "coming home," which is fitting as the tree springs into being in the redhead's room. The words "right in front of you" are significant because the leaf has heretofore been behind, below, above, or otherwise away from the protagonist. Having been out in the world and having faced its perils, s/he has returned home capable of spotting sudden surprises; somehow the journey has jogged her/his consciousness awake.

The redhead is breaking free of the insanity of the single vision, alienation, and brutality that appear to govern the human world.

The fantasy of the red tree springing from a single leaf stem into a full, vibrant, pulsing tree is very compelling. It suggests becoming attuned to what really matters, to true needs. To say the tree represents hope leaves too much unsaid and unexplored. For those who feel their lives are hopeless, such a reading is also likely too trite. It's all very well to be told there's always reason to hope, but if you are not in a position to imagine it, then you'll never see the red tree. The plural vision afforded by ecological perception acknowledges the pain of social prescription and proscription and the inner freedom and power of being, which is independent of all physical and worldly restrictions. The change within the protagonist is represented by the red tree, for which the narrative provides no explanation—suddenly the tree is there and readers are left to account for it: how should the tree be read? Ecological perception might lead us to conclude that the redhead has achieved some form of enlightenment. Because this is a writerly text, other conclusions are left to be drawn. Perceptive readers will voluntarily and cooperatively pull these readings together into an anarchic assembly, thereby making sense of the writerly metaphors and overall text.

The Red Tree is in some ways a counter to the much touted "don't worry; be happy" mentality that would have us deny our own true feelings about ourselves and the perilous state of the world and of our planet Earth. The book can be read as a counterstory wherein readers make up the "morally abnormal" community that views the protagonist with a loving eye and marshal the moral resources to counter the master narrative of standardized normalcy through the recognition that every person has his or her own version of normal rather than adhering to the social decree that normal behavior fits within a narrow range of acceptability. In this way Tan's writerly text doesn't "merely *reflect* a shift in understanding. [It sets] out to *cause* a shift" (Nelson 156). Because "perception is a participatory act" and because "the ultimate power of vision [is] the ability to co-create the world we see and act upon" (Sewall, *Sight and Sensibility* 15–16), Shaun Tan's *The Red Tree* is a powerful example of postmodernism and "the re-emergence of a relational way of seeing" and of "our developing consciousness of the relationships that constitute a woven, interdependent world" (Sewall, *Sight and Sensibility* 52). By embracing the challenges of this text with all manner of readers in the ideal practice of sensible anarchy, we stand a good chance of emerging from our "collective myopia" (Sewall, *Sight and Sensibility* 66), accepting our emotions, and honoring our perceptive capabilities. What better place to begin this process than with picture books, all of which lay the foundations and possibilities for storytelling and reading in a variety of ways. The boundaries of possibility are continually being recast in picture-book publishing. Although Tan is not the only one pushing those boundaries, *The Red Tree* is a book that will mark the genre of children's literature and the field of children's publishing. *The Red Tree* shifts our understanding of what picture books can be and can do and therefore of what narrative can be and can do; the words are only a fraction of the meaning, and much of that is conveyed by how they look and where and how they are positioned on the page. A picture-book opening would reveal much more about the classic distinction between plot and story featuring the queen's demise and the king's subsequent grief and death, and if it were illustrated by Tan or someone equally courageous, it, too, could foster ecological perception. Books like *The Red Tree* are beacons lighting the way to a new awareness of the possibilities in picture-book storytelling for all ages.

"Narratology" and "children's literature" are terms that either can lead to myopic views of picture books or, if you are willing, can combine to enable remarkable perceptions of theory, literature, and your life. Tan's book reminds us that these are all connected. It is no accident that the red tree grows in the protagonist's bedroom: anything is possible.

Works Cited

"Anarchy." *The Random House College Dictionary*. 1980.
Barthes, Roland. "Style and Its Image." *Literary Style: A Symposium*. Ed.

and trans. Seymour Chatman. London: Oxford University Press, 1971. 3–15.

McCloud, Scott. *Understanding Comics: The Invisible Art*. New York: Harper Perennial, 2004.

Nelson, Hilde Lindemann. *Damaged Identities, Narrative Repair*. Ithaca NY: Cornell University Press, 2001.

Nodelman, Perry. *The Hidden Adult: Defining Children's Literature*. Baltimore: Johns Hopkins University Press, 2008.

Poe, Edgar Allan. "*Twice-told Tales*: A Review." *Graham's Magazine* May 1842. Rpt. in *Edgar Allan Poe: Essays and Reviews*. The Library of America. New York: Literary Classics of the U.S., 1984. 569–77.

Scholes, Robert. "Afterthoughts on Narrative II: Language, Narrative, and Anti-Narrative." *On Narrative*. Ed. W. J. T. Mitchell. Chicago: University of Chicago Press, 1981. 200–08.

Sewall, Laura. *Sight and Sensibility: The Ecopsychology of Perception*. New York: Tarcher, 1999.

———. "The Skill of Ecological Perception." *Ecopsychology: Restoring the Earth Healing the Mind*. Ed. Theodore Roszak, Mary E. Gomes, and Allen D. Kramer. San Francisco: Sierra Club, 1995. 201–15.

Tan, Shaun. Home page. 7 July 2008. http://www.shauntan.net.

———. *The Red Tree*. 2001. South Melbourne: Lothian, 2002.

Thompson, Colin. *Falling Angels*. 2001. London: Red Fox, 2002.

———. *Looking for Atlantis*. 1993. New York: Dragonfly Books, 1997.

8

Now Playing

Silent Cinema and Picture-Book Montage

NATHALIE OP DE BEECK

In 1926, after illustrating an edition of George MacDonald's *The Light Princess*, children's artist Dorothy P. Lathrop compared the artistic imagination and film spectatorship: "To think in terms of illustration is to put one's self in a projection room, where the story unfolds in a series of pictures which leap into the mind as complete and as silently as if falling upon a moving picture screen. 'The princess was lying motionless on her bed'—and suddenly there she is for the drawing. There are no 'experiences.' Only an intense effort to make tangible the intangible [. . .] . At any rate there is something very like magic back of it all" (38). Lathrop idealizes the imaginative process and with it the flickering cinematic image. Her projection-room metaphor likens the artist's consciousness to a projection booth and the artist's physical process to cinematic recording and projection technology. Using an affirmative modernist analogy between body and machine, Lathrop indicates the pervasiveness of cinema in 1926. She also implies the creative uses to which technological apparatuses could be put, materially and metaphorically. She offers a utopian vision of production in which "an intense effort to make tangible the intangible" makes for a realization of "magic."

Lathrop compares an interrelated series of pictures, produced by book illustrators like herself, to a set of film stills, parts of an indivisible sequence. When she refers to the unfolding of a fairy tale, her remarks suggest the pleasurable immediacy of film spectatorship. If the story requires a princess, Lathrop says, "Suddenly there she is for the drawing," projected on the imagination as in the movie house and consequently spooled out upon the page. Lathrop's artist is as much recorder as imaginative creator, her human ingenuity allied with the mechanical. Her comments acknowledge early cinema's influence on artists' and storytellers' vocabularies, cinema's fascinating ability to put even inanimate things in motion, and the reader's ability to make sense in and of the gaps between still images. The imagination animates illustrated texts.

As Lathrop indicates, modern picture books and illustrated texts parallel emergent technologies and early twentieth-century modes of communication, including animated cinema. Animation was by no means new in 1926, the era of the talking revolution in cinema, and neither were the sequential modes of comic strips, photoplays, and picture-book narratives. But American picture books came into their own in the early twentieth century, helped along by an increasing book-industry commitment to profitable juvenile publishing and by educators' fears of a decline in storytelling and material folk traditions. At the time, picture books offered a comforting nod to read-aloud, tangible print culture, while representing the latest developments in printing, the current multimedia modes of storytelling, and the pleasurable distractions of modern life. The picture book, as it developed in the late nineteenth and the early twentieth century, was not (or not just) a throwback to premodern times.[1] Instead, the modern picture book reflected and influenced the multiple media waxing and waning.

By the time Lathrop made her remarks, people already had fully developed picture-book sequences at their fingertips.[2] Readers could choose from books by Randolph Caldecott, Beatrix Potter, W. W. Denslow, L. Leslie Brook, and William Nicholson, to name a few memorable examples.[3] What remains, then, is to re-present sequential communication as it crossed over into newer technologies and to acknowledge changing modes of perception. Every transformative or new media provides the necessary contexts for the emergence of a new—although not necessarily improved or somehow better—media. As Tom Gunning writes, "The century-long pursuit of 'animated pictures' reveals cinema's imbrication within new experiences of technology, time and visual representation" ("Animated Pictures" 318). One might make a similar statement about developments in comics and picture books. Like animation the picture book evolved as a narrative medium and art form, reflecting the ways its producers and consumers perceived temporality, interpreted imagery, and used the latest technical means of expression.

This essay establishes a comparison between silent cinema and pictorial literature of the modern era, while acknowledging the limits to any comparison among media and urging attention to context (of picture books especially). Both silent cinema and pictorial literature deal in immediacy, montage, and early twentieth-century narrative forms, suggesting what fascinated popular audiences of the early twentieth century. Some of the ideas here might be extended to live-action cinema with intertitles or paratextual written signs, subtitled films, comics and graphic narrative, or picture books of later decades. But I want to emphasize the modern context of early twentieth-century animation and picture books. Although some of my observations may be read as formalist, I wish to historicize my examples and dispute reductive claims that a picture book of today is directly analogous to an animated piece of a century ago (or, for that matter, a picture book of a century ago). Both texts involve visual play and rely on their audience's imagination to close gaps. Yet too often critics attempt to universalize familiar media and childhood, proclaiming them easy to understand or divorcing them from salient cultural-historical contexts.

It is not uncommon to find a picture book of, say, the 1920s mentioned in the same breath with one of the 1940s, despite the fact that picture-book conventions and concepts of childhood continually shift and change.[4] Formal analysis needs to take into account the socioeconomic and political conditions in which texts are produced and consumed, the ways in which texts are fabricated, and the implicit and explicit stories texts tell. Although a picture book and an animated short may have formal similarities, I would not discount the ideological implications of these captivating media, which remain attached to their originating spatiotemporal contexts even when they become accessible to audiences today. Further, I would not argue any direct equivalence between the animated feature and the picture book—or, for that matter, between animation and comics. Viewing a film variety program at a storefront movie house or nickelodeon is unlike handling a material book, sharing a book one to one, reading in a small group, or reading alone. Picture books do not belong in the same media categories as live theater or motion pictures but instead are related to and emerge alongside technologies of the moving image and synchronized sound, whether live or recorded. As modes of production that developed concurrently, cinematic animation and the picture book share similar subject matter and a focus on sequentiality that became possible with changing print technologies and with dissolving boundaries between multiple media.

Also, while picture-book examples of the period often address a young readership, cinematic pieces are not necessarily "for" children at all—although picture books, comics sequences, and animated work often feature young protagonists. Silent animated cinema and pictorial texts exist in complex relation to each other. Certain aesthetics of animated films, which like the Sunday funnies were not for children exclusively, appear in children's picture-book storytelling and vice versa. My research indicates neither a strong division nor a close equation, but rather a blur between picture books, their sequential counterparts in comics and graphic narrative, and animation.[5]

Rather than align animated films or pictorial books with childhood exclusively, we might say we associate them with childhood or align them with a youthful (not to say juvenile) imagination.

As Ian Wojcik-Andrews writes, paraphrasing Perry Nodelman, "Not all children's films are just about children, and not all films children see are just children's films" (7). Noting intersections between early twentieth-century newspaper comics, animation, and children's literature, Wojcik-Andrews encourages a recognition of ambiguities among media. He designates a category of "countercinematic" films—for example, the one-reelers and feature comedies of Charlie Chaplin, Vittorio De Sica's neorealist *The Bicycle Thief* (Italy, 1948), or Albert Lamorisse's *The Red Balloon* (France, 1956)—that are child oriented but not child specific in their appeal. According to Wojcik-Andrews, "The action of countercinematic children's films—if action is the right word— often takes place in real rather than movie time" (7), highlighting the pleasure of experience in the now, whether humorous or serious. This approach questions the concern with "action," which implies linear narrative, and links the countercinematic to a perception of immediacy. For him the countercinematic invites plural or crossover audiences of children and adults and relates to the pleasure of suspense.

Suspense likewise originates for readers who want to find out what lies on the next page of a picture book. The much-referenced "drama of the turning of the page" cited by Rémy Charlip, Barbara Bader, and William Moebius (among others) is associated with picture-book storytelling. Yet it can be understood more broadly as a drama related to modernity and the shock of the new. Because picture books make use of distraction and surprise, they constitute an eminently modern storytelling form. Some picture books offer so many lively distractions and payoffs along their seemingly linear paths that we can argue whether the journey or the ending is the thing. Just as readers focus on imaginative experience and revelation rather than the completion of a task when reading work by Gertrude Stein, James Joyce, or Marcel Proust, readers exist in a transformative moment while experiencing a popular modern text like a picture book. Rather than proceed to a distinction between so-called high or low modernism, or highbrow and lowbrow aesthetics, we might acknowledge the similar experiences of absorption that diverse texts make possible for modern audiences.

Within a visual-verbal narrative framework, picture books create the kind of spontaneous effects that characterize the "cinema of attraction"—the trick-centered, carnivalesque cinematic modes contemporaneous with early twentieth-century picture books. According to André Gaudreault's and Tom Gunning's accounts of the cinema of attraction, early audiences were not as gullible as some midcentury scholars assumed. Apocryphal tales aside, audiences did not look at the black-and-white moving image of a locomotive and think they would be hit by a real train, nor did they look down the barrel of an outlaw's gun in *The Great Train Robbery* and fear real bullets shooting from the screen. Given their knowledge of photographic technologies like magic lanterns and rotoscopes, they were surprised and impressed by the new modes, but not naive about the projected moving image. Gunning establishes that crowds were aware of the cinematic apparatus but willing participants in the spectacle. "This is a cinema that displays its visibility, willing to rupture a self-enclosed fictional world for a chance to solicit the attention of the spectator," Gunning explains ("Cinema of Attraction" 64). Cinema audiences suspended disbelief to take extra pleasure in filmmakers' winking displays of their own trickery.

Just as an audience is aware of the mechanical apparatus required to produce and project the animated film, then, readers of a picture book cannot help but be aware of the artifice of the book's pictorial sequence and reproducible paper package. Considering picture books in relation to the cinema of attraction enables critics to explore how picture books invite performativity and participation. The twentieth-century development of animation and trick cinema parallels concurrent developments in the modern picture book, comics, and graphic narrative. All these reproducible media interpellate and reinforce a mass audience. They rely on sequential exposition, limited words and phrases, and pantomimic gestures.[6] They are produced through creative enterprise and technically skilled labor. They often deal in comic or absurd subject matter, typically associated with immaturity and popularity rather than with a realist or ostensibly serious, literary quality. Indeed, after 1908 many film creators hoped to upgrade from morally ambiguous burlesque shows—focused on the performing body and low comedy—to material that could appeal to a middle-class audience with greater spending power and, allegedly, more refined tastes.[7]

Moreover, modern perception of pictorial entertainment—including picture-book storytelling and other games and diversions—changed in response to photography and cinematic production. The picture-book sequence, like the animated one-reeler, foregrounds jokes, surprises, optical trickery, and the mechanical apparatus. Reflective readers grasp that the print format itself is produced mechanically and the finished book serves the reader as a sort of tangible, manipulable apparatus. To mime a Derridean attention to words and phrasing, we might say that picture books—like cinematic features—are *now playing*.

Early animation inevitably alludes to print culture and pictorial modes of communication. Animators did emerge from and borrow from print publishing (and vice versa) while experimenting in newer media. Animation built on established entertainment features like the magic-lantern lecture, the vaudeville act, stop-motion onscreen magic, and journalistic pictorial sequences like the photoplay. With the passing of time and changes in publishing, picture-book creators—that is, readers, filmgoers, modern consumers—poached in early animation as well, imitating its iconic characters, plotting, and techniques of suspense.[8]

As late nineteenth- and early twentieth-century media developed, intertextuality was a given. Animation historian Donald Crafton writes, "The early cinema in all its forms had a craving for narrative, dramatic situations, visual motifs, and iconography [. . .] that could only be satisfied by foraging in other media" (35). At the same time, Crafton cautions against "a widespread misconception that comics were somehow intimately related to the inception of animation" (36), since by his reckoning "the early producers were just not all that interested in comic-strip graphics. They viewed the strips only as a mine of story material and ready-made characters with appeal for the [. . .] huge middle-class audience" (44). Crafton prefers to link animation to vaudeville, particularly the theatrics of the lightning sketch artists who amused audiences with swiftly drawn caricatures on blackboards and paper. He cites lightning sketchers and animators like James Stuart Blackton who claimed to have "outgrown" their fascinations with animated cartoons. Blackton, for instance, quit animation around 1909 and took an ostensibly more mature interest in the business of film production (46). Allusions to vaudeville stunts that were going out of fashion and animators' eventual decisions to distance themselves from cartoon-style trickery imply a growing stigma around animation as mainstream culture, a division between adult and child diversions, and a gradual redefinition of mass popular entertainment as juvenile amusement. This trend helps us rethink the printed visual sequence, aimed at entertaining a youth market and miming the special effects of animation.

Before the 1915 invention and patenting of the cel method of animation (in which changing foreground material is painted on transparent overlays, so that background material need not be redrawn for each frame), creators traced and inked individual drawings on separate sheets of paper, then photographed them in sequence. They reverted to the familiar materials at their disposal, pen and ink on paper, to begin creative work in a new mode. An effective and often cited example is Winsor McCay's *Little Nemo* (1911), which opens with McCay's self-assured lightning sketch of three characters. The live-action portion of the film focuses first on his confident hand movement as he inks the characters, then shows him betting with his jolly, cigar-chomping male friends that he can bring the sketch to life. Afterward, in a montage exaggerated for comic effect, men deliver literal barrels labeled "ink" and enormous boxes labeled "paper" to McCay's art studio, where he laboriously draws his individual frames one by one; in a slapstick moment a curious boy leans on a completed, apparently arranged stack of drawings and sends them cascading to the studio floor. Against these odds McCay wins his bet. He places the original sketch of Little Nemo and friends on an easel, an intertitle directs viewers, "Watch me move," and the illustrated characters flow into motion, observed through the hand-cranked camera's eye and hand-tinted in color on a white ground.

Others among McCay's contemporaries retold well-known tales with stop-motion special effects, as in Thomas Edison's *The "Teddy" Bears* (1907) and Howard S. Moss's Motoy Films (1917, using dolls, stuffed animals, and intertitles in doggerel rhyme), thus adapting puppeteers' methods to cinema.[9] The increasing competition and borrowing among media was not lost on book illustrators themselves, as we see in the opening quotation from Lathrop or, for that matter, in examples of artists who involved themselves with marionettes, books, and animation. In a 1939 *Horn Book Magazine* appreciation of German cut-paper animator Lotte Reiniger, Eric Walter White, who coauthored three illustrated books with Reiniger in the 1930s, celebrates the way Reiniger's stop-motion filmmaking—in *The Adventures of Prince Achmed* (1926) and other animated films—brings together "two old and honourable art forms [. . .] the puppet play and the silhouette" (45). Reiniger, whose work was shown on American screens, created elaborate two-dimensional paper cutouts. She hinged their limbs and accessories, manipulated each tiny piece, photographed the silhouettes frame by frame, then hand tinted the empty backgrounds for a kind of color film that could flash or dim depending on the desired effect. The results resemble Thai shadow puppetry, minus strings or sticks to produce motion. White describes Reiniger's work as "kinetic rather than static" and admires her ability to transform material puppets into celluloid fantasies. Attentive to developments in montage, he urges readers "not to forget [Reiniger's] passages of brilliant editing, such as the Magic Fight in *Achmet* [*sic*] with its positive-negative lightning effect that anticipated Eisenstein's celebrated machine-gun sequence in *October* by two or three years" (47–48). Reiniger's experiments in multimedia storytelling and tendency toward bricolage in artistic production characterize the modernist mentality, which found inventive ways to manipulate old media such as paper.

If animators relied on print conventions, producers of print media used metaphors of animation to explain the interplay of words and pictures on the page, although Crafton argues that "the word 'cinematic' is often carelessly used to describe comic-strip art" and warns against it (93). The sequential still images in a picture book and the moving frames or cels of a film stand in different relations to time, of course, because under ordinary conditions a film cannot be halted, reversed, skipped over, or hastened to a close the way a book can. Scott McCloud, in his well-known definition of comics as "juxtaposed pictorial and other images in deliberate sequence" (9), duly considers the relation of comics and film. "Isn't animated film just *visual art in sequence?*" asks a skeptical character in McCloud's metacomic, to which McCloud (i.e., the comics character representing McCloud) replies, "Animation is sequentially juxtaposed in *time* but not spatially *juxtaposed* as comics are. / Each successive frame of a *movie* is projected on exactly the *same* space—the screen—while each frame of *comics* must occupy a *different* space. / *Space* does for *comics* what *time* does for *film!*" (7). McCloud's concise statement—with its bold and italic emphases for enhanced visual and verbal impact—applies just as well to picture-book space as to comics space; picture books do differ from comic strips, based on the conventions of panels and multipage format, but picture books relate to forms of graphic narrative in that they emerge alongside broadsheets, illustrated newspapers, photoplays, and comic strips, so that we can understand the place of picture books in modernity. McCloud qualifies his answer on space for comics and time for film—"You might say that *before* it's projected, film is just a very very very very *slow* comic!" (8)—indicating that the experience of the medium depends on its presentation (that is, whether we turn pages, flip a flipbook, or look at individual animation frames in a row, for example).

In any event it remains necessary to discriminate among media. As Maria Nikolajeva and Carole Scott note in *How Picturebooks Work*, "Unlike film, the picturebook medium is discontinuous, and there is no direct way to depict the flow of movement. However, unlike decorative art, the picturebook medium is narrative and sequential, and intends to convey a sense of movement and of duration [. . .] . Different graphic codes, many borrowed from comics and photography, have been adopted by picturebook authors" (139). This ahistorical and formalist statement covers many cases and acknowledges the influence of mass-reproducible modes like cinema, photography, and comics. Similarly, Perry Nodelman writes that "picture books are more like theater in their storytelling conventions than they are like films," based on how picture books stage their visual and verbal material in space and time (231). Nodelman investigates the "ironic relationship between the sequential storytelling of words and the series of stopped moments we see in a sequence of pictures" (239) and concludes that picture books differ from both novels and films in their ability to operate simultaneously in spatial and temporal registers. "According to [cinema critic George] Bluestone, novels create space by using time, and films create time by using space [. . .] . Picture books do both, but in ways that seem to contradict each other," says Nodelman (241), echoing McCloud's dictum that "*Space* does for *comics* what *time* does for *film!*" (7). Thus, critics alternately align picture books with cinematic, theatrical, or comic-strip media.

These critical examples seem persuasive, but an investigation of each era's graphic codes is in order. Critics must ask how and why the picture-book sequence developed as it did during the modern era, and why populations fascinated with the moving image, cinematic duration, and flickering immateriality would continue producing and consuming cumbersome, materially hefty, self-reflexively theatrical narrative sequences of still images. The same questions could be addressed, in reverse, to silent animation, which trades in pictorial narrative conventions like the comic-strip voice bubble. The picture book developed in relation to animation in the early twentieth century, just as animation became feasible and comprehensible through analogies to comics.

Some projected animation mimes comic-strip material viewed at a leisurely pace, with big-screen bonuses.[10] Wallace Carlson's *Dreamy Dud—He Resolves Not to Smoke* (1915), based on Carlson's *Dreamy Dud* comic strip, depicts a boy who steals and smokes a pipe. As the title implies, this includes a dream segment related to McCay's more famous *Little Nemo in Slumberland* comics and animation. Donald Crafton calls Carlson "as dependent on McCay for ideas as for technical inspiration" (279), but *Dreamy Dud* still provides worthy examples beyond the better-known and widely distributed work of McCay.[11]

Besides the flimsy plot about smoking, the film lingers on the way Dud's pet dog, Wag, does tricks for Dud, dances, and chats with an amiable cat, which remains friendly until Wag whispers something behind his paw, causing the offended cat to arch and bristle. Using a commonplace technique known as cycling (i.e., repeating a series of frames forward and/or backward), animator Carlson primes the audience's level of amusement. Similarly, McCay's *Gertie the Dinosaur* (1914) reiterates sequences of a dinosaur shifting its weight back and forth, back and forth, in a silly dance. (Most animation of the period includes some cycling, a time-saving device that predated less-laborious cel animation.) Audiences today watch *Dreamy Dud* with some impatience, aggravated by its need to repeat Wag's backflips. Yet we recognize that the animator wanted to replay visual tricks purely for spectatorial pleasure and unrelated to advancing the slender plot.[12] Rudimentary techniques notwithstanding, we can look beyond the superficials and consider the mode of amusing an audience in the second decade of the twentieth century with antic line drawings. Crafton makes much the same point about stop-motion trick filmmaking: "Although some may view this [the trick film] as 'primitive,' it demonstrates that even at the beginning the makers of animated films were, like earlier romantics, fascinated with the material of artistic creation. These subjects [. . .] were also representations of animators' enduring concern with autokinesis, movement in itself, the stuff of animation" (32–33).

Conventions of print media—for example, the cat's offstage "Mee-ow!" to signal its presence before it is shown, Wag's quick turn of his head toward the voice-bubble meow, and a dotted sight line connecting the dog's gaze to the cat—show that film creators did not yet trust audiences to understand montage and film editing. They also found creative ways to imply sound, which might or might not be synched with a feature, depending on the piece's budget and the popularity of the venue. Voice bubbles acknowledge the absence of recorded voices, although cinema scholars hasten to point out that silent film (with its live score, sound effects, and occasional voice actors or lecturers) was never really silent but always participatory in a present-tense manner that spectators seldom experience any longer. "It was quite exceptional, in the silent period, for a film to be projected in complete silence," comments Gaudreault. "The filmic spectacle, even in those days, was nearly always an *audio*-visual one like (for example) circus or theatre" (274). Norman King likewise writes, "Live sound actualised the image and, merging with it, emphasised the presentness of the performance and of the audience" (43). Early silents were often accompanied by lecturers, related to magic-lantern slide-show lecturers of the past, who explained the screened goings-on or pretended (like McCay in *Gertie the Dinosaur*) to interact with onscreen action.[13]

In the five-minute *Dreamy Dud* sequence, Dud plays with Wag, sneaks into a house to steal a sleeping man's pipe, and puffs on the pipe while sitting (unwisely) outside the man's window. "Here's where I make Pittsburg [*sic*] look like a million dollars worth of sunshine!" Dud says in a voice bubble, lighting the pipe and implying the mass audience's awareness of industrial pollution. The words in the voice bubble appear a few at a time, accounting for the audience's reading speed and acknowledging their source in comic strips. As Dud smokes, the puffs resolve into figures, including the grouchy old man from whom he stole the pipe and an imploring woman (who resembles a neoclassical Fate but also the famous Princess Nicotine of earlier trick films and variety-show cigarette ads). The smoke forms the words "You're a bad boy!" an insult that makes Dud giggle. At last the Spirit of Smoke lifts Dud into space and maroons him on the crescent moon, where he sits and swings a bit. Dud gets his comeuppance in this fantasy sequence, brought on by the effects of nicotine or whatever else might bring on a pipe dream (and here again we cannot help but think of Little Nemo and McCay's *Dreams of the Rarebit Fiend* comic strips, on the ill effects of eating before bedtime).

Carlson's animated visuals reside very much in the foreground of his sketchy "set" for the piece. The horizon line or picture plane is only implied, and the caricatures are developed. Later in the film the side of the house lends vertical stability to the setting (Crafton 110), while an outer-space, presatellite-age view of the planet Earth provide the illusion of Dud telling a joke to the Man in the Moon, then free-falling through clouds to the ground below. Mimetic visual excursions alternate with Dud's comical spoken remarks, which write themselves into thin air at a comfortable reading pace and rest there while the characters freeze, as if the audience needs time to say the words aloud. We might think of *Dreamy Dud* as a hybrid of animated cartoon and comic strip, complete with setups for Dud's droll one-liners. Building on McCloud's remark ("*before* it's projected, film is just a very very very very *slow* comic!" [8]), we might call this a very very very very *slow* projection that presumes a measured reading speed. An animated film like *Dud* reasonably may be associated with childish entertainment while interpellating a much broader readership, including adults nostalgic for simpler times and easy jokes in their modern world.[14] Certainly students and conference audiences, upon seeing *Dreamy Dud* today, still find it funny if unsophisticated—and sophisticated it was never meant to be.

Another animated example, *Krazy Kat and Ignatz Mouse Go to the Circus* (1916), comes from the comic strip by George Herriman, animated by Leon Searl. Some elements of *Dreamy Dud* recur. Again we have voice bubbles—there is more dialogue in this one—and are left to imagine or read aloud the voices of familiar comic-strip characters. The characters do not move while the dialogue writes itself into place, implying a concern that readers could focus their attention on either words or movement, but not both at once.

Krazy Kat orders "a ticket and a half" to the circus—the half is for Ignatz Mouse, who's not there yet—then sways back and forth a few times. Krazy's cycled swaying is a nonessential activity, but one that plays up the animator's art, lengthens the viewing time, and establishes the spaciness of Herriman's wistful character. The picture plane and background are somewhat more detailed than in Carlson's work—audiences can read the circus signs and more easily grasp the horizontal ground of the animated plane—though the action happens in the foreground, and there are marked transitions between spaces, without visual "pans" across space.

The film follows a narrative logic, but Searl, the animator, cycles certain pleasing details—like Krazy Kat's ambling walk and flexible tail—for their humor value. Searl frames Krazy's twisting, jerking tail in an iris-eye shape, directing spectators to watch. Based on later animation, audiences today might expect the arriving Ignatz, whose puzzled thoughts are represented as a big question mark, to chomp Krazy's fidgety tail or otherwise tease the cat. But nothing happens; the filmmakers linger on the tail just for the antic way it moves. The unlikely couple also goes to the circus, but spectators never see the circus acts. Instead, viewers see only the bleachers, where Krazy and Ignatz sit on their date. The cinema spectators are in the space where the circus ring would be, observing the audience, and we can make of that what we will.

Drama ensues when another character, a bulldog named Lynxie, strolls by Krazy and expresses hunger for a fat mouse or even one that "ain't so fat." Krazy cheerfully pretends not to have seen any mice, and Lynxie moves on. Ignatz emerges from behind Krazy, his knees quivering, and Krazy asks him, "Why is mice sech cowards?" "Fool I ain't a coward," Ignatz responds, in unpunctuated vernacular. He boldly strides away, heading for a building labeled Dressing Rooms, where he looks through the keyhole. At this an onscreen keyhole silhouette gives spectators an Ignatz-eye view: he sees a busty woman in her underthings, from the chest down. This lowbrow moment is followed by a still portrait of Ignatz, in close-up, winking broadly at the audience and breaking the fourth wall. Ignatz successfully frightens the woman to prove mice are not cowards. In the denouement Krazy gets a broom on the head when she or he tries to do the same.

Gunning provides ways of reading films like these in his article "Now You See It, Now You Don't," which details the "now playing" presence of the cinema of attractions. Gunning contrasts classical narrative cinema—based firmly on advancing a plot—with the nonnarrative form that calls attention to its technological components and promises sensational surprises without insisting on a strictly linear plot (e.g., the films of Blackton, McCay, Georges Méliès, and Emil Cohn). Gunning's essay largely concerns live-action cinema from 1895 through about 1910 and thus is not at all restricted to drawn animation, which developed after stop-motion animation of actual objects like furniture, appliances, and other household items. But Gunning's conclusions apply to the earliest cinema, to trends in filmmaking during the second decade of the twentieth century, and potentially to the picture book. For instance, Gunning outlines three assumptions that apply to both the cinema of attractions and the early picture book: the "evolutionary assumption" that sees early cinema as a "primitive" stage in the full development of true cinema as we know it; the "cinematic assumption" that depends on conventions of theater to explain montage and critiques the term "cinematic" in a manner contrary to Crafton's; and the "narrative assumption [...] that cinema only truly appeared when it discovered the mission of telling stories" ("Now You See It" 72). Gunning complicates these assumptions based on the inventiveness of nonlinear/nondiegetic early film or the nonnarrative elements calculated to surprise a spectator rather than to advance any plot.

Repeatedly, the theses evoke comparisons with picture-book

experience. "Rather than desire for an (almost) endlessly delayed fulfillment and a cognitive involvement in pursuing an enigma [i.e., what we pursue when enjoying classical narrative]," Gunning writes, "early cinema [. . .] *attracts* in a different manner. It arouses a curiosity that is satisfied by surprise rather than narrative suspense" ("Now You See It" 75). Here again I would assert that picture books set up *narrative* suspense, but many (and certainly didactic A B C s and counting books) rely on quick payoffs followed by new tricks to appeal to the reader and on numerous moments of closure instead of a buildup to one conclusion. Gunning adds, "Time in narrative [. . .] is never just linear progression (one damn thing after another), it is also the gathering of successive moments into a pattern, a trajectory, a sense. Attractions, on the other hand, work with time in a very different manner. [. . .] In this intense form of present tense, the attraction is displayed with the immediacy of a 'Here it is! Look at it'" (76). Certainly we could say the same of picture books that we believe might appeal to a fidgety prereader.

Comparisons like these enable us to draw connections between disparate media and place children's texts within a wide and distinctly modern context that includes animation and silent cinema. Based on critical theories of the cinema of attractions and the debatable relationship of comics to cinema, I propose that the use of comic strips and lightning sketches as the bases for animation is evidence of the desire to explore and extend verbal-visual pleasure beyond the newspaper comic-strip gag. Thus we need not make the direct, one-to-one analogy between pictorial narrative and animation that Crafton rejects. Instead, we can consider the comic strip or the picture book as just one avenue for telling a story or a joke, one option for directing spectatorial attention at a particular time and place (e.g., in the portable, material, home-use format). We could say that examples of silent animation supplement comic-strip or visual-sequence entertainment with orchestral or voiced sound and with amusing motion. But we also could argue that a mode like the picture book offers supplements to the animated piece, including wordplay or rhyme, the voice of the reader, pleasurable but not necessarily diegetic illustrations, and tactile packaging that could be said to mimic the conventional book, the newspaper, and the rectangular movie screen.

Notes

1. David Lewis traces the conventional Western picture-book format to "the chapbook, the development of toys and games in the [late eighteenth and] nineteenth century, and the rise of caricature" ("Pop-ups" 8–9). Brian Alderson recognizes a "long-standing urge to formalize the relationship between words and pictures" and links British Victorian picture books to "amateur 'family' books and magazines" (14–15). Scott McCloud connects contemporary comics, a close relative of picture books, to discrete sources like Egyptian paintings (as distinct from hieroglyphics), the Bayeux tapestry, and pre-Columbian screenfolds (10–17). All these origin stories acknowledge picture books' multimedia bases.

2. Maurice Sendak writes that Randolph Caldecott's *The Three Jovial Huntsmen* "has the vivacity of a silent movie, and the huntsmen are three perfect Charlie Chaplins."

3. In "Suspended Animation: Picture Book Storytelling, Twentieth Century Childhood, and William Nicholson's *Clever Bill*," I detail Nicholson's indebtedness to multimedia modes of the 1920s and to the commodification of children's entertainment.

4. For instance, Wanda Gág's *Millions of Cats* (1928) informs Virginia Lee Burton's *Mike Mulligan and His Steam Shovel* (1939) and *The Little House* (1942); Walt Disney's short *Steamboat Willie* (1928) informs *Fantasia* (1940). Yet these quick examples plainly demonstrate the changing technical standards and shifting cultural attitudes across the span of twelve years. The picture books may make for effective comparisons, yet I want to ensure that cultural and historical gaps are given their due.

5. For information on early twentieth-century graphic narrative and criticism on its development, see David A. Beronä's *Wordless Books* on the wordless novels of Lynd Ward, Milt Gross, and Frans Masereel in the twenties and thirties.

6. On the merits of pantomime and brevity in communication, see Charles Chaplin's discussion of pantomime in his "A Rejection of the Talkies." In this 1931 editorial, Chaplin argues, "The lift of an eyebrow, however faint, may convey more than a hundred words [...] . We hear a great deal about children not going to the movies any more, and it is

undoubtedly true that hundreds of thousands of prospective film patrons, of future film-goers, young tots who formerly thrilled to the silent screen, do not attend any more because they are unable to follow the dialogue of talking pictures readily. On the other hand, they do follow action unerringly. This is because the eye is better trained than the ear." Chaplin is distinctly concerned with the narrative content of the film but meanwhile conscious of the effect of the visual gag. He also expresses concern about entertainment for all ages at the movie theater, preferring a universal appeal to a more exclusive sort.

Chaplin's 1931 assumptions about modern reception reflect not only the novelty of talking pictures but the familiarity of "silent" media formats besides film—for example, page-turning picture books and comics—in which the visual had primacy among the senses. Chaplin rejects *sound* (and the radio play, griping that "nonvisual drama leaves altogether too much to the imagination"), while making an analogy between silent cinema and other media. Further, he acknowledges that the silent film is not a "primitive" form at all, as Gunning and others argue. Chaplin was averse to excessive captioning too, which could disqualify some of the short comic-strip-based animations that set up a verbal joke and likely required more experienced spectators to read the joke aloud to preliterate ones.

7. André Gaudreault, in "Showing and Telling," and Charles Musser, in "At the Beginning," discuss the analogies made between literary subject matter and highbrow categories, perceptions of film as a degraded medium, and attempts by filmmakers to enrich their audiences with narratives based on, for instance, famous novels.

8. On the concept of poaching in the text, see Michel de Certeau's "Reading as Poaching" and Henry Jenkins's *Textual Poachers*. Certeau writes, "The elite upset about the 'low level' of journalism or television always assumes that the public is moulded by the products imposed on it. To assume that is to misunderstand the act of 'consumption.' This misunderstanding assumes that 'assimilating' necessarily means 'becoming similar to' what one absorbs, and not 'making something similar' to what one is, making it one's own, appropriating or reappropriating it" (166). He argues that the reader "invents in texts something different from what they 'intended'" (169) and says, "Far from being writers—founders of their own place [. . .]—readers are travellers; they move across lands belonging to someone else, like nomads poaching their way across fields they did not write" (174). Certeau discusses books and other consumable texts as sites for action and urges a valuation of the immediacy and *pro-*

ductivity of the reading act itself (which relates to the "now playing" concept). I contend that picture-book creators of the early twentieth century, like fans or cultural producers of any era, incorporated new media forms and reapplied them creatively to an older form, the book.

9. George Latshaw writes, "The animated film cartoons posed the first real threat to the puppet domain of fantasy. Live puppets were outclassed in every way by cartoon characters who blinked their eyes, cried tears, shaped their mouths to suit the words, wiggled fingers, squashed themselves flat as pancakes only to rise up and fill out again" (18). He cites animator and picture-book creator Tony Sarg—"for years his name was a synonym for the marionette"—as one puppeteer who successfully crossed over into cinema and publishing (17).

10. The *Dreamy Dud* and *Krazy Kat* examples are available in the vhs collection *Origins of American Animation: 1900–1921* (Washington DC: Library of Congress/Smithsonian Video, 1993).

11. Carlson is far from alone in imitating McCay's dream-sequence trope. Peter Newell's *Polly Sleepyhead* comics (ca. 1906–07), to name one prominent example, rely on catnaps and rude awakenings as routes to and from modern forms of reverie.

12. Hank Sartin writes that "cartoons of this period, like many vaudeville acts, deployed 'a fractured use of story,' and they emphasized carnivalesque rather than narrative pleasures" (Sartin 70, quoting Klein 29).

13. Audiences initially resisted recorded, synchronized sound. "The transition from silence to sound [. . .] was as difficult for audiences as it was for technicians [. . .] . Filmmakers, under pressure to find a formula that would win audiences, engaged in an extended period of experimentation in the uses of sound" (Sartin 69).

14. In "Of Mice and Ducks," Miriam Hansen investigates the aesthetics of animation and unpacks the debate whether mass enjoyment of Mickey Mouse promoted cathartic collective laughter (per Walter Benjamin) or fascist conformity and barbarism (per Theodor Adorno). Hansen explains how the Disney films of the twenties and early thirties "became emblematic of the juncture of art, politics, and technology debated at the time. The key question for critical theory in the interwar years was which role the technical media were playing in the historical demolition and restructuring of subjectivity: whether they were giving rise to new forms of imagination, expression, and collectivity, or whether they were merely perfecting techniques of total subjection and domination" (28). In hindsight and given the continued popularity of Mickey Mouse, these concerns remain relevant to children's storytelling and subject formation.

In a later essay, "Room-for-Play," Hansen further explores how Benjamin posits the category of *Spiel* or play as utopian potential in children's cinema spectatorship: "Even if Benjamin [. . .] withdrew from imagining film [and Mickey] as a play-form of technology and cinema as a site for collective and homeopathic innervation, he was willing to wager the possibility of a technologically mediated aesthetics of play capable of diverting the destructive, catastrophic course of history" (30).

Works Cited

Alderson, Brian. *Sing a Song for Sixpence: The English Picture Book Tradition and Randolph Caldecott*. Cambridge: Cambridge University Press, 1986.

Beeck, Nathalie op de. "Suspended Animation: Picture Book Storytelling, Twentieth Century Childhood, and William Nicholson's *Clever Bill*." *The Lion and the Unicorn* 30.1 (Jan. 2006): 54–75.

Beronä, David A. *Wordless Books: The Original Graphic Novels*. New York: Abrams, 2008.

Certeau, Michel de. "Reading as Poaching." *The Practice of Everyday Life*. Trans. Steven Rendall. Berkeley: University of California Press, 1984. 165–76.

Chaplin, Charles. "A Rejection of the Talkies." In Chaplin's "Pantomime and Comedy." *New York Times* 25 Jan. 1931: sec. 8, 6.

Crafton, Donald. *Before Mickey: The Animated Film, 1898–1928*. Chicago: University of Chicago Press, 1993.

Gaudreault, André. "Showing and Telling: Image and Word in Early Cinema." *Cinema: Space Frame Narrative*. Trans. John Howe. Ed. Thomas Elsaesser and Adam Barker. London: BFI, 1990. 274–81.

Gunning, Tom. "'Animated Pictures': Tales of Cinema's Forgotten Future, after 100 Years of Films." *Reinventing Film Studies*. Ed. Christine Gledhill and Linda Williams. London: Arnold, 2003. 316–31.

———. "The Cinema of Attraction: Early Film, Its Spectator, and the Avant-Garde." *Wide Angle* 8.3–4 (1986): 63–70.

———. "'Now You See It, Now You Don't': The Temporality of the Cinema of Attractions." *Silent Film*. Ed. Richard Abel. New Brunswick NJ: Rutgers University Press, 1996. 71–84.

Hansen, Miriam Bratu. "Of Mice and Ducks: Benjamin and Adorno on Disney." *South Atlantic Quarterly* 92.1 (Winter 1993): 27–61.

———. "Room-for-Play: Benjamin's Gamble with Cinema." *October* 109 (Summer 2004): 3–45.

Jenkins, Henry. *Textual Poachers: Television Fans and Participatory Culture*. New York: Routledge, 1992.

King, Norman. "The Sound of Silents." *Screen* 25.3 (May–June 1984). Rpt. in *Silent Film*. Ed. Richard Abel. New Brunswick NJ: Rutgers University Press, 1996. 31–44.

Klein, Norman M. *Seven Minutes: The Life and Death of the American Animated Cartoon*. London: Verso, 1993.

Lathrop, Dorothy P. *Horn Book Magazine* 3 (Nov. 1926): 38.

Latshaw, George. *The Complete Book of Puppetry*. Mineola NY: Dover, 2000.

Lewis, David. "Pop-ups and Fingle-Fangles: The History of the Picture Book." *Talking Pictures: Pictorial Texts and Young Readers*. Ed. Victor Watson and Morag Styles. London: Hodder, 1996. 5–21.

McCloud, Scott. *Understanding Comics: The Invisible Art*. New York: Harper Perennial, 2004.

Musser, Charles. "At the Beginning: Motion Picture Production, Representation and Ideology at the Edison and Lumière Companies." *The Silent Cinema Reader*. Ed. Lee Grieveson and Peter Krämer. London: Routledge, 2004. 15–30.

Nikolajeva, Maria, and Carole Scott. *How Picturebooks Work*. New York: Garland, 2001.

Nodelman, Perry. *Words about Pictures: The Narrative Art of Children's Picture Books*. Athens GA: University of Georgia Press, 1988.

Sartin, Hank. "From Vaudeville to Hollywood, from Silence to Sound: Warner Bros. Cartoons of the Early Sound Era." *Reading the Rabbit: Explorations in Warner Bros. Animation*. Ed. Kevin S. Sandler. New Brunswick NJ: Rutgers University Press, 1998. 67–85.

Sendak, Maurice. "Caldecott Medal Acceptance." *Caldecott & Company*. Farrar, 1988. 149.

White, Eric Walter. "Lotte Reiniger and Her Art." *Horn Book Magazine* 15 (Jan.–Feb. 1939): 45–48.

Wojcik-Andrews, Ian. *Children's Films: History, Ideology, Pedagogy, Theory*. New York: Garland, 2000.

PART THREE

Narrators and Implied Readers

As Chris McGee's essay in the previous part considers the blending of forms from different times, the opening essay in this part, Holly Blackford's "Uncle Tom Melodrama with a Modern Point of View: Harper Lee's *To Kill a Mockingbird*," considers the implications for the interplay of a Victorian story pattern of reform with the modernist strategy of using an alienated narrator. The unique combination of courtroom racial melodrama and naive child narration makes *To Kill a Mockingbird* what it is and keeps the novel both empowering and interesting to contemporary young adult readers. The second essay, Maria Nikolajeva's "The Identification Fallacy: Perspective and Subjectivity in Children's Literature," considers the gap between children's literature and literature for adults regarding the importance of authorial intention as well as the literary and pedagogical importance of a child reader's identification with characters in children's books. Finally, Dana Keren-Yaar's "The Development of Hebrew Children's Literature: From Men Pulling Children Along to Women Meeting Them Where They Are" examines the role of gendered narrative voice in Israeli children's books in the service of recruiting boys for military service.

The voice of the narrator is a major topic of discussion in the fields of children's and young adult literature for the simple reason that who speaks and to whom are the first elements that many people examine in their attempts to determine what constitutes a children's book. In short, narrative voice and the implied reader of those voices are foundational issues in the poetics of literature for young people. This part variously addresses multivoiced narration, perceptible narration, voice as a distancing tool as well as a device to draw readers in, ironic and melodramatic delivery, real and implied readers, and fundamental questions about child readers' identification with fictional characters.

9

Uncle Tom Melodrama with a Modern Point of View

Harper Lee's To Kill a Mockingbird

HOLLY BLACKFORD

It's not necessary to tell all you know. It's not ladylike—in
the second place, folks don't like to have somebody
around knowin' more than they do. It aggravates 'em. You're
not gonna change any of them by talkin' right,
they've got to want to learn themselves, and when they
don't want to learn there's nothing you can do
but keep your mouth shut or talk their language.
—CALPURNIA, in *To Kill a Mockingbird*

Because of Harper Lee's carefully controlled narrative strategy, young readers feel a great sense of pleasure and accomplishment when reading *To Kill a Mockingbird*. My recent interview project involving sixty-eight readers of *The Adventures of Huckleberry Finn* and *To Kill a Mockingbird* reveals that teens speak of being able to laugh at Scout's childishness and at their own past selves through her, yet they enjoy the feelings of suspense generated by her unusual combination of objectivity and local color. They proudly speak of how they have to figure out matters for themselves, "feeling through Scout," as one fifteen-year-old African American reader describes it. The scenes of the lynch mob, Calpurnia's church, and the trial are universally acknowledged by readers as scenes in which Scout does not understand the significance of events, and thus "through her not understanding, it kind of helps you understand" (fifteen-year-old Lisa), because "you have to figure things out for yourself." Lisa compares Scout's style to someone who might be able to describe an apple without knowing the word for it, thus using "an outsider's perspective" on its shape, color, and texture, "whereas an insider would look at it just like an apple." Why is *To Kill a Mockingbird* so accessible, and why do young readers feel such a sense of mastery when they "figure out" the trial and relate its theme of exclusion to the presumed otherness of Boo Radley? The answer is the novel's unique blend of two literary traditions: popular melodrama, which defines the trial, and sophisticated modern narration, which controls the reader's experience before and after the trial.

Published just over a century prior to Lee's 1960 *To Kill a Mockingbird*, Harriet Beecher Stowe's *Uncle Tom's Cabin* is an important intertext to Lee's novel of social reform. Stowe's tropes inform Lee's use of racial melodrama. Like *Uncle Tom's Cabin*, *To Kill a Mockingbird* features the crucifixion of a virtuous and innocent African American character named Tom. In melodramatic fashion Lee depicts this persecution as the fall of the black family and home, calls upon us to restore Christian ethics and combat the sin of white law, equates evil with lower-class characters who refuse domestic order and live beyond the boundaries of civilization, and yet admits that these lowly characters are merely scapegoats for what the law encodes. As Linda Williams writes in *Playing the Race Card: Melodramas of Black and White from Uncle Tom to O. J. Simpson*, Stowe's protest novel almost immediately became a touchstone for Victorian melodrama on the stage, and it certainly became a framework by which all subsequent racial melodrama on stage, screen, and television would be understood.

However, while Stowe tells her story with a masterful and judgmental omniscient narrator, Lee deploys the multivoiced narration of Scout, invoking a different literary tradition: that of the modern, alienated narrator, a type of narrator born of authors who were reacting against the secure and stable narrative conventions of the Victorian novel. The younger Scout's consciousness focalizes the story, but she neither perceives the melodrama in a conventional manner nor allows us to rest satisfied with the heroic deeds of her father, who, like Stowe's narrator, in effect crusades for justice and pleads for universal rights directly with the reader. In trial fiction, Carol Clover argues, the reader becomes a juror.

The character Scout becomes our naive eyewitness to the melodramatic persecution of the innocent and even disabled Tom Robinson. But the intrusive presence of an older narrating Scout in scenes before and after the trial tightly controls our experience of the story, tempering our relationship with young Scout and providing a southern critique of melodrama. The novel vacillates between deploying the distancing type of ironic, colorful child voice first glimpsed in Mark Twain's *Adventures of Huckleberry Finn* and the more immediate, unmediated stream-of-consciousness technique pioneered by later modernist writers. Lee deploys the former style for everyday scenes in Scout's world, to construct comic distance from the young Scout and to set up a contrast in scenes that take Scout beyond her everyday world. In other words Lee uses the young Scout to acknowledge what white eyes can and cannot see, continually negotiating between local and transcendent perspective.

In the novel we effectively meet three different Scouts. There is a six-year-old Scout revealed to the reader, without narrative comment, in action and dialogue. *This* Scout is complex enough. She is passionate, headstrong, impulsive, childish, feisty, and endearing. She craves affection, gets easily upset, distorts and misunderstands situations, shows her brains and resourcefulness, hates restriction, notices far more than she can explain, and both reasons and applies her prior knowledge and experience. She changes with her social context, following the model of Calpurnia, who exemplifies liminality and marginality with her code- and style-shifting, as Natalie Hess argues. With Atticus, Scout is an innocent questioner; with Jem she is assertive and grumpy;

with Miss Maudie she is respectful; with Walter Cunningham and Cecil Jacobs she is a bully; and with her new teacher she is superior and wise. But then a more sophisticated side of Scout is revealed through the narrator's rendition of the six-year-old's immediate thoughts. With Scout as focalizer, or what Seymour Chatman argues should be more properly termed "filter" (144), Lee places the unique attentions, thoughts, and interpretations of Scout alongside a more direct transcription of adult behaviors and dialogue that are beyond her understanding. For example, Scout's thoughts might focus on how something Atticus is doing differs from his usual custom, upon which she is an anthropological expert, placed alongside snippets of conversations that she overhears, allowing the reader to put it all together.

There is also the distinct presence of an older, reflective Scout, who introduces the novel and intermittently inserts herself throughout the story. This narrator-Scout provides background on people, places, and customs, often disrupting an immediate scene. She offers humorous commentary on the young Scout's behaviors, through a gentle irony revealed in description. She manipulates narrative time, deploying flashbacks and foreshadowing the significance of a scene with a summary. Her slant (Chatman 144) typically directs our understanding of Scout's everyday contexts, but then she fades into the background when the young Scout confronts new adult behaviors and scenes that she cannot easily understand.

The presence of the older Scout is sometimes perceptible and sometimes not, depending on how seriously she wants us to take the young Scout's interpretations. Philippe Lejeune characterizes narratives of childhood as indirect free style (60). The style, pioneered by Jules Vallès, creates "a perpetual 'dissolve' or a 'double exposure' between the two voices" of older narrator and child filter, "so subtle" a transition that different readers may not agree on which voice is which (56). For example, on Scout's first day of school, the narrator's slant and the young Scout's sensory experience complicate the event: "Jem condescended to take me to school the first day, a job usually done by one's parents, but Atticus had said Jem would be delighted to show me where my room was. I think some money changed hands in this transaction, for as we trotted around the corner past the Radley Place I heard an unfamiliar jingle in Jem's pockets" (16). The present "I" who "thinks" money changed hands echoes the senses and intuition of young Scout, who "heard" but could not interpret the bribe. The young Scout knows Atticus's words about Jem being "delighted" are suspect, and she knows both Jem and Atticus intimately enough to detect a change from their usual tones. The vocabulary of "condescended" and "this transaction" suggests an interpretation by the older narrator. But the phrase "a job usually done by one's parent" and the knowledge of custom implied by the line could be observations of either of these locally trained Scouts. The irony derives from the older Scout's interpretation of what the young Scout could hear and suspect but could not place in a broader meaning—that she has been "dumped" on Jem, who has been bribed. We laugh but feel sympathy because the two Scouts blend so smoothly, and we feel simultaneously "with" and "beyond" the young Scout.[1]

This technique implies a reader who remembers childhood and can empathize with someone of limited experience, but also one who appreciates wit. Throughout the novel Lee, who wished to be the Jane Austen of the South (Shields 64), uniquely multiplies the character remembered as Scout to be both a product of her town and a being who transcends it with her adult self's language, intuition, and irony, a mode that enjoys a special place in young adult literature (see Cadden). The older narrating agent both attaches and detaches from the young Scout, just as that narrator loves and hates the town and its small-minded childishness. The implied audience is one both "inside" and "outside" the small town of childhood, ready for ironic reflection on roots dialogically internalized by the self: older children, teens, and young adults. The unique effects of the doubled narration emerge most fully when we separate story from discourse or melodrama from detached irony. The latter counters the former's appeal to passion and sympathy, but it also provides a critical viewpoint on the purely detached stance of Atticus, who "could make a rape case as dry as a sermon" (169).

Melodrama: Uncle Tom's Cabin
and To Kill a Mockingbird

Melodrama fuses the Greek word for song, *melos*, with "drama," a theatrical form. The term was originally used to denote musical plays, according to M. H. Abrams. Stylized melodrama evolved from pantomime and a variety of theatrical influences in eighteenth-century France and England, particularly through the illustrious career of Guilbert de Pixerécourt (see Rahill). Over time, however, melodrama has evolved into a more general term that encompasses a mode or sensibility, according to film critics like Christine Gledhill and Linda Williams (Mercer and Shingler 93–94). We use the term "melodrama" to denote dramatic plots that privilege emotional excess, intrigue, action, and violence over complex character: "The hero and heroine are pure as the driven snow and the villain a monster of malignity" (Abrams 99). Concerned with mimed action, spectacle, suffering heroines and heroes, misunderstood virtue, unregenerate villains, improbable coincidences, and "in the nick of time" saving and punishment, melodrama renders emotion through external and therefore mute means (Mercer and Shingler 22–23), expressed in the mute but legible "pantomime" (178) of Tom Robinson on trial, easily read by the child characters "from as far away as the balcony" (186).

The character of Uncle Tom, brutally used and eventually murdered by the evil Simon Legree, sings and preaches the gospel throughout his sojourn from Kentucky to Louisiana and down the Red River. The singing Uncle Tom is the hero "as pure as the driven snow"; his Christian song symbolizes what to Stowe was the purest relationship to God, uncorrupted by worlds of writing or formal churches—a kind of direct and instinctive faith from the heart. Stowe equates Uncle Tom with Eva, who similarly can read but cannot write, to indicate the purity and simplicity of the

Christian affected by, but not authors of, cultural prejudices. Lee similarly dwells on the preliterate faith of the black community, glimpsed in the practice of "linin" and in the inaccessibility of the Bible to Tom, whose crippled arm slips off the Bible as he is being sworn in. The Finch children find it striking that Atticus, who is not inclined to speak of sin, claims that it is a sin to kill a mockingbird. Critics such as Isaac Saney object to the equation of mockingbirds and African Americans, but it is probably an allusion to Uncle Tom as well as to the variously titled poems by Walt Whitman about two mockingbirds from Alabama, one of whom loses his mate and sings his grief, pain intimately witnessed by the child speaker.

In both *Uncle Tom's Cabin* and *To Kill a Mockingbird*, we are to understand the suffering of the black characters named Tom as a ritual sacrifice for the sins of white culture: "They've done it before and they did it tonight and they'll do it again and when they do it—seems that only children weep," argues Atticus in his home court (213). Williams points out that melodrama performs a particular cultural function by identifying suffering and pain as virtue (29). Both novels maintain a Christian stance, invoking a Genesis plot in which the sin of racism corrupts the innocence of children. Uncle Tomism has become virtually synonymous with passivity and the desexualization of the black man, yet the innocence of the Toms in both novels is a choice, thus virtuous, and both Toms voice their resistances and actively testify to their innocence. Both authors introduce the physical appeal of the Tom characters; Stowe introduces Tom as "a large, broad-chested, powerfully-made man, of a full glossy black" (68) before describing his grave face and suggestion of simplicity, and focalizer-Scout's first glimpse of Tom includes a focus on his "powerful shoulders" (186): "Tom was a black-velvet Negro, not shiny, but soft black velvet [. . .] . If he had been whole, he would have been a fine specimen of a man" (192). They do not threaten the status quo, but they could; Tom could certainly have become the overseer Legree wants him to be, for example. Both undergo temptation scenes; temptation comes in the form of women who tempt them into the slovenly yards of lowly white characters, Simon Legree and Bob Ewell.

With similar melodramatic emphasis on good and evil topography, the novels place Simon Legree and Bob Ewell in chaotic and dilapidated spaces that indicate their hopeless, heathen condition. Both narrators help the reader visualize decayed residences and unruly yards, cluttered with objects and remnants of slovenly living. Although the lowly yards are literally and symbolically dumping grounds for all that civilized cultures consider abject, they harbor struggling flowers. In Legree's yard "some solitary exotic reared its forsaken head" (10), and in Ewell's yard "against the fence, in a line, were six chipped-enamel slop jars holding brilliant red geraniums" (11). These flowers are Mayella and Cassy, who have similar functions in testing the Toms. For Scout, a young girl, Mayella suggests how female flowering and passion could be occurring in an abject yard beyond Scout's world, explaining why the Ewell yard is imaged as "the playhouse of an insane child" (170). The Ewell yard echoes the variety of yards in which the Finch children play and supports Laura Fine's assertion that Mayella and Bob Ewell function as "dark doubles" for Scout and Atticus. Scout is attracted to Tom's body and "husky voice calling in the night" (169) from prison, amid the smells of alcohol emitted by the old Sarum men, just as she is curious about rape.

The women tempt the pure, untainted Toms to cross into their yards of evil. Mayella tempts Tom into a sexual relationship, while Cassy tempts Tom into killing Legree. Both Toms resist but are damned the moment that the women select them for temptation. However, it is really sympathy for the women that gets the Toms into trouble, a sympathy that Stowe's narrator and Scout encourage us to share. Scout repeatedly ponders what Mayella's life might be like, a life that (unlike Stowe's mature narrator) she can only render through clues such as the geraniums. Both women symbolize miscegenation and they cause the fall of black cabins, settings equated with innocence, as opposed to the miscegenation implied by the hybrid household of the Finches and the entwined history of Cal and Atticus at Finch's Landing.

Thus comparison with Stowe's novel reveals how Lee's child focalizer revises the concept of innocence at home. As Williams argues, melodrama typically begins by constructing home as a space of innocence and "virtue taking pleasure in itself" (28). Stowe titles her novel *Uncle Tom's Cabin* and introduces the cabin setting of Chloe and Uncle Tom to equate the "purest" black family with a New England sense of the origin of the nation's Christian goodness. Uncle Tom's cabin features a portrait of George Washington, tapping into cultural foundations, and gives us an image of domestic bliss. Chloe's cooking, Tom's cabin preaching, young Master George's reading, and all the children filling the home evoke an image of a temporary Garden of Eden that the institution of slavery contradicts and causes to fall. The novel particularly dwells on the presence of a female baby who unselfconsciously plays with Tom's face even on the very day he is to be handed to the trader. Similarly, Lee dwells on the family image of Tom's residence when Atticus has to tell Helen that Tom has been murdered. Atticus carefully assists Tom and Helen's baby girl down the stairs, just before Helen "drops to the ground" upon news of Tom's death. The baby girl emphasizes the destruction of innocence and Atticus's role in easing the fall, which can be interpreted as also causing the fall of the white gentlemen's houses, Augustine St. Clare's and Atticus Finch's.

Atticus is actually a problematic role model for his daughter, just as Augustine is problematic for Eva. Atticus and Augustine voice liberal sentiments but are overwhelmed by a system much larger than they. Consider the weightiness of Finch's Landing, the plantation from which Atticus comes: "Finch's Landing consisted of three hundred and sixty-six steps down a high bluff and ending in a jetty. Farther down stream, beyond the bluff, were traces of an old cotton landing, where Finch Negroes had loaded bales and produce, unloaded blocks of ice, flour and sugar, farm equipment, and feminine apparel" (80). Eva and Scout pepper their fathers with questions about why things are as they are, both stand accused by aunts and cousins of "loving Negroes" and thus not accepting things as they are, and both learn of black oppression through female sexuality—Eva of Prue, Scout of Mayella. The two novels feature parallel scenes in which a trip to the home of cousins, where in Eva's case a slave is whipped and where in Scout's case she herself is whipped, serves to highlight the liberal difference of Atticus and Augustine. With Augustine, Stowe paints a unique portrait of a southern gentleman whose rhetoric against slavery embodies a rare burst of passion but whose life signifies laissez-faire detachment, which eventually causes him to suffer the loss of his daughter and his own life. Strikingly similarly, narrator-Scout takes great pains to give us background on Atticus and demonstrates how intrinsically bound he is to a system that was once slaveholding and hence holds certain attitudes. Like Augustine, Atticus spends most of the novel reading and offering ironic commentary to his family; both men let servants and children do as they please and thus leave them free to lead a more public existence. The presence of aunts Alexandria and Ophelia, who are both racist and both opposed to the child-rearing practices of the men, provides a critical view of the St. Clare and Finch households.

Both Eva and Scout must navigate three different worlds governed by different sentiments: the sentiments espoused by their fathers, the sentiments defined by their larger community, and the sentiments espoused by aunts who have come to live with them and revise domestic management and values. While Eva cannot continue to live in such a divided landscape, Lee found a more inspirational, disruptive force in the changeling Topsy. The relationship between Aunt Ophelia and Topsy offered a template for Aunt Alexandra and Scout, who continually resists Alexandra's lessons and who revels in topsy behavior, complicit with the many references of the Finch children as "passin'" and acting like blacks (Calpurnia accuses them of "nigger-talk"; Mr. Radley mistakes them for blacks in his yard; and they cross boundaries into the black church and the black section of the courthouse to view the trial). Michelle Ann Abate has argued that the figure of Topsy mutates into "topsy Jo" of *Little Women*, changing into a possibility for white female resistance to femininity. Like Topsy, Scout with her tough demeanor emerges the most unscathed in the end; although continually chastised by her aunt, particularly for boundary crossing (see Johnson), she is practically adopted by her in the Missionary Society scene. Just as watching Cal teaches Scout "there was some skill involved in being a girl" (116), Scout learns "if Aunty could be a lady at a time like this, so could [she]" (237). Like Scout, Topsy is the only child to emerge unscathed from the decadent St. Clare household; she is adopted by Aunt Ophelia, who like Scout's "Aunty" is somewhat transformed.

Scout's aunt even brings Scout a clean pair of overalls toward the end, just as, in the final scene, Atticus reads Jem's melo-dramatic books instead of his own genres, cuddles Scout and prepares her for bed himself, and waits anxiously at his child's bedside. Less the public gentleman, a part never accessible to her, Atticus is finally the parent that I believe Scout has wanted all along. Lee updates the clarity of Stowe's vision—her divisions between innocence and evil—by refocusing punishment of the villain, emphasizing not Ewell's undoing but changes in Atticus and Atticus's world. In *To Kill a Mockingbird* Atticus is threatened with losing his children and fully becoming Augustine, revealing that the novel is Scout's story after all. Scout is Topsy's disciple because she is not merely Atticus's child and Jem's sister.[2] Motherless, Scout is also a composite of black and white women whose voices she has internalized. She speaks in multiple voices quite unlike, and quite critical of, the transcendent eloquence of her father, who speaks in Standard English and is renowned throughout the community for being the same in public as in private. As a hybrid, Scout is Cal's child, too. Cal's code-switching, boundary-crossing, passin', and passion, symbolized most effectively by "her hand [. . .] as wide as a bed slat and twice as hard" (6), does indeed teach Scout how to write and thus do more than detach and read—something Eva could never achieve.

A Topsy Point of View on Melodrama

To Kill a Mockingbird establishes the colloquial and colorful speech of the young and older Scout, whose language is both an earthy product of her community and an exercise in sophisticated vocabulary. The language of the six-year-old becomes a point of contention in the novel when she agitates her family by swearing and, as always, tests the feasibility of her father's policy of tolerance and patience. Slang also peppers the narrator's voice. In the beginning the narrator introduces at length the circumstance of her family and its southern history; in describing the history of Atticus's practice, she establishes her mocking voice, which will freely wander in and out of other people's viewpoints in a parodic fashion, as if mocking her father's lessons in seeing from the eyes of others: "[Atticus's] first two clients were the last two persons hanged in the Maycomb County jail. Atticus had urged them to accept the state's generosity in allowing them to plead Guilty to second-degree murder and escape with their lives, but they were Haverfords, in Maycomb County a name synonymous with jackass. The Haverfords had dispatched Maycomb's leading blacksmith in a misunderstanding arising from the alleged wrongful detention of a mare, were imprudent enough to do it in the presence of three witnesses, and insisted that the-son-of-a-bitch-had-it-coming-to-him was a good enough defense for anybody" (5). The older narrator combines colloquial language and legal concepts, establishing that she is both an insider to the local community and a transcendent being with more global knowledge. She establishes her insider and outsider position in relation to the community, parodying how "the Haverfords" would view the matter (stupidly) versus her own legalese, "a misunderstanding arising from the alleged wrongful detention of a mare." She establishes her authority to make claims about the sentiments of Maycomb County in earthy language but also parodies how she feels about the town and the stereotypes that even she holds. She continually vacillates between these voices to show that she is both a product of the environment she describes and has somehow transcended it.

The narrator establishes the young Scout as an authority on the county and its families. Scout, ironically like Aunt Alexandra, whose worldview we are supposed to reject, equates behavior with families. When she first attends school, we see her educating the teacher about the Cunninghams, based on lessons gleaned and somewhat simplistically applied from Atticus. Her first-grade class seems to recognize the young Scout as an eloquent authority on the community; when the teacher does not understand Cunningham behavior, the narrator reports, "I turned around and saw most of the town people and the entire bus delegation looking at me. Miss Caroline and I had conferred twice already, and they were looking at me in the innocent assurance that familiarity breeds understanding. I rose graciously on Walter's behalf" (20). The young Scout sees the crowd's eyes upon her and intuits their expectations, but the narrator's vocabulary ("delegation," "conferred," "innocent assurance that familiarity breeds understanding") and parody ("graciously on Walter's behalf") suggests a parallel between Scout's appointment in this scene and the town's appointment of Atticus to argue on behalf of those in need of representation. The entire forthcoming narrative, however, underscores the gap between the skills of Atticus and Scout, as she tries to explain why Walter Cunningham will not accept the teacher's quarter for lunch. In the middle of the scene, the narrator gives us background on how the young Scout knew about the Cunninghams from her father's lessons. The flashback distances us from the young Scout, but we are simultaneously distanced from and appreciative of Scout's succinctness: "It was beyond my ability to explain things as well as Atticus, so I said, 'You're shamin' him, Miss Caroline'" (21).

The narrator-Scout establishes a command of the story by calling attention to the way she orders its presentation and controls the flow of information, while the younger Scout disrupts the whole idea of control and command. For example, the beautiful transition of the older Scout's summative narration, "That was the summer Dill came to us" (6), greatly contrasts with the skills of the six-year-old, who is told to hush after prying into Dill's life:

"Then if [your father's] not dead you've got one, haven't you?"
(8). The narrator offers background when she wishes us to have
context, but she presumes that we are outsiders and that she must
translate for us: "The misery of that house began many years
before Jem and I were born [. . .] . I never knew how old Mr.
Radley made his living—Jem said he 'bought cotton,' a polite term
for doing nothing" (9). Her position as a translator demonstrates
that she expects her reader to need her insider information—her
expertise on local language.

In fact in many ways both older and younger Scout establish
themselves as cultural anthropologists, explaining what different groups will and will not do, given their belief systems: "A
Negro would not pass the Radley Place at night, he would cut
across to the sidewalk opposite and whistle as he walked. The
Maycomb school groups adjoined the back of the Radley lot;
from the Radley chickenyard tall pecan trees shook their fruit
into the schoolyard, but the nuts lay untouched by the children:
Radley pecans would kill you" (9). Scout tells us what is part of
children's "ethical culture" (35) and what its limits are. The older
and younger Scout use legal language throughout the novel to
describe the systems of informal law that govern particular social
groups.[3] The older Scout's role as a folklorist greatly contrasts with
the young Scout's prejudices and misunderstandings, as she discovers truths about others; however, the young Scout is in some
ways a distillation of melodrama *and* the regional novel, which
serves to demonstrate how character is a product of a particular
environment.[4] The narrator-Scout offers a scathing view of the
Dewey school curriculum because it is a set curriculum void of
students' life context, which the regional novel seeks hard to make
understood. Learning can take place only in a specific context
from specific points of view that have been developed over time
and in a particular place.

The older Scout liberally mocks her younger self's sense of
proportion, heightened sense of imagination, and attention span:
"Without [Dill], life was unbearable. I stayed miserable for two
days" (116). Yet the purpose of this self-irony is only to suggest

the point of the novel: the white characters are entirely trapped in their skewed sense of self-worth and proportion: "Maycomb was interested by the news of Tom's death for perhaps two days" (240). *Mockingbird* is saturated with the self-irony of Twain's character Huck, with a similar purpose of social satire. One technique the books share is misplaced emphasis: the Radley blanket receives more attention and emphasis than Miss Maudie's fire; the presence of Arthur Radley receives greater emphasis at the end than the fact that Bob Ewell is dead and tried to kill the children. Only after Scout meets "Boo" does she admit to learning; only her encounter with Boo, a view from a close neighbor's porch, resolves the melodrama. However, upon reflection it is easy to see Lee's point; skewed perspective is not a limitation of the child but a problem of the human being. Tom dies and little changes in the town. The Boo Radley plot, a commonly used plot of the strange neighbor, is in many ways a means for Scout and young readers to understand the trial and an encounter with difference, the persecution of innocence. However, Boo is also a darker symbol for Scout and the closeted condition of human perception. The intimate connection between Scout and Boo, whom Scout also compares to Mayella, demonstrates that although growth can occur, one can really only cross the street in perspective, after all.

The technique established in the initial school scene, interrupted yet deepened by a flashback to Atticus's lessons on the Cunninghams, becomes a pattern for how the naive child-Scout and her everyday world are disrupted and complicated by her father's world. Lee manages information in the Cecil Jacobs scene similarly, beginning the chapter with her words in the schoolyard: "You can just take that back, boy!" (74). The narrator then provides a flashback to the scene in which Atticus patiently and rationally explains Cecil's challenge that "Scout Finch's daddy defended niggers," then abruptly switches back to the schoolyard: "With this in mind, I faced Cecil Jacobs in the schoolyard next day: 'You gonna take that back, boy?'" (77). The narrator-Scout is literally asking the reader to "keep in mind" how young Scout misapplies Atticus's lessons because of the gaps between her worlds—the gap between Scout's Emersonian training at home and passionate response to peers, a gap similar to Cal's "modest double life" (125). The narrator-Scout then puts further distance between us and the young Scout with a sentence about Scout's limited sense of time and the impending doom of a scene to come: "I felt extremely noble for having remembered [not to fight], and remained noble for three weeks. Then Christmas came and disaster struck" (77). The older Scout in effect foreshadows the importance and drama of the following Christmas scene, in which Scout will strike her cousin. The narrator-Scout achieves omniscience at the expense of the limited child-Scout, who does not know herself well enough to know she cannot remain noble. But both speak different languages in different contexts, indicating that they are the same personality. The older is a more refined revision of the younger. Together they indicate the essential fact that any one person is multiple, both because any local subject speaks with the different voices of cultural influences and because at any given point an individual embeds all her past selves within, as both interpolated subjects and objects of perspective. We are continually shown how Scout is and is not Atticus, Jem, Calpurnia, and others, a continual negotiation of identities through voices internalized in the self.

In contrast to the tightly controlled flow of information of scenes in which Lee visibly inserts the presence of the narrator-Scout, we find that the younger Scout's unfiltered and uninterpreted impressions take precedence when the six-year-old experiences adult-run events, formalizing the idea that these scenes fall outside the purview of her expertise. In such scenes the focalizing effect is similar to the stream of Maisie's consciousness in Henry James's *What Maisie Knew* or the raw impressions governing Benjy's perceptions in William Faulkner's *The Sound and the Fury*. Upon heading to Calpurnia's church, the young Scout emphasizes what she sees and smells—raw impressions. The narrator emphasizes the point, "I sensed, rather than saw" (119). But Scout's close observation of Calpurnia and her speech patterns at church is characteristic of the way that Scout can find a point of entry into adult settings. She relies on reading the people whom she knows well, very similarly to the way Maisie learns to read people to understand the significance of adult scenes and conversations. Scout's intimate knowledge of those she loves becomes her lone knowledge in scenes that challenge her, but also the source of our trust of her. For example, during the scene in which the sheriff calls Atticus outside and expresses reservations about Tom's safety, Scout reads Atticus and presents in raw form snippets of the adult conversation occurring outside, which she does not understand. What she does understand is Atticus's question—his "Do you really think so?" addressed to the men. She knows that this is something he characteristically says just before "the checkerboard was swept clean of [her] men" (146). When Atticus heads to the jail, she knows something is amiss because he drives rather than walks; similarly, she knows Jem isn't getting ready for bed that night because she knows his go-to-bed noises so well.

The lynch mob scene presents to her, in contrast, an inscrutable and illegible situation; she transcribes what she sees and hears but her consciousness focuses on the "mutual defiance" (152) between Atticus and Jem and then on Atticus's prior lessons in politeness, which she then applies to Mr. Cunningham. With this interplay between Scout's six-year-old actions and the representation of her consciousness, we notice an absence of the intrusive, older narrator-Scout. In such scenes we are suddenly in the position of becoming an immediately engaged (as defined by Andrea Schwenke Wyile 191) eyewitness. We perceive the serious tone because the narrator's usual self-irony is absent. The child-Scout is no longer the subject, and thus we experience broader possibilities than a local, embedded one. We are *almost* the transcendent eyeball that parallels the democratic ideal of Atticus's speech. But such moments never last, just as Maycomb's attention span for Tom cannot last. Humans are habit-forming creatures.

Ironic self-commentary *almost* disappears during the trial, which is transcribed through Scout as a quasi-objective filter rather than focalizer, achieving the effects that Clover equates with courtroom fiction. Clover analyzes the adversarial structure of trial fiction—the prosecution versus defense—and suggests that we are never given details about the jury because the jury is a blank space that we inhabit as readers and viewers before whom the adversaries and testimonies unfold (265). We weigh points of view, we judge character, we compare story versions, and we always have the sense that there is more to know, a facet of trial fiction that grabs our attention and heightens our suspense. Scout, in and out of sleep throughout some of the trial, is located beyond the all-white section and thus beyond the limited perspective of the prejudiced jury. She is thus a stand-in for a better juror or a more objective witness, insofar as she becomes a means for the reader to experience the trial as it unfolds in the tension of the moment. Her sleepiness is also an asset; an unreflective consciousness puts irony and detachment temporarily to rest.

The distance between the young Scout and the narrator-Scout returns in a much fuller way outside the trial, where we are again within her everyday life, and thus we again feel distance from the young character Scout. In fact Lee forces us to disconnect from the young Scout and the immediacy of the trial quite abruptly; the children leave because Dill cannot stop crying over Tom's treatment by the prosecuting attorney, and Scout, after witnessing this trial relatively neutrally, quite callously says, "Well, Dill, after all he's just a Negro" (199). It is not an appropriate response, but it is characteristic of her tone with Dill, whom she often "one-ups" and belittles. In other words the requirements of her relationship with Dill take precedence over her impressions of the trial. After closing arguments, narrative intrusion returns with full force. Scout dwells on hearing Calpurnia yell at Jem for taking her to the trial: "I was exhilarated. So many things had happened so fast I felt it would take years to sort them out, and now here was Calpurnia giving her precious Jem down the country—what new marvels would the evening bring?" (207). The idea that the young Scout can be pleased about Jem's fall from grace at such a time heightens the sense that she might be oblivious to the racial melodrama in the court yet egocentrically reacting to the racial melodrama of Cal and Jem. Yet she is clearly not merely a child either; consider what follows—her ironic summary of the rape statute: "We were subjected to a lengthy review of evidence with Jem's ideas on the law regarding rape: it wasn't rape if she let you, but she had to be eighteen—in Alabama, that is—and Mayella was nineteen. Apparently you had to kick and holler, you had to be overpowered and stomped on, preferably knocked stone cold. If you were under eighteen, you didn't have to go through all this" (209). The voice of the beginning narrator returns here, showing an unusual combination of transcendent legalese ("a lengthy review of evidence") and local color ("kick and holler," "knocked stone cold"). The narrator-Scout's voice is a combination of Atticus's dry cynicism and Calpurnia's code switching; the combination offers her the ability to proffer a biting critique of the law and of Jem, whose impending adolescent status has been the one thing as illegible and mysterious to her as the rape case itself. In fact the trial section begins with the words "Jem was twelve" (115), as if life's, and the town's, trial is developmental.

Thus the unique combination of racial melodrama and multi-voiced narration makes the novel what it is. The former is Victorian, stemming from an era of social reform, and the latter is modern, stemming from an era obsessed with consciousness and the flawed yet universal nature of human bias. While the innocence-versus-evil melodrama of the trial is crucial to the novel's ability to speak to young and popular audiences, the narrative strategy creates a paradoxical relationship with melodrama, which is neither ironic nor tolerant of the deconstruction of innocence. The way that melodrama operates is by asking the reader to feel rather than to reason—to passionately respond to persecuted innocence and become angry enough to protest the plight of the victim. The child characters in both *Uncle Tom's Cabin* and *To Kill a Mockingbird* are models for reader response to melodrama in that they are distinctly passionate and feeling. They are opposed to the detached, analytical stances of the adults—

particularly Augustine St. Clare and Atticus Finch, who are parallel tragic heroes who eloquently voice liberalism through logic and argument. The adult Scout is rather like these detached beings, particularly in her irony, but her voice is rooted in the young Scout, who is everything Atticus is not; she embodies and craves passionate reactions that exceed the rational. She exemplifies the very dangers of passion. The community charges the Finch family and Scout in particular with "nigger-loving," something that is a virtue in Stowe's Eva but problematic in Maycomb's distaste for miscegenation and in Atticus's general distaste for the emotional. The dry comment "[Atticus] could make a rape case as dry as a sermon" (169) reveals a narrator who can match his dryness but who does not completely want to, as revealed by her next comment: "Gone was the terror in my mind of stale whiskey and barnyard smells, of sleepy-eyed sullen men, of a husky voice calling in the night, 'Mr. Finch? They gone?'" (169).

If the young Scout bears the very dangers of Eva's passion in a way similar to Topsy's, Eva's dark double, then *To Kill a Mockingbird* simultaneously asks for and warns us against feeling the melodrama too strongly. The novel wants us to mediate our feeling by seeing, but its paradoxical "insider" and "outsider" point of view deconstructs Atticus's plea for universal equality, a plea *embodied by who he is*—detached, courteous, and gentlemanly, regardless of whom he is with. Almost a parody of Atticus's philosophy, of detaching from self and seeing through the eyes of others, young Scout continually and melodramatically misapplies his lessons. She is a communally rooted changeling, a composite of voices, and ultimately a critical lens on the possibility of universal justice.

Notes

1. In his biography of Lee, Charles Shields reviews the criticism launched at Lee for switching between narrator and focalizer. For example, "W. J. Stuckey, in *The Pulitzer Prize Novels: A Critical Backward Look*, attributed Lee's 'rhetorical trick' to a failure to solve 'the technical problems raised by her story and whenever she gets into difficulties with

one point of view, she switches to the other'" (qtd. in Shields 128). Shields agrees that Lee might have "floundered" since she wrote the original draft in third person, the second in first person, and later blended the two (128). I find the blend unique, compelling, and well executed—a way to complexify the simplicity of the trial. I agree with William T. Going (28) that the technique is Jamesian, but it also makes interpretation of irony tricky, similar to the trickiness of interpreting irony in Vallès's narratives of childhood, as Lejeune finds (64–66). It is difficult to sort out whether the irony depends on a secret between narrator and narratee, at the expense of the child, or between child and narratee.

2. When asked who made her, Topsy famously claims, "I spect I grow'd. Don't think nobody never made me" (356). Scout neither remembers nor misses her mother, and she cannot remember being taught to read, especially by Atticus, who, she tells her teacher when questioned, is too busy. These children are not specifically made—others detach from them—so they grow as cultural productions and thereby expose the cracks of the system that neglected to make them.

3. On law in the novel, see Johnson's chapter "Legal Boundaries" (94–106).

4. Perhaps the best symbol of the way in which the community "produces" Scout is her dressing up as a ham for the pageant. Importantly, the ham costume endangers her safety and protects her; it glows in the dark and thus makes her a walking target for Ewell, but its sturdy wire mesh shields her from his knife. Environment is both a blessing and a curse of Ham, if you will.

Works Cited

Abate, Michelle Ann. "Topsy and Topsy-Turvy Jo: Harriet Beecher Stowe's *Uncle Tom's Cabin* and/in Louisa May Alcott's *Little Women*." *Children's Literature* 34 (2006): 59–82.

Abrams, M. H. *A Glossary of Literary Terms*. 5th ed. New York: Holt, 1998.

Cadden, Mike. "The Irony of Narration in the Young Adult Novel." *Children's Literature Association Quarterly* 25.3 (Fall 2000): 146–54.

Chatman, Seymour. *Coming to Terms: The Rhetoric of Narrative in Fiction and Film*. Ithaca NY: Cornell University Press, 1990.

Clover, Carol. "'God Bless Juries!'" *Refiguring American Film Genres: History and Theory*. Ed. Nick Browne. Berkeley: University of California Press. 255–77.

Faulkner, William. *The Sound and the Fury*. New York: Jonathan Cape and Harrison Smith, 1929.

Fine, Laura. "Gender Conflicts and Their 'Dark' Projections in Coming of Age White Female Southern Novels." *Southern Quarterly* 36.4 (1998): 121–29.

Going, William T. *Essays on Alabama Literature*. Studies in the Humanities 4. University: University of Alabama Press, 1975.

Hess, Natalie. "Code Switching and Style Shifting as Markers of Liminality in Literature." *Language and Literature* 5.1 (1996): 5–18.

James, Henry. *What Maisie Knew*. 1897. New York: Penguin, 1986.

Johnson, Claudia Durst. *To Kill a Mockingbird: Threatening Boundaries*. New York: Twayne, 1994.

Lee, Harper. *To Kill a Mockingbird*. New York: Warner, 1960.

Lejeune, Philippe. *On Autobiography*. Ed. Paul John Eakin. Trans. Katherine Leary. Theory and History of Literature 52. Minneapolis: University of Minnesota Press, 1989.

Mercer, John, and Martin Shingler. *Melodrama: Genre, Style, Sensibility*. New York: Wallflower, 2004.

Rahill, Frank. *The World of Melodrama*. University Park: Pennsylvania State University Press, 1967.

Shields, Charles J. *Mockingbird: A Portrait of Harper Lee*. New York: Henry Holt, 2006.

Stowe, Harriet Beecher. *Uncle Tom's Cabin or, Life Among the Lowly*. 1852. New York: Penguin Classics, 1986.

Twain, Mark. *The Adventures of Huckleberry Finn*. 1884. New York: Bantam, 1981.

Williams, Linda. *Playing the Race Card: Melodramas of Black and White from Uncle Tom to O. J. Simpson*. Princeton NJ: Princeton University Press, 2001.

Wyile, Andrea Schwenke. "Expanding the View of First-Person Narration." *Children's Literature in Education* 30.3 (1999): 185–202.

10

The Identification Fallacy

Perspective and Subjectivity in Children's Literature

MARIA NIKOLAJEVA

In *Winnie-the-Pooh*, chapter 3, "in which Pooh and Piglet go hunting and nearly catch a Woozle," the two characters, one of which is a Bear with a Very Little Brain, follow some tracks in the snow. They think they are hunting first a Woozle, then two Woozles, then "two Woozles and one, as it might be, Wizzle, or two, as it might be, Wizzles and one, if so it is Woozle" (Milne 35).

As usual, Christopher Robin the Almighty comes to the rescue, saying:

"Silly old Bear [. . .] what *were* you doing? First you went round the spinney twice by yourself, and then Piglet ran after you and you went round again together, and then you were just going round a fourth time—"

"Wait a moment," said Winnie-the-Pooh. (37–38)

Let us consider the reading competence that is necessary to understand this chapter. For unsophisticated readers *Pooh* books are about the teddy bear called Winnie-the-Pooh. As critics we can develop other, sophisticated interpretations (Kuznets 47–53; Nikolajeva, *From Mythic to Linear* 93–103), but for the young reader Pooh is the only option. The world is presented through Pooh's eyes, through a naive, curious, and inquisitive view that all children possess until we adults impose our own clever ideas on them. A young reader will be engaged with Pooh, feel his joys and sorrows, his fear of Heffalumps, and his admiration for Christopher Robin. Yet, in chapter 3 young readers have a problem. If they entirely share Pooh's perception, they will, together with Pooh and Piglet, believe that the two friends are tracking fierce and dangerous animals. On hearing Christopher Robin's comment, they will feel as "Foolish and Deluded" (38) as Pooh. Naturally, there are illustrations to help; a reader still needs to feel at least slightly superior to Pooh to appreciate the scene.

In my thirty-year career in children's literature, I have repeatedly and in various situations encountered the firm belief that young readers should be encouraged to "identify" themselves with one of the characters, normally with the protagonist. A teacher may express this urge by asking: "Who would you like to be in this story?" Students of children's literature warmly embrace texts that offer identification objects. This perplexing phenomenon can be called "identification fallacy," in analogy with the famous "intentional fallacy" of New Criticism (Wimsatt and Beardsley 1954). Perhaps more than any other critical stance, identification fallacy reveals a striking inconsistency between children's literature research and literacy education. The conviction that young readers must adopt the subject position of a literary character is, however, totally ungrounded and in fact prevents the development of mature reading.

Contemporary scholarly studies, especially those leaning on narratology and reception theory, emphasize the importance of the readers' ability to liberate themselves from the protagonists' subjectivity in order to evaluate them properly (see Stephens 47–83). This ability is an essential part of reading competence, which enhances sophisticated readers' ideological and aesthetic appreciation of the text. Interestingly enough, identification compulsion is seldom, if ever, discussed in general literary studies. How could we possibly read Dostoyevsky if we were supposed to identify with Raskolnikov? Yet teachers and even critics insist that young readers must necessarily find an identification object in the text, while children's book reviews often include in their evaluation something like: "This book is very good because it is easy to identify with the main character." There is no empirical research about how and at what age identification fallacy is surmounted, yet young readers must be extremely resistant to teachers' pressure to be able to switch from object to subject, from the passive acceptance of the literary character's fixed subjectivity to an independent and flexible one.

Similarly, children's writers must apparently develop intricate strategies in order to deceive adult critics, teachers, and librarians and, behind their backs, subvert identification compulsion. Moreover, writers certainly teach their readers how to feel *empathy* with other people (cf. Keen). Yet to be able to feel empathy, young readers must separate themselves from literary characters, just as they in real life must learn to abandon solipsism and start interacting with other individuals. It is therefore essential to understand how subjectivity is constructed in literary texts and how children's writers can either promote or hamper the readers' deliverance from identification compulsion.

The opposition between the literary and the pedagogical approaches is reflected in the terms used. Pedagogy prescribes identification *object*, a reader's passive role, following whatever the text provides. Literary studies emphasize the importance of the *subject*, the reader as an active participant interacting with the text but independent of its imposed ideology. The difference can further be described in Mikhail Bakhtin's terms as the author's monologic versus dialogic construction of subjectivity, which also suggests different reading strategies (see McCallum and Wilkie-Stibbs). Identifying with characters, readers are limited to a single position. A detached reader can enter a dialogue with the character. We often subscribe to teaching children to be critical readers, but as long as they are encouraged to be objectified alongside literary characters, they can hardly be expected to learn to be critical toward what they are fed.

After a very brief glance at a few classic texts, we can clearly see that the subjectivity provided by a literary text (or recognized through reading strategy) is seldom fixed and tied to a character or even a number of characters to choose from. Rather, subjectivity is constructed through the narratee and especially the implied reader, and these agencies manipulate real readers in interpreting the text. The word "manipulate" is not used here pejoratively; "manipulation" can imply assistance as well as interference, and further, both assistance and interference may be more or less desirable from different viewpoints. In any case, the subject position of the text is played against the textual construction of the implied reader, and it is exclusively in this sense that the word "reader" will be used henceforth, unless otherwise specified.

Terror and Idealization

The most elementary case of children's literature that destroys rather than supports identification is the cautionary tale, such as *Struwwelpeter*. What children in their right minds would want to identify with Little Suck-a-Thumb or Augustus Who Would Not Have Any Soup? Heinrich Hoffmann has been severely criticized for his brutal stories, while other scholars have equally ardently stated that *Struwwelpeter* is a parody (see Zipes 147–69). As a cautionary tale the story's purpose is to frighten its reader. Since all the characters are punished for bad behavior, they are supposed to evoke repugnance rather than empathy. The book offers no counterbalance; child characters are evil because of their deeds, while adults are evil because they subject children to cruelties. The cautionary tale creates an insurmountable distance between the characters and the readers. If, on the other hand, Hoffmann's evergreen should be perceived as an ironic reply to his contemporary children's writers, young readers' subjectivity becomes still more complicated. It is asserted occasionally, based on limited empirical research, that children do not appreciate irony. If this is true, young readers will be unable to grasp Hoffmann's irony in the first place. If they somehow do, they would all the more need to step back from the stories and avoid identification. As it turns out, this equally popular and despicable book efficiently challenges identification. Perhaps this is the secret of its undying attraction.

The opposite of Hoffmann's crime-and-punishment stories are the instructional stories with model, idealized children that often appear in nineteenth-century children's fiction; these children not only improve themselves but preferably reform the adults around them. *Heidi*, a textbook example of child idolatry, has a title character so perfect, sweet, nice, and obedient that a sensible reader is rather disgusted if compelled to identification. To enjoy this angelic child, readers are expected to shift their subjectivity so that they perceive idealization as a deliberate characterization device; moreover, the text invites readers to recognize that they are not like the character and should not strive to be. Viewed in this manner, *Heidi* is just another cautionary story. Malcolm Usrey interprets the novel as being in actual fact the story of the grandfather rather than the child. Such interpretation is symptomatic. Unable to identify with the female five-year-old child, the critic starts searching for another identification object and, finding it, builds his argument against all reason.

Diamond in *At the Back of the North Wind* is not only idealized; he appears within an ambivalent genre and an ambivalent world. Like Heidi—and dozens of other perfect and innocent children of nineteenth-century children's literature—Diamond converts adult sinners, radiates messages of joy and love, and demonstrates intrinsic wisdom and impeccable morals. The synergy of idealization and the liminal dreamworld makes it completely impossible to appreciate the story unless readers really take a step back and judge it from there. Diamond's parents and friends believe him to be mentally disturbed, which is verbally expressed as being "God's child." Unless readers understand the implication, they are caught in Diamond's subjective view of himself and the world.

However, a book can be rather direct in order to shatter the reader's identification. In *The Secret Garden*, the narrator from the beginning repeatedly tells us that Mary, the protagonist, is a horrible person. It is partially *shown* to us through Mary's behavior and the reactions of those around her, but the narrator is trying to convince the reader that Mary is "the most disagreeable child ever seen [. . .] sickly, fretful, ugly" (Burnett 7); "tyrannical and selfish [. . .] little pig" (8); "plain and fretful" (18); "thin, sallow, ugly" (46); "languid and weak" (67). For a young reader Mary is the only identification object in the novel. She is instrumental to the plot, and she is the only child character until later in the story. Colin does not appear until halfway through the plot, and he is, if possible, still less agreeable than Mary. Dickon is too unreal, almost a mythical figure, and is only a secondary character. It is therefore easy to accept the narrator's perspective and subjectivity. Who wants to identify with a nasty, lazy, spoiled, and uneducated brat? Yet the text equally invites readers to consider Mary's predicament with sympathy. If readers can overcome the aversion expressed by the narrator toward Mary, they will soon see, for one thing, that Mary is not as nasty as the narrator states and, second, that she is improving much faster than the narrator is prepared to admit. Further, readers are supposed, together with Mary, to recognize a mirror reflection of her previous self in Colin and understand her behavior toward him, without the narrator's explanation. While the perceptible narrator seems to alienate the character, the implied author does the opposite, and an interesting tension is achieved. The subject position will thus be neither tied to Mary nor to the narrator, but rather emerge from an active, dialogical response to what the narrator tells the readers and what they can infer themselves. Unless this happens, readers will be irritated either by the abominable character or by the intrusive narrator.

Multiple Choices

One of the favorite texts in the identification argument is *The Lion, the Witch and the Wardrobe*. If you are oldest, brave, and responsible, choose Peter. If you are careful and reasonable, choose Susan. If you are gullible, joyful, and loyal, Lucy is your figure. If you are nasty, evil, and have a sweet tooth, press for Edmund. This procedure is indeed reminiscent of the choice of your character in a computer game.

In pedagogical contexts stories with multiple characters or protagonists are proclaimed desirable in children's literature since they presumably provide identification objects for readers of different ages and of both genders. Translated to a more advanced terminology, the text allows a variety of subject positions, each firmly tied to one of the characters. A closer investigation of collective characters in children's literature demonstrates that they are used mostly as pedagogical devices (see my *Rhetoric of Character* 67–87). Instead of portraying one complex character, the author splits the personality traits between several actors, getting the brave Peter, the sensible Susan, the treacherous Edmund, and the honest Lucy rather than one character possessing many and sometimes contradictory features. While collective characters may be viewed as a part of the conventional poetics of children's literature, this presents a difficulty exactly because the subject position of the text is steadily attached to one of the characters. Particular real readers may, for some reason, choose to identify with the "wrong" character, Edmund, since the text allows this strategy; they can equally identify with the cowardly Piglet in *Winnie-the-Pooh* because they recognize traits they possess themselves. Such choices are not more advanced since they still presuppose fixed subjectivity.

The postmodern concept of intersubjectivity allows readers more freedom since it makes the subject position deliberately fluctuant, which in turn renders the text more challenging.[1] In the concrete example of the four children in *The Lion, the Witch and the Wardrobe*, rather than sharing the characters' perceptional and conceptual point of view, mature readers are assumed to choose a subjectivity somewhere in between, which will enable them to assess all four characters from equal premises, at the same time avoiding the judgmental subject position of the narrator.

It is otherwise quite natural to suggest that the most suitable candidate for subjectivity in a text is the main character. This may, however, present a dilemma when the decision on the protagonist depends on the level of sophistication (Pooh or Christopher Robin?) (see Kuznets 51; Nikolajeva, *Rhetoric of Character* 82–84).

The fictive child can be abused by the author to the degree that identification becomes entirely out of the question. In *Alice's Adventures in Wonderland*, the young protagonist finds herself in a strange world in which she is rendered helpless and is denied use of her common sense (which is of no use in Wonderland), her education, and her willpower. She even loses control of her body, and most of the time she is physically inferior to creatures and inanimate objects that normally would be smaller and thus less powerful. She is ordered about, humiliated, and denied agency until just before the end of the book.

Readers have the option of distancing themselves both from Alice and from Wonderland and enjoying the book for what it is, with its lack of proper plot, its bizarre figures, its linguistic brilliance, and its disappointing closure. Yet it is not uncommon for real readers, even adult readers, to put away the book with aversion. The problem is obviously that these readers cannot recognize themselves in Alice; they are unable to free themselves from the identification pressure and painstakingly seek an identification object.

In Western children's literature, *Alice's Adventures in Wonderland* is one of the rare texts that instead of empowering the fictional child through displacement in an alternative world, disempowers and even humiliates her. It is only on waking up that Alice regains the relative power she has before falling down the rabbit hole, which isn't much: she returns to being ordered about by her elder sister, much in the same manner she has been ordered about by rabbits and caterpillars in Wonderland. Alice is hardly a role model, and her adventures are nightmares rather than pleasant dreams. Her constant bodily transformations are not merely disturbing and uncomfortable; they reflect abjection, a young girl's dissatisfaction with and fear of the imminent changes in her body. Readers adopting Alice's subjectivity will feel the same discomfort and frustration that the character goes through; in contrast, from an external subject position they will see Alice's experience as a marvelous depiction of a lonely, confused child in the perplexing and absurd adult world. To enjoy *Alice* readers must be mature enough to interact with the text by stepping out of it rather than passively following the character's similarly passive engagement in the story.

Contrary to Alice, the title character of *Pippi Longstocking* has full control over her situation, physically as well as mentally: she is the strongest girl in the world, rich beyond imagination, endowed with power that in real life is only reserved for adults, and not restricted by any rules. This makes her radically unlike any child reader, real or implied. Like Tommy and Annika within the text, readers are supposed to understand that Pippi is one of a kind and that they cannot be like her or behave like her. This does not prevent Pippi from being a highly subversive figure, yet readers are hardly encouraged to copy Pippi by sleeping with their feet on the pillow, watering flowers under pouring rain, eating toadstools, or talking sense with sharks. Thus the character construction as such presupposes a shift in subjectivity. The narrative perspective of the *Pippi* books amplifies the subjectivity shift away from Pippi; she is actually not the subject to whom the story happens but its engine.

In the penultimate Harry Potter novel, *Harry Potter and the Half-Blood Prince*, the text consistently pushes the reader toward the dark wizard Voldemort's subject position. The text's quite candid intention may be to explain that evil can grow out of the ordinary, but this is a dangerous or at least an irresponsible stance, since readers can start feeling sympathy for the poor, abandoned, and maltreated orphan and seek roots of evil in his unhappy childhood or in social injustice. Somehow this perspective shift makes his malicious deeds more justified. The inexplicable and therefore especially threatening evil, presented in the previous volumes of the series, is de-demonized, and Voldemort, or rather his more human image, Tom Riddle, is brought closer to the orphaned hero Harry. It requires extremely strong reader integrity to continue feeling the same loathing for the lonely and miserable youth who resents his parents' neglect that we felt for the unscrupulous murderer and villain in the earlier novels.

For some reason it is commonly held that animals, especially anthropomorphic animals, are suitable characters in children's literature. The assumption is based on a rather vague belief that children love animals, one of those many ungrounded prejudices about children's literature. Some scholars have been rather skeptical about this stance, pointing out the contemptuous attitude of bundling together animals and children as small, inferior, and basically not human (see Schwarcz 9).

Yet animals in the vast majority of stories are used to empower the readers who do not identify with the characters but rather feel superior to them. Readers are provoked to feel sorry for the disobedient protagonist of *The Tale of Peter Rabbit*, especially since he is not only defeated and humiliated on his heroic quest but also further punished by his mother. The little hero, naturally breaking his mother's prohibition, ventures into a new, unknown, and exciting territory. He does what every folktale hero has done before him, and what many children's literature characters have been doing after him. The author, however, anticipates the failure of her protagonist by condemning him from start: "Peter, who was very naughty" (Potter 18). Here identification is encouraged by the hero's bold actions yet hampered by the development of events. Upon entering the enemy's territory, he is not, as the mythical or fairy-tale hero, allowed to revenge his father's untimely and horrible death. He is not allowed to show courage or wit; he does not find any treasure. On the contrary he is repeatedly humiliated, first being sick because of his gluttony, then chased by Mr. McGregor, caught in a net, and finally, and perhaps most significantly, losing his clothes, which transforms him from an intelligent, anthropomorphic creature into an ordinary, dumb animal.[2] Instead of returning home as a glorious hero, he returns exhausted physically and defeated morally. Readers may feel compassion for the character; however, sympathy is not the same as empathy. Even a very young reader is counted upon to infer that Peter is acting wrong, and the didactic narrator supports this view by declaring that Peter was "naughty." The reader is thus free to choose a wide spectrum of subject positions in between the narrator's didacticism and the character's striving for independence. Moreover, readers can go further yet than the narrator in condemning the character (for instance by saying that Peter's punishment is insufficient: he should have been caught by Mr. McGregor and put into a pie, similar to the penalty suffered by the *Struwwelpeter* characters), or, on the contrary, judge the character as too cowardly: he should have challenged his opponent rather than have fled from him. In either case the use of a zoomorphic child character as a design seems more likely to subvert identification rather than support it since the animal shape creates alienation and enhances an independent subjectivity.

Both anthropomorphic animals and animated toys in symbiosis with a human child have excellent premises for undermining identification. In the company of toys and animals, the child can feel strong, clever, and protective. *Winnie-the-Pooh* is an excellent example. Christopher Robin feels stupid and uneducated in the fictive reality of the book, a frightened child exposed to rules and regulations, allowed for a short while to visit his omnipotent father in his study and then promptly exiled back to the nursery. In his own realm he is a king and a god, appearing each time that his small, silly subjects have entangled themselves in unsolvable problems. While it is difficult to identify with the oppressed Christopher Robin of the frame narrative, it is perhaps still more challenging to share subjectivity with the godlike sovereign of the forest. Therefore, the most natural choice for a young reader is Pooh.

Flying Dutchmen and Wandering Jews

Fantasy as such works as an alienation strategy and thus encourages the reader to adopt an independent subject position. Just as nobody could seriously identify with Jack the Giant Killer, readers cannot fully adopt, for instance, Frodo Baggins's subjectivity, not only because he is not human, but in the first place because they lack his experience of a magical world. Readers are supposed to feel compassion when Frodo is anguished; they are allowed to make their own judgments, perhaps even try on the situation themselves, yet identification is strongly hampered. Incidentally, if we compare *The Hobbit* with *The Lord of Rings* in terms of identification and subjectivity, the former, addressing younger readers, has one main character and thus encourages identification. The latter addresses teenage and adult audiences and offers a wide range of characters that split and have their own plots. Presumably, Tolkien falls into the identification pit when writing for children but not for adults.

In quite a few fantasy novels, the subject position of the text promptly demands that identification be abandoned. In *Tuck Everlasting* the dream of immortality, a recurrent theme in children's literature, is transformed into a nightmare. While the Tucks may discuss among themselves whether their situation is a blessing or a curse, the narrator is quite explicit about the tragedy of their fate. The novel focuses sharply on the human suffering connected with the dilemma of eternal life. It also underscores the alienation of the cursed: the Tucks cannot make friends or generally get involved with the outside world. Behind the narrative a mature reader will recognize the universal motif of the Wandering Jew. The Tucks, however, are not punished for any specific wrongdoing or vice. Neither have they had any choice. This may be a disturbing thought, since the Tucks are paying a terribly dear price for a mere accident. Yet the anguish of the curse is shifted from the child protagonist, apparently to protect the reader, who is likely to adopt Winnie's subjectivity rather than that of any of the Tuck family. This position is subverted by the epilogue of the novel, which features the Tucks visiting Winnie's grave. Identification is seriously impaired, even though the novel follows the children's literature conventions, allowing the child to win over evil merely by virtue of her innocence.

By contrast, in *Homeward Bounders* the text abandons all earlier practices of children's literature, making the protagonist, rather than a secondary character, the bearer of the curse. The book declares its intertextuality openly: "Have you heard of the

Flying Dutchman? No? Nor of the Wandering Jew?" (Jones 7), thus setting the informed reader's expectations. When Jamie finally finds his way home, he discovers that a hundred years have passed in his own universe, and everyone dear to him is dead. A recognizable feature from the fairy tale of immortality, the ending is significantly more disturbing than the Tucks' visiting Winnie's grave. In fact this kind of ending is by definition impossible in conventional children's fiction since it shatters the child's intrinsic belief in the stability of the world. *Homeward Bounders* interrogates this illusory stability. Jamie must shoulder the burdens that no adult could endure, which makes him such a tragic character that one can only relate to him from a distance.

Alienated Place and Time

Some other examples of exotic setting are the historical novel, Orientalism, utopia or dystopia, and the closely related counterfactual novel.[3] Each of these genres in its own way erects a barrier between the protagonist and the reader, persuading the latter to adopt an independent subject position. Once again, unless this happens, readers will be strapped to the characters that, especially in dystopian and counterfactual texts, are completely blind toward their own behavior as well as the surrounding world. Among other things readers' resistance to disempowering endings is a common phenomenon; for instance, many real readers of *The Giver*, even adult readers, prefer to interpret the ending optimistically, claiming that the protagonist has indeed reached a better place and will live happily ever after. A more sophisticated reading of the novel excludes such an interpretation: throughout the novel the Elsewhere, which Jonas is trying to reach, is used as a euphemism for death.

Contemporary dystopias for young readers, for instance, *The Denials of Kow-Ten*, *Feed*, or the counterfactual *Noughts and Crosses*, display several stereotypes that are gratifying to investigate from the identification point of view. Dystopia is built around the double estrangement effect: while the reader is not familiar with the rules of the society presented in a novel, the characters are not aware of the "normal" world. Already this makes dystopian fiction an excellent strategy for subverting identification. The chronotope, or time-space, of dystopia is an enclave, distanced from the reader by a span of the future. This temporal and spatial isolation is already a powerful factor to create alienation. There is always a world beyond the dystopia, such as "Elsewhere" in *The Giver* or "Outside," the landscape beyond the Wall in *The Denials of Kow-Ten*, but the characters are either happily unaware of it or likewise happily convinced that the outside world is evil. The discrepancy between the characters' and the readers' knowledge, understanding, and physical as well as mental experience is the axis of all dystopian fiction, yet for a young reader, additional effort must be made to grasp the significance of the protagonists' ethical choices. The protagonists' epiphany can cause several actions that all demand the reader's ethical standpoint: they may attempt to change their society, escape from it, or conform to it. Forced conformity may occasionally take extremely violent forms, reminiscent of Orwell's *1984*; however, it can equally be a matter of simple cowardice. In this case moral judgment is left wholly to the reader, who must disengage from the protagonist to be able to judge. Dystopia is then a powerful vehicle to alienate readers, making them aware of either the characters' naïveté or their failing morals. The ending of *The Giver* spares the protagonist—and the reader—the humiliation of being brainwashed all over again. Jonas's death echoes the nineteenth-century practice of killing off fictive children before they have an opportunity to sin.[4]

The Detached Self

The most unexpected discovery in investigating identification fallacy is perhaps that first-person narration is an exceedingly successful strategy for subverting identification. This may sound like a paradox: many textbooks and critical works on juvenile fiction claim that personal narration is more engaging, allowing a total penetration into the protagonist's mind. Yet, again, engagement is not the same as identification. Contemporary young adult novels frequently employ first-person narration, which ostensibly creates an authentic teenage voice, especially when youth jargon is used. First-person perspective encourages the reader to share the character/narrator's point of view. The subject position prompted by the text becomes restricted when the narrator and the protagonist fulfill the same agency. However, in most cases first-person narratives demonstrate a dialogical nature by the very fact that subjectivity is split between the experiencing and the narrating self. Can readers possibly understand the disturbed state of mind in which Holden Caulfield of *The Catcher in the Rye* roams the New York streets if they choose to identify with this disoriented teenager? They must certainly let the dialogic interaction with the one-year-older Holden's ironic comments come into their evaluation, as well as their position toward both of the agents. Thus the dissonance between the narrative voice and the point of view in personal narration has exactly the opposite effect than might seem natural.

While in *The Catcher in the Rye* the time scope between narrative and narration is explicitly stated, and the two agencies are more or less separated, in *Jacob Have I Loved* the relationship between Louise the character and Louise the narrator is highly ambiguous and indistinct, which strongly affects our perception of the narrator's reliability. Louise the narrator constantly distances herself from Louise the character, for instance, by saying: "As a child, I . . ." (Paterson 3, 22).[5] In *Dance on My Grave*, the purpose of the temporal detachment is not so much to illuminate the gap between experience and narrating as to show the narrator's interrogating his own capacity of finding adequate linguistic means to convey his experience. Concerning the breach between the experiencing and the narrating self in *Dance on My Grave*, it is important to bear in mind that the time span between the events and the narration is considerably shorter than in *Jacob Have I Loved* and even that in *The Catcher in the Rye*. The poignantly exact time account emphasizes the intensity of Hal's experience, when each second was significant. Hal's memories are quite fresh, and unlike Louise he is eager to describe the events as accurately as possible. This does not mean that his narrative is less subjective than Louise's, but Hal does not win anything by lying or explaining away his actions; on the contrary, he tries to sound as candid as he can. By the end of the novel, story time and discourse time are synchronized, that is, the gap between experience and narration diminishes and eventually disappears.

In all these cases, if readers fall into the identification trap and share the protagonists' inevitably limited point of view, they will never be able to comprehend what is actually going on in the novels and become so confined to the protagonists' subjectivity that they will ignore the repeated cracks that the texts offer. A mature reading of any first-person narrative presupposes liberation from the character/narrator's subject position, even though personal narration does allow the reader to enter the characters' minds and thus stand as close to them as possible.

Yet the personality split can be much more concrete and complex than detachment in time. In *Surrender* two personal narrators tell the same story antiphonically through alternating chapters, each literally in dialogue with the other, complementing the events to which the other had no access and, more significant, correcting the erroneous inferences of the dialogue partner. Time oscillates between then and now, yet neither is clearly delineated. Readers are successively allowed to realize that one of the characters/narrators, the feral boy and the arsonist Finnigan, is entirely the product of the mentally sick Gabriel, his dark side, created to hold his vicious dreams and painful memories. The now of the story appears to be a short time before Gabriel's self-inflicted death by starvation; the then is his whole short life made up of disparate pieces, all of which focus on parental abuse and humiliation. The ambivalent meaning of the title refers not merely to the character's final capitulation but also to the name of his dog, brutally killed by his father. Together with Finnigan, Surrender becomes the character's scourge, yet by the time Gabriel opens his memory to the day he murdered his parents, he is unable to distinguish between his many selves, between then and now, between dark and light. Needless to say, identification with the character is out of the question.

Narrator Dissolved

In Gérard Genette's theory no distinction is made between personal and impersonal narration: impersonal narrators focalize a character, while personal narrators focalize themselves. Instead, Genette stresses the importance of mood, including the narrator's presence in the narrative, the narrator's distance to the narrative, and focalization patterns. Strong internal focalization in many ways works similarly to personal narration, and just as readers need to stand free of the personal narrator, they also need to liberate themselves from the focalizing character. For instance, in *Bridge to Terabithia*, the protagonist, Jess, refuses to admit his friend Leslie's death and goes through several stages of acceptance that readers can only observe from a distance, even though the strongest imaginable sympathy is evoked. The title character of *The Great Gilly Hopkins* is similarly unable to judge her own position, and her alleged greatness is deeply ironic.[6]

In *The Devil Latch* multiple internal focalization amplifies the split subjectivity, since neither character's perception is presented as more reliable. Aimee seems to be enchanted by Kitten and totally oblivious to his ruthless behavior, while Kitten initially appears to be merely a confused young man, but successively the reader notices a complete disintegration of the mind, which neither he himself nor Aimee are able to assess. Like multiple narration, internal multifocalization does not allow readers to make a definite choice of subjectivity and forces them to stand somewhere in between. Yet unlike collective characters that commonly appear in action-oriented novels, multiple focalizers invite strong sympathy without imposing fixed subject positions.

Internal focalization has become widespread in all genres, not exclusively in the realistic adolescent novel. The *His Dark Materials* trilogy exhibits a number of alienation strategies. Lyra, the protagonist, lives in a world that is very similar to our own but not quite identical. Thus certain facts, either mentioned directly or implied, that are self-evident for Lyra are strange and unfamiliar for the reader, and the other way round. Not least, in Lyra's world all human beings' souls or personalities are externalized in the form of animal companions. Further, Lyra, who functions as focalizer in the larger part of the trilogy, demonstrates several quite unpleasant traits: she lies and cheats, and although unknowingly, she causes the death of her closest friend. Readers are supposed to see Lyra's negative sides as well as her anxieties and fears. In the second and third volumes, a number of other focalizers are added, and this intricate multifocalization creates a complex intersubjective rather than collective protagonist. None of the characters offers a self-evident subject position. Taken all together these narrative strategies allow readers to detach themselves from characters as well as the narrator and make their own, independent judgments.

Making the protagonist unsympathetic, like Lyra, is a very efficient way of alienating the reader. *The White Mercedes* (later released as *The Butterfly Tattoo*) starts with a breathtaking line: "Chris Marshall met the girl he was going to kill on a warm night in early June." After this opening readers will have problems identifying with Chris but will hopefully still follow his fate with engagement. There is, however, a subtle boundary beyond which the lack of subjectivity may become problematic. The tremendously popular *Artemis Fowl* series portrays a protagonist of low morals, evil by nature, whose adversaries are equally unpleasant. Alternating focalization offers the readers different ideologies, all indiscriminately corrupt. It is doubtful that all readers of Artemis Fowl are sophisticated enough to adopt an independent subject position and see both Artemis and his opponents for what they are. Thus the readers are enticed into identification, and since Artemis is the title character and carries the glory of the hero, he becomes the natural choice.

All my examples point to the discrepancy between the desire to evoke empathy, if not merely a strong sympathy, and the need to subvert the subject position tied to a fictive character. The notorious didacticism of early children's literature implies, among other things, fixed subjectivity in which the characters are either models or cautionary examples. In both cases the reader is seemingly encouraged to adopt the narrator's position, that is, admiration or contempt. The reader's freedom of independent subjectivity would appear to be limited, yet paradoxically, repulsion and perfection equally subvert identification.

In contemporary children's literature the tendency is to make protagonists more like ordinary people, which implies that the subjectivity of the text shifts from the narrator to the character. It is natural that authors want the reader to be engaged in their characters' trials and quests; otherwise the reader will simply put the book aside. However, if the subject position inflicted by the text is too strong and there are no narrative devices that displace subjectivity, readers are likely to be trapped. The various strategies outlined in this essay can support a mature subject position.

It can be argued that young readers can enjoy books even though they share the protagonist's subjectivity. I would certainly agree that they can, just as they can enjoy reading for the plot exclusively, ignoring characterization, psychological implications, ideology, and style. However, character-tied position endorses solipsism, an immature child's conviction that the world rotates around himself or herself. As mediators of literature we want children to be able to place themselves in other people's life situations, to develop understanding and compassion, to be self-reflective, and not least, to be able to assess ideology. As suggested earlier independent subjectivity is one of the major constituents of reading competence. If we want to foster our children as mature readers, the first and most important step is to make them aware of identification fallacy.

Notes

1. For a more detailed discussion, see Nikolajeva, *Rhetoric of Character* 88–109.

2. On Peter's transformation, see Scott.

3. A counterfactual novel is based on the premise that human history has at some point developed differently from the course we know, for instance, that Hitler died in his early childhood. Some of these genres are often discussed together. See, for example, Jameson; Hintz and Ostry.

4. See Plotz for more on this nineteenth-century practice.

5. For more on this in Paterson's novel, see Nikolajeva, "Art of Self-Deceit."

6. See my discussion of this in "The Art of Self-Deceit."

Works Cited

Anderson, M. T. *Feed*. Cambridge MA: Candlewick, 2002.

Babbitt, Natalie. *Tuck Everlasting*. New York: Farrar, 1975.

Blackman, Malorie. *Noughts and Crosses*. 1969. London: Doubleday, 2001.

Burnett, Frances Hodgson. *The Secret Garden*. 1911. London: Penguin, 1995.

Carroll, Lewis. *Alice's Adventures in Wonderland*. 1865. *The Penguin Complete Lewis Carroll*. Harmondsworth, England: Penguin, 1982.

Chambers, Aidan. *Dance on My Grave*. 1982. London: Random, 1995.

Colfer, Eoin. *Artemis Fowl*. London: Viking, 2001.

Hartnett, Sonya. *The Devil Latch*. Sydney: Penguin, 1996.

———. *Surrender*. Sydney: Penguin, 1995.

Hintz, Carrie, and Elaine Ostry, eds. *Utopian and Dystopian Writing for Children and Young Adults*. New York: Routledge, 2003.

Hoffmann, Heinrich. *Struwwelpeter*. 1845. New York: Dover, 1995.

Jameson, Fredric. *Archaeologies of the Future: The Desire Called Utopia and Other Science Fictions*. London: Verso, 2005.

Jones, Diana Wynne. *The Homeward Bounders*. New York: Greenwillow, 1981.

Keen, Suzanne. *Empathy and the Novel*. New York: Oxford University Press, 2007.

Kuznets. Lois. *When Toys Come Alive: Narratives of Animation, Metamorphosis, and Development*. New Haven CT: Yale University Press, 1994.

Lewis, C. S. *The Lion, the Witch and the Wardrobe*. 1950. Harmondsworth, England: Penguin, 1959.

Lindgren, Astrid. *Pippi Longstocking*. 1945. New York: Viking, 1950.

Lowry, Lois. *The Giver*. New York: Doubleday, 1993.

MacDonald, George. *At the Back of the North Wind*. 1871. Harmondsworth, England: Penguin, 1984.

McCallum, Robyn. *Ideologies of Identity in Adolescent Fiction: The Dialogic Construction of Subjectivity*. New York: Garland, 1999.

Milne, A. A. *Winnie-the-Pooh*. 1926. London: Methuen, 1965.

Nikolajeva, Maria. "The Art of Self-Deceit: Narrative Strategies in Katherine Paterson's Novels." *Bridges for the Young: The Fiction of Katherine*

Paterson. Ed. Joel Chaston and Sarah Smedman. Lanham MD: Scarecrow, 2003. 10–33.

——. *From Mythic to Linear: Time in Children's Literature*. Lanham MD: Scarecrow, 2000.

——. *The Rhetoric of Character in Children's Literature*. Lanham MD: Scarecrow, 2002.

Orwell, George. *1984*. Secker, 1949.

Paterson, Katherine. *Bridge to Terabithia*. 1977. New York: HarperCollins, 1987.

——. *The Great Gilly Hopkins*. 1978. New York: HarperCollins, 1987.

——. *Jacob Have I Loved*. 1980. New York: HarperCollins, 1990.

Plotz, Judith. "Literary Ways of Killing a Child: The 19th Century Practice." *Aspects and Issues in the History of Children's Literature*. Ed. Maria Nikolajeva. Westport CT: Greenwood, 1995. 1–24.

Potter, Beatrix. *The Tale of Peter Rabbit*. 1902. London: Warne, 1987.

Pullman, Philip. *The Amber Spyglass*. London: Scholastic, 2000.

——. *Northern Lights*. London: Scholastic, 1995.

——. *The Subtle Knife*. London: Scholastic, 1997.

——. *The White Mercedes*. London: Macmillan, 1992.

Robson, Jenny. *The Denials of Kow-Ten*. Cape Town: Tafelberg, 1998.

Rowling, J. K. *Harry Potter and the Half-Blood Prince*. London: Bloomsbury, 2005.

Salinger, Jerome D. *The Catcher in the Rye*. 1951. Philadelphia: Chelsea, 2000.

Schwarcz, Joseph H. *Ways of the Illustrator: Visual Communication in Children's Literature*. Chicago: American Library Assn., 1982.

Scott, Carole. "Between Me and the World: Clothes as Mediator between Self and Society in the Works of Beatrix Potter." *The Lion and the Unicorn* 16.2 (1992): 192–98.

Spyri, Johanna. *Heidi*. 1880. Ware: Wordsworth, 1993.

Stephens, John. *Language and Ideology in Children's Fiction*. London: Longman, 1992.

Tolkien, J. R. R. *The Hobbit*. 1937. Boston: Houghton, 1997.

——. *Lord of the Rings*. 1954–55. Philadelphia: Chelsea, 1999.

Usrey, Malcolm. "Johanna Spyri's *Heidi*: The Conversion of a Byronic Hero." *Touchstones: Reflections on the Best in Children's Literature*. Ed. Perry Nodelman. West Lafayette IN: Children's Literature Assn., 1985. 3:232–42.

Wilkie-Stibbs, Christine. *The Feminine Subject in Children's Literature*. New York: Routledge, 2002.

Wimsatt, William K., and Monroe C. Beardsley. "The Intentional Fallacy." *The Verbal Icon: Studies in the Meaning of Poetry*. London: Methuen, 1954. 3–18.

Zipes, Jack. *Sticks and Stones: The Troublesome Success of Children's Literature from Slovenly Peter to Harry Potter*. New York: Routledge, 2001.

11

The Development of Hebrew Children's Literature

From Men Pulling Children Along to Women Meeting Them Where They Are

DANA KEREN-YAAR

Jewish women began writing in Hebrew not long before the birth of Hebrew children's literature. Hebrew children's literature, that is, texts for children written in the Hebrew language, was born in the framework of the modern revolutions of the Jewish Enlightenment and Hebrew nationalism (Ofek 12–24). The first stage, which took place in Europe from the end of the eighteenth century until the second half of the nineteenth century, reflected an enlightened Jewish ambition to mold Jewish society anew through a change in the educational orientation and study program. In the second stage, the Palestine–the Land of Israel stage, Hebrew children's literature functioned as a didactic, ideological tool in the service of an evolving modern Hebrew education system (Shavit 11). In this essay I focus on the two waves of women writing for children from near the end of the first stage until the end of the second stage in 1950.

From a feminist narratological perspective, Hebrew children's literature developed in two waves. The first wave includes pioneer women Hebrew writers at the turning point from Jewish Enlightenment to the birth of Hebrew nationality. It began in Europe in 1886 with *Children's Way*, by Sara Foner—the first children's book written in Hebrew by a woman—and continued in Palestine–the Land of Israel at the beginning of the twentieth century with stories by Hemda Ben Yehuda.[1] The second wave (1930–50) was consolidated in Palestine–the Land of Israel during the decades surrounding the foundation of the state of Israel (1948). This division will help to demonstrate the move from writing in a "father's tongue" to writing in a "mother's tongue" in Hebrew children's literature.

The First Wave of Women Writers

The first wave was influenced by developments from the Jewish Enlightenment in Eastern Europe in the late eighteenth century through the European Jewish migration to Palestine in the late nineteenth century. During the period of the Jewish Enlightenment and even at the transition to Hebrew nationalism, Hebrew children's literature could be described as a masculine creation and written in the "father's tongue," an apt description of the Hebrew language during this period. In contrast to "mother's tongue," it was neither acquired from birth nor spoken at home but rather practiced in prayers and religious studies and used mainly by Jewish male scholars. In the Enlightenment period in Europe, Hebrew was considered a "father's tongue" because canonical Jewish holy texts (e.g., the Talmud) were created, as in most patriarchal societies, by men to express their worldviews and were read and thus studied by men (Cohen 71). Moreover, during the ensuing period of Hebrew nationality and in the first Jewish national immigration to Palestine–the Land of Israel, Hebrew was not yet used widely among settlers (Bar-Adon 13).

Under a patriarchal gender-role division, women were responsible for child care while men were charged with child enculturation, a role passed from the domain of the traditional rabbi to that of the enlightened teacher. Very few fathers gave their daughters a private Hebrew education; therefore, traditional women in general had hardly any knowledge of Hebrew. Not only did most

Hebrew women not have the cultural knowledge that granted professional authority to write for children, but also women's knowledge and life experience were not considered worthy subjects for instilling and spreading Enlightenment values. Hence, Hebrew children's literature of the Jewish Enlightenment period was both about and created for European Hebrew males.

During the resettlement of Palestine the revival of Hebrew as a spoken modern language became one of the first national means to realize the vision of forming modern Jewish life in the historic land of Israel, then under Ottoman rule. In that period Jewish immigrants wished not primarily to found a state but rather to revive Hebrew. Eliezer Ben Yehuda, the reviver of the biblical language as modern Hebrew, regarded motherhood and childhood as crucial institutions. He considered his life's endeavor to be turning Hebrew from a father's tongue into a mother tongue, the term meaning here the language used by those closest to and caring for the infant, whether women or men. Ben Yehuda wished to impart Hebrew as a mother tongue, used as the main mode of communication between children and mothers, so that the language would take root and spread. Moreover, he claimed that women's lack of traditional Jewish education made women particularly suitable for turning the holy language into a modern one, free of Talmudic context (Berlovitz 114). It would be women, not the *Schull* (religious teaching to toddlers held in a traditionally clustered group), who would engage children in the Hebrew language and promote its normalization on national lands.

The pioneer women writers of Hebrew children's literature—Hemda Ben Yehuda, Nechama Puchachevski, Nechama Gisin, Miriam Pepermister, Rachel Newman, and Dvora Baron—immigrated from Eastern Europe to Palestine–the Land of Israel. Hebrew was not their mother tongue but rather a language revived by Eliezer Ben Yehuda. They had no feminine Hebrew models to lean on. It is no wonder that as they immigrated to Palestine and wrote for children at the service of a developing national project, their literature did not reflect intimate communication and presymbolic communication between the parent and the child. Instead, they wrote in a Hebrew that was largely a "father tongue" amplified and elaborated by Eliezer Ben Yehuda. Their dedication to a national linguistic project didn't leave much space for poetic flexibility, and very often the writing tone was didactic and stringent.

Yet the Hebrew writing for children by pioneer Hebrew women can be valued as a women's achievement in another way. The writers often used the didactic axis in their stories as a vehicle to express opinions in public matters. Along with attempting to phrase themselves in public, they demonstrated an ability to use the symbolic "father tongue" and participated in the public cultural discourse.

The Second Wave of Women Writers

The second wave of Hebrew women who wrote for children appeared around the time when the State of Israel was established (1930–50). The road to independence was paved with both internal and external struggles. The population in Palestine was ruled by the British Mandate from 1922 to 1948. Among all those living in Palestine in the 1930s, the Jews were a minority. As the Nazi Party rose to power in Germany (1933), masses of Jews from Eastern and Central Europe escaped to Palestine, making their national presence there more and more prominent (Chalamish 43–46). This wave of immigration faced restrictions imposed by British rule as well as objections from the Palestinians, who feared Jewish Zionist hegemony in Palestine (Pappe 93–107). Nevertheless, the Jews generally aligned themselves with Britain, while Arab leaders saw in Germany a potential ally. The separation between Jewish and Palestinian communities grew, and militias on both sides began preparing for an armed struggle. A Palestinian flare-up materialized into the Arab revolt in 1936 against the British Mandate and Hebrew nationalism and was brutally suppressed by the British army in 1939 (Porat 301–02).

As thousands of men joined underground defense forces, scores of women began writing for children. As opposed to men, who received fighting roles and were understood actually to be soldiers, women were allocated secondary roles, mainly outside the military realm: they were to provide support for men and both education and care for children. Chief among such women were Leah Goldberg, Miriam Yalan-Shteklis, and Yemima Avidar-Tchernovitz. As will be discussed, the children's literature of the time ought not to be characterized simply as militaristic. Indeed, we must focus on a process whereby militarization and normalization were interwoven almost paradoxically. The term "normalization" denotes differentiation, in the framework of which Hebrew children's literature was becoming a separate system in its own right (Shavit 15). I propose that normalization began with these two moves: a shift of Hebrew from father's to mother's tongue as discussed earlier and a later process of professionalization. Following teachers, who were the first writers for children in Hebrew, came professional children's authors, and an individual thematic and style was added to the national thematic.

According to Shavit this process started at the end of the 1950s (16), but one can argue that it began with the wave of creative women who were known as professional writers for children. Children's writers such as Miriam Yalan-Shteklis and Yemima Avidar-Tchernovitz created a "drawing close" style of writing whose poetic element strove to shrink distance and to bridge gaps between the adult writers and the target child. Although not only women used this more private and intimate writing tone, the professionalization of children's literature—a basis for a wider normalization in coming decades—can be attributed to the massive wave of women writers and their works.

However, professionalization has a political aspect that leads to a paradox. The buds of individualism indeed blossomed on the grounds of the newly established national state without abandoning nationalism. Interactive, "drawing close" writing sometimes served as a pedagogical means of inculcating national ideology in a friendly and personal manner. But its strength lay in hiding the political power from the target audience: the child. Breaking through narrow national representation and adding personal and "feminine" aspects to the text allowed doubling of the recruiting effect on the readers.

The political facet of literary professionalization is known for practices of stabilization and regulation and therefore can also be considered as a disguised ideological, political mechanism. A militant attitude emerged as the State of Israel was established (1945–47). One of the narrative models was the recruiting narrative (Darr, "Military Recruitment" 165–71). This national narrative recruited Hebrew children to be citizens of a state in the making and even future partners in military activity. The narrative strove to create homogeneity and described the consolidation of a children's group around a leader for the purpose of fulfilling a joint action of defending the borders of the land from German spies and Arab natives.

It may appear paradoxical that along with the militaristic aims of new narratives, professionalization eventually retreated from a direct national preaching tone in favor of a more intimate and friendly style of writing. The national theme of militarization was enhanced by combining with it personal and emotional themes. That interactive poetic element shifted from the preaching tone that had prevailed in previous generations to a different consideration of the implied reader, the Hebrew child. In contradistinction to the small proportion of Hebrew women who wrote for children in the first wave with the "father tongue" and a direct didactic tone, the second wave of Hebrew women authors elaborated a "drawing close" style.

Those using this "drawing close" style considered the developmental stage of the young reader and his or her ability to absorb information, tried to diminish the distance between him or her and the adult, and even invited the child for joint reading and discussion; all this was done with the help of the communications media most appropriate for children according to their specific developmental stage.

The dominant poetic approach of the hegemonic men writers (Bialik and Shlonsky, for example) demanded that those writing for children raise the level of the reader. Bialik, who had acquired his learning in the Wolozin Yeshiva, used biblical and Talmudic expressions in some of his works for children; he argued that this was needed to enrich and elevate the child's language: "The children will teach their teeth to crack somewhat hard nuts and they will become strong."[2] The following generation of such male writers developed the language of children's books as a poetic rich in sophisticated word games and verbal challenges meant for readers with an extensive knowledge of cultural and canonic language. This elitist approach did little to acknowledge a difference between child and adults readers.

In contrast, from the end of the 1930s the second wave of female authors developed a different stance and enhanced it together with male educators, editors of children's newspapers, and male writers for children (such as Levin Kipnis and Aharon Zeev). Through the work of the most outstanding women writers—Goldberg, Yalan-Shteklis, and Avidar-Tchernovitz—children's literature became more conscious of the implied reader and employed a more intuitive style in an attempt to ease the encounter between the child and the text.

The experience of marginality, as part of the terms of Hebrew feminine existence, contributed to fashioning a way of addressing the child. The main "drawing close" technique involved breaking loose from the grip of Hebrew as a symbolic father tongue and from the tough tone customarily used by women in the previous wave. Women would begin to fashion an intimate tone that was friendlier to the reader. For instance, women writers of this generation often interwove childlike language with cultural and symbolic language. In this way their writing was more accessible and drew from the language familiar to the child.

New techniques of drawing close relied simultaneously on accessibility and empowerment. For instance, in order to teach the language to a child without overburdening her, the women authors used clear, correct, but simple language (in contrast to the "father tongue," which pulls the child along with difficult Hebrew terms). As a means of bridging the gap between the adult and the child and adapting the story to the person addressed, they emphasized musicality and tonality over content. To hold the attention of young listeners, they wrote game poems for toddlers that were accompanied by physical signs, particularly finger motions. To fashion text relevant to the child's life, they used illustrative means and tried to adopt the viewpoint of the marginal. To make absorption easier, they used repetition. To hold the listener's attention and to help him follow the sequence of events, they wrote short and minimalistic or narrative associative stories whose plots' progress is mainly emotional. To impart to the child a feeling of strength and security in a world ruled by grown-ups, they chose appropriate narrative structures of escape and control, such as the carnivalistic story, the adventure story, and the fantasy story.[3] Other means employed to create an intimate, caring experience were writing from a position of empathy with the child; using a confessional, personal, or humble tone; self-mockery; dialogue writing, and sentimentalism, which emphasizes the importance of emotions.

"Drawing close" increasingly appeared to connote personal and interpersonal messages in various writings (as in texts by Miriam Yalan-Shteklis). However, professionalization—which always avoids a preaching, paternalistic tone—did not necessarily abandon nationalistic or even militaristic attitudes. In fact it served as a persuasive device. Given the military forging of Hebrew settlements into a national state, the professionalization of writing can be seen as a normalizing national strategy. "Drawing close" writing nurtured in the reader an aspiration to take active part in military conflict for national independence. Its friendly strategies motivated the young to national action; it camouflaged political and forceful aspects and emphasized personal aspects in a way that produced the impression that national action is essentially apolitical, voluntary, and natural. In other words replacing the previous preaching, overtly didactic tone with a soft, normalized one reflects not a change in the goal but a new strategy to achieve it. The second wave's writing tightened the affinity between the implied reader and the national public interest.

The Case of Avidar-Tchernovitz

Yemima Avidar-Tchernovitz (b. Vilna, 1909; d. Israel, 1998) belongs to the second wave of professional women authors for children, credited with promoting the normalization process. Her book *Eight on the Track of One* (1945), written close to the establishment of the State of Israel (1948), became one of the most admired and popular children's books of the time in Israel. Avidar-Tchernovitz also won the esteem of the establishment and later the prestigious Israel Prize, awarded to her "as a pioneer of modern children's literature in Israel," and is recognized for the literary practices by which the author conveyed social and national messages.[4]

From a critical perspective Darr describes *Eight on the Track of One* as a recruiting text that was structured as a model intended to prepare that generation of Hebrew children for a military struggle and to actively resist enemies opposing the establishment of the State of Israel (Darr, *Called Away* 166–73). It is also possible to read *Eight on the Track of One* subversively and skip the enlisting ideology. I wish to demonstrate the congruence in the text between a personal, confession-like style and ideologies.

When *Eight on the Track of One* was conceived, Yemima's husband, Yosef Avidar, was serving as a member of the Hagana command and was one of the first generals of the Israel Defense Forces.[5] The division of roles between fighting men and supportive women is characteristic for national societies preparing for armed conflict to establish a national state and defend their borders (Nagel 249). Thus, during the period of conflict before the establishment of the State of Israel, the book was written as a powerful text offering consolation and inspiration. Avidar-Tchernovitz imbued the text with these qualities, which she personified in supporting the officer she stood beside. (It is worth noting that the writer occupies a more prominent place in Israeli public memory than her husband, who rose to the rank of general.)

The conditions that determined Avidar-Tchernovitz's consciousness of modesty and marginality, including her acceptance of her traditional gender role, her Hebrew Zionist education, and the national situation, informed her narrative decisions.[6] For instance, she fashions the narrator in *Eight on the Track of One* as a marginal, humble figure who narrates from the side and admires the fighting hero and through his admiration nurtures the reader's admiration for the fighter.

The story takes place close to the establishment of the State of Israel, and its plot describes the city boy Haggai's stay in a kibbutz. (A kibbutz is a type of settlement that combines socialism and Zionism and played a major role in the creation of the Israeli state. The children growing up in this collective community sleep in a communal nursery room and eat in a communal dining room.) Haggai is sent there by his mother, who wants to get him away from the air battles in the city between the German and British armies. In the kibbutz Haggai grows attached to a group of children, in particular to their leader, Amos. Together they pursue a detective adventure, which develops into a security matter when a German guest is found to be a Nazi spy who draws maps of Palestine–the Land of Israel and reports military activity. The children's self-assigned mission is to capture the spy, but the spy traps Amos when he discovers their mission. The group of children engages in a military-like operation in which they rescue Amos and capture the German spy.

The narrator, Haggai, is a city boy who is just a visitor at the kibbutz. He does not characterize himself as the hero; he documents the deeds of the kibbutznik hero, Amos, and the group consolidated around him. Even if the narrator aspires to be a hero ("Actually," the narrator observes, "every child wants to be something of a hero" [41]), when he is close to the action he suggests to the other kids, "Perhaps we ought to return" (100). Nevertheless, he overcomes his fear, participates in the action, and even earns a kind of reward of excellence—a scar he gets when thwarting the spy's attempt to stab Amos.

The voice of the child narrator is shaped through internal monologues but in addition turns to and addresses a narratee that is also the implied reader. Haggai shares with the reader his innermost emotions, which he tries to hide from those around him, and thus is constructed as a narrator friendly to the reader. First, he confesses, in an apologetic tone, his weaknesses:

> I do not live peacefully with grammar. This grammar does not at all want to enter my brain and when it does it sits there and does just the opposite of what it should, and this war with grammar is seen mainly in my Hebrew notebook, where you will find broad fields sown with slain "alephs" and "ayins" [letters of the Hebrew alphabet], wallowing in the red ink of the teacher. And I, when I sat writing the story, saw that the matter is bad, because a book must be written properly, without mistakes. Therefore, I took my notebook and went to my uncle [...] and told him: Uncle, please make some order in the pages in front of you! (4)

The confession and the humility of a credible character narrator lend the story the force of authenticity. Moreover, the humble tone produces a calming effect since the confessing narrator who shares his fears with the reader demonstrates the process of over-coming fear. Speaking about his fears characterizes Haggai as a brave boy with a sense of humor. In the act of rescuing the leader, Haggai admits, "From the time I entered that cave, I felt that my heart had rolled down to the soles of my shoes [...]. To tell the truth I was really scared!" (67). Of note, what was premeditated as scary and evolved as such is told in hindsight with some humor, mitigating the buildup of horror. In a different scary occurrence, fear is overcome during the action, as told by the narrator: "And suddenly a cry sliced through the air, as if the world had been destroyed and this crier is bewailing it [...]. What happened? I asked and I was immediately embarrassed. How can you not recognize the voice of a braying donkey? Are there so few don-keys in Israel? [...] But I told you: At night everything seems so strange. Even the voice of the donkey is not its voice" (30). The detective adventure described from the point of view of a narrator who overcomes his weaknesses provides readers with a process of coping and inner strengthening. Haggai, who admires Amos—the active, cool-headed leader—and strives to emulate him, contends with feelings of fear and marginality that are expressed in his internal monologues throughout the entire story. In these he addresses himself, as can be seen from the sentence "'Haggai, pay attention!' I said to myself" (20). This practice returns many times and in different variations (10, 27, 86, 123). Haggai's self-address and his observations from the margin finally prove to be a real advantage, for they keep the narrator focused. Haggai indeed is afraid before going out to capture the spy ("I was really sweating. . . . I couldn't sit quietly for one minute. . . . In my dream I struggled with the paratroopers and with spies and I screamed and yelled, until Amos finally woke me and told me that if I didn't stop screaming he would put me outside" [118]). While the other children are distracted by a passing combat airplane, only Haggai is focused on the leader ("'Haggai, pay attention!' I told myself" [123]), and he notices the spy's attempt to take a knife out of his pocket and stab Amos in the heart. Haggai strikes the spy on his hand. Thus without any plan of action, military tactics, weapons, or great physical strength, but just using his body for protection and relying on a kind of resourcefulness or "motherly" instinct of concern for the other, the narrator becomes a hero ("and only the scar remained as a soldier's decoration of excellence for his action. And I am very proud of it" [127]).

In addition to internal monologues the narrator turns to the narratee, the implied readers who happen to be Israeli children, the same age as he: "And why I thought so you will find out only after you read about Amos and about the kibbutz. And don't be angry if my description of Amos is lengthy, because he is essentially the hero of my story and not me, as you certainly may have thought at the beginning" (10). The narrator's appeals to his readers are always friendly and often intimate and confessional. This is how he opens himself up: "And you will certainly ask, what was I doing at that hour [. . .] ? Actually I wanted to keep that from you, but since I promised to write the truth I am revealing it to you: I didn't do anything, only sat and really trembled" (100).

Later on as he finally contests the German, the character narrator overcomes his fear and in this way demonstrates to the implied reader the possibility of moving from marginality to action.

The "drawing close" strategy overshadows the issue of Palestinian presence and absence in Palestine–the Land of Israel. In *Eight on the Track of One*, beyond the overt defensive activity against the invasion of the Nazi army, there is an additional covert activity disguised in the story's plot. It constitutes taking control of an Arab house. The plot describes Hebrew children, weak and without an army, keeping track of a German spy and coping with a Nazi threat from outside the fledgling country. They also confront a problem from the inside, only hazily expressed, which is the emptying of the country of its Palestinian residents. It is briefly stated in the exposition that the German spy aroused the Hebrew children's suspicion and anger because he seized an Arab house, "abandoned by its dwellers" (25). But this "abandonment" has neither a place in the plot nor is it explained. Apparently Palestinian presence in the country is blurred: "At the foot of the hill stands a small house. In this house lived an Arab family last year, and after the house was abandoned by its dwellers, we children would play around there and in the courtyard. This was our supreme command post, where we kept our secret weapons [. . .] and then a few days ago Dr. Berg appeared and cut us off from our base" (25). Behind the defense in the face of a foreign power hides the desire of the Hebrew children to take control of the Arab house and make it their own "headquarters" and "base." When the German spy settles in the Arab house, the children are portrayed as those whose inheritance has been robbed. What the Hebrew children are struggling with as they confront the German is not only security but also the Arab house, a symbolic Hebrew sovereignty over Arab living space. Hebrew bravery in the process of making the State of Israel is presented in a softer context of self-defense (not full-scale aggression).

Until now we have seen how Avidar-Tchernovitz played the part designated for her in the framework of gender-role division and created nondidactic, friendly strategies for enlisting child readers. *Eight on the Track of One* also shows traces of parental concern; it prepares its boy readers to participate in military-like action but depicts the feelings of a mother regarding her son's future enlistment. In addition to appealing to children, this children's story neutralizes the fear and objections that might be felt by mothers. On the one hand, it cheers on the children to seek challenges and act; on the other, it succeeds in comforting and heartening the mothers about the children's fate.

The text opens with a description of Haggai's mother, who also "fought hard with life" during the period of national struggle (6). Above the city in which she lives, an air battle takes place between Rommel's German army and the British Mandate army. While the father is serving in the British Mandate army and is absent from home, the mother continues to work in the workers' kitchen and in the house, caring for her son. She is frustrated because of the multiple tasks: to work at home and outside and somehow take care of her wild son: "Mother works in the Workers' Kitchen. She serves food there, and in the evening she returns home with a very tired face. And in the house her son awaits her, that is: me. And you have to know that I am not such a quiet child" (6). Sending her son to a kibbutz makes it easier on the mother, who is concerned for her son during the bombing in the city and hopes to protect him: "Mother started to complain as mothers will: 'What will happen to the child' (the child is me, in my mother's eyes I, of course, am still a child, and that is quite maddening), 'the child' (that is, me) 'doesn't sleep nights, he is pale and run down and will, God forbid, get sick. He has to be sent to a safe place where he can rest a little'" (10).

Even though she intended to distance him from a scene of battle, it turns out that Haggai's mother has sent him to a more "combative" place: a German fighter plane that fell in the area of the kibbutz arouses the children to national action. It is her son's plot that conceals a promise that the children will be excellent fighters—fast and resourceful. Humorous anecdotes present them as even more fit for war than the adults, and with the happy ending the mother finds both pride and the restoration of normal order.

Looking beyond the boundaries of the text, one might ask if following the founding of the state, life in Israel became more peaceful. Three years after *Eight on the Track of One* appeared, Israel was established as a sovereign state. However, gradually a routine of preparedness and emergency prevailed. In the field of children's literature, professionalization has widened gradually to a fuller process of normalization in which a universal thematic has taken the place of the local and the national, while Hebrew children's literature has come to resemble Western children's literatures (Shavit 16–18). "Drawing close" writing is used less and less as a vehicle for propaganda.

But as literature evolved, the geopolitical realities in the Middle East has shown increasing potential for armed conflicts. If the region's agenda is not to shun peace, it may be well to ponder how literature can allow the drawing together of disparate parties; such a possibility would involve drawing close not only the *Hebrew* narrator to a *Hebrew* implied reader but also the adversarial characters within the text. The aim could be to establish a virtual meeting space for literary characters of different nationalities whose real-life counterparts find it hard to make their children sit together. How could this be done without leaning toward disingenuous solidarity, without intruding while reaching out to touch? *Eight on the Track of One* utilized self-deprecating humor (narrative admissions of weakness and imperfection) as a basis for drawing close. It thus offers reaching out to the other party through a softer approach, rather than saving face at all cost.

Children's literature has two courses to offer: either show obligation to a universal child in place of a national one or rehabilitate the body politic and promise plurality. Both courses share the goal of blurring antagonism between "us" and "them." Instead of planting fear of the Other in children and educating them toward separation and defense of their borders, they can be encouraged to examine the near and the "strange" through recognition and discussion.

When the universal thematic overtakes all-binding nationalism, it obscures local conflicts such as the one at hand between Israelis and Palestinians. Universalism effects depoliticization, limiting the function of Hebrew books for children to the private realm. But what will they offer beyond accomplishment of private goals? How will the literature foster plurality? In order for it to offer more and to a wider public, local affairs should not be neglected. Shaping a political space in which the welfare of certain groups is not acquired at the price of the suffering of others is a challenge. The future challenge may be the return of the political in a way that would nurture children's ability to act out of free choice in the public space, a multifaceted human environment.

Avidar-Tchernovitz's "drawing close" writing, while propelling children to activism at the time of the establishment of their state, focused on the singular Hebrew nationality. Anxieties reflected in the text are wholly of the Jewish inhabitants in Palestine–the Land of Israel. Protection is therefore meant for Hebrew children and is not considered for their Arab neighbors. Reflecting internal monologues and realizing personal capabilities were among Avidar-Tchernovitz's significant devices. If we wish in our times to draw together protagonists with different perspectives, fears, and desires, then we perhaps should rely on dialogism and recognition of one another's weaknesses and capabilities. More generally, if adults could allow children to seek and follow dissimilar paths, but not exclusively normalization, new political opportunities may ensue.

Notes

1. Sara Foner (b. Riga, 1855; d. Harlem, 1937) belonged to an extraordinary group of Jewish women in Eastern Europe who received a Hebrew education and are considered Jewish women scholars (see Cohen and Feiner). Yet as a woman, marginalized by the cultural system, Foner considered her children's book not only a textbook but also a tool for

expressing her opinions in public. Her book is a national allegory criticizing the way in which the emerging Hebrew nationality is handled by men. Its implied readers were not only young pupils but the general public in Eastern Europe. A mocking review by David Frishman published around the same time criticized her as a woman and described *Children's Way* as "women's way" (Ofek 170). Women did not follow in Foner's footsteps and did not write much for children until the first Jewish national immigration to Palestine. Even in that pivotal time they produced mainly paternal stories. Hebrew was not yet the spoken language of any Jewish community (the main spoken languages were Yiddish in the Ashkenazi Jewish community and Arabic or Ladino in the Sephardic Jewish community; see Shilo) because of the traditional attitude that regarded use of Hebrew in day-to-day circumstances as a sacrilege.

2. From a letter of Bialik (dated ca. 1920) to Bat-Sheva Grabelsky, the editor of the New York children's paper *Eden*. The letter was attached as an explanation of poems that Bialik sent and included clarifications of the difficult words in the poems.

3. The carnivalistic is that which overturns the existing social organization and gives the exceptional preference over the conventional (see Goldberg). The adventure story is one in which coping with danger and the ensuing victory imparts to the child a sensation of control and independence (see Avidar-Tchernovitz, *Eight on the Track of One*). The fantasy story uses magic and wonder as tools of the small and the marginal for influencing reality and glorifying ideals that at the time are seen as inferior (see Yalan-Shteklis).

4. Defined this way by the judges' committee of the Israel Prize awarded to her in 1984: "The author uses her books as an instrument for transferring an education message to her reading audience and to impart humane, social, and national values, but in a natural way, and as part of a dialogue with her readers. Thus, for example, some of her works focus on problems of absorption of immigrants, leaving the country, the help of children at a time of siege and war, helping fellow-men, Diaspora Jewry—all these while weaving a living, somewhat detective-like, real, and very actual plot" (Friedlander, Hadas, and Cohen 48).

5. Among his military roles he served as commander general of the Northern Command (1949–52) and of the Central Command (1952–53) and afterward in the representative national role of ambassador to the Soviet Union and to Argentina.

6. In interviews in which she was asked about her writing process, Avidar-Tchernovitz described it in terms of traditional women's work,

such as baking a cake: "Writing a book is like baking a cake—to keep the book from being boring, you need good ingredients, spices of adventure and a lot of humor" (Avidar-Tchernovitz, "Writing a Story" 56). Regarding her education, her father, Shmuel ("Samuel" in English) Tchernovitz, who was counted in the circle that initiated and spread Hebrew culture, worked as the secretary of *Olam Katan* (Small World), one of the first Hebrew children's newspapers, and encouraged her to write. "You know that I am not only your father but also your follower when it comes to your talents, and I have great expectations for your future. You only have to promise me that when you finish the gymnasium, you will resume your literary work. I think that only literature can give man satisfaction and pleasure in life" (Zur 209). At the age of nine Yemima had already fulfilled these educational expectations when she began writing a diary and short stories in Hebrew and even published several of these in children's newspapers. Her story "On the Mount of Olives" appeared in 1925 in the children's newspaper *Eden*, which was published in New York, and one year later her story "Son of My Country" was published in the Tel Aviv weekly *Haaretz*. At the age of twelve she immigrated with her family to Palestine–the Land of Israel, which was under British Mandate rule, studied in the Hebrew gymnasium, and immediately afterward began to work as a teacher in a school for workers' children. (Schools of the labor stream were established in the days of "the State to Come" by the labor movement, the workers' settlement, and the Histadrut. This independent educational stream sought to plant in the heart of its students the values of the labor movement.)

Works Cited

Avidar-Tchernovitz, Yemima. *Eight on the Track of One*. Tel Aviv: Tversky, 1945. [Hebrew].

———. "On the Mount of Olives: A Legend." *Eden* [children's newspaper supplement] 11 (1925). [Hebrew].

———. *Secret Diaries: From the Years 1919–1936*. Ed. Rama Zuta. Or Yehuda: Dvir, 2004. [Hebrew].

———. "Writing a Story Is like Baking a Cake." Interview with Yaron Golan. *Naʾamat* 70 (1984): 56–68. [Hebrew].

Bar-Adon, Aharon. "The Founding Mothers and Their Part in the Revival of Hebrew and Its Coming into Being (1882–1914)." *Language and Hebrew* 3 (1990): 4–26. [Hebrew].

Berlovitz, Yaffah. "The Woman in the Women's Literature of the First Aliyah." *Cathedra* 54 (1989): 107–24. [Hebrew].

Chalamish, Aviva. *A Dual Race against Time: Zionist Immigration Policy in the 1930s*. Jerusalem: Yad Ben-Zvi, 2006. [Hebrew].

Cohen, Tova. "Inside and Outside Culture: On the Appropriation of the 'Fathers' Tongue' as a Means for Intellectual Characterization of Female Self." *Saddan* 2 (1997): 69–110. [Hebrew].

Cohen, Tova, and Shmuel Feiner. *Voice of a Hebrew Maiden: Women's Writings of the Nineteenth-Century Haskalah Movement*. Tel Aviv: Hakibbutz Hameuchad, 2006. [Hebrew].

Darr, Yael. *Called Away from Our School Desks: The Yishuv in the Shadow of Holocaust and in Anticipation of Statehood in Children's Literature of Eretz Israel, 1939–1948*. Jerusalem: Magnes, 2006. [Hebrew].

———. "Military Recruitment of the Native-Born Israeli: Hebrew Children's Literature Is Recruitment to Enlist Its Readers, 1939–1949." *Sadan* 5 (2002): 254–86. [Hebrew].

Foner, Sara. *Children's Way*. Vienna, 1886.

Friedlander, Yehuda, Yardena Hadas, and Adir Cohen. "The Arguments of the Judging Committee." *Journal for Children's and Youth Literature* 41.1 (1984): 48–49. [Hebrew].

Goldberg, Leah. *Miracles and Wonders*. Merchavia: Sifriat Poalim, 1954. First published in the children's paper *Davar Liyladim* 4–9 (1938–39). [Hebrew].

Nagel, Joane. "Masculinity and Nationalism: Gender and Sexuality in the Making of Nations." *Ethnic and Racial Studies* 21.2 (1998): 242–70.

Ofek, Uriel. *Hebrew Children's Literature: The Beginning*. Tel Aviv: Porter Institute for Poetics and Semiotics, 1979. [Hebrew].

Pappe, Ilan. *A History of Modern Palestine: One Land, Two Peoples*. Cambridge: Cambridge University Press, 2004.

Porat, Yehoshua. *The Palestinian Arab National Movement: From Riots to Rebellion (1929–1939)*. London: Routledge, 1977.

Shavit, Zohar. "Hebrew Children's Literature." *Olam Katan* 1 (2000): 11–21. [Hebrew].

Shilo, Margalit. *Princess or Prisoner? The Female Experience of the Old Settlement in Jerusalem*. Haifa: University of Haifa Press, 2002. [Hebrew].

Zur, Shmuel. "The Tree and Its Fruits." Avidar-Tchernovitz, *Secret Diaries* 206–13. [Hebrew].

PART FOUR

Narrative Time

This last section, devoted to narrative time, begins with Susan Stewart's "Shifting Worlds: Constructing the Subject, Narrative, and History in Historical Time Shifts," a study of the ways children's historical time-shift narratives make visible the constructedness of storytelling to the child reader. The role of the metafictive continues in Martha Hixon's discussion of how the nonlinear nature of Diana Wynne Jones's *Hexwood* performs as a model of the recursive writing process for young readers. As Jones's book forces the reader to revise notions of character identity, so Angelika Zirker's essay "'Time No Longer': The Context(s) of Time in *Tom's Midnight Garden*" discusses the ways that Pearce's novel shifts contexts throughout the story so that the young reader is asked to consider ghosts, magic, time travel, and dream as explanations for temporal (dis)order.

Narrative time in literature for the young is, contrary to popular assumption, hardly limited to either singularity or linearity. These different techniques used by writers for the young show confidence in the implied reader's ability to navigate different temporal arrangements. Perhaps of most interest is the way each essay points to a relationship between the temporal experiments in the novels and the construction of identity within the text. To what extent are temporally sophisticated novels for the young necessarily novels that comment on (and model?) identity development for young readers?

12

༝❀

Shifting Worlds

*Constructing the Subject, Narrative, and
History in Historical Time Shifts*

SUSAN STEWART

There are generally two ways in which time is handled in historical fiction written for young readers. Perhaps the most common
occurs when the plot is fully positioned in the past. That is, the
characters are born and stay in that time period, and the plot
reflects their world. There are no explicit intrusions from the present. While the present informs these novels and readers might see
similarities, this type of historical fiction works in something of
a vacuum and is separate from the present even though readers
might come to a better understanding of how the past affects the
present and the future. In this type of fiction history appears fixed
and closed in the sense that the past does not change.

The second type of historical fiction incorporates time shifts
wherein a character or characters travel from one time period
to another. This approach is distinctly metafictive in nature. As
Patricia Waugh explains, "*Metafiction* is a term given to fictional
writing which self-consciously and systematically draws attention
to its status as an artefact in order to pose questions about the
relationship between fiction and reality" (2, author's emphasis).
Metafiction for Waugh "becomes a useful model for learning
about the construction of 'reality' itself" (3). Since historical fic-

tion generally offers a perspective on reality, narratives incorporating time shifts offer an interesting approach to fiction and history. David Lieby explains that protagonists in time-travel narratives are preoccupied with "the structure of time [. . .] . In order to survive, protagonists must come to understand the physical laws of their fictional world" (38). Because "the main characters focus on the order of events in the story, readers will focus on the order of events" and "will be forced to focus on the activity of plotting" (38). Ultimately for Lieby, time-travel narratives "encourage readers to think about the construction of narrative" (38). This approach, says Lieby, contributes to the metafictional nature of time-travel narratives for it emphasizes how time and plot, both of which are connected, are constructed.

Time shifts, though, also offer readers an unusual opportunity to examine other aspects of fiction, for the inclusion of a time shift potentially brings readers' attention to the manner in which subjects form and develop as a result of history and context, particularly when an author depicts a character who seems divided between past and present. This is particularly relevant for adolescents in that one of their main preoccupations is subject formation—identifying who they are and their place in the world. Robyn McCallum suggests that fiction incorporating a character that is split, as in a double or doppelgänger, "is used to represent intersubjective relationships between self and other as an internalized dialogue and the internal fragmentation of the subject—the split subject" (68). In some instances, though, this "split subject" becomes what I refer to as an "amalgamated subject," wherein we see an individual constructed through history, culture, and circumstances making the retelling or reconstruction of history more transparent.

Although McCallum is not necessarily speaking of time shifts, she suggests that displacing characters, which includes spatial, temporal, cultural, and ideological factors, serves several functions. Most important for this discussion is her assertion that "to displace a character out of his/her familiar surroundings can destabilize his/her sense of identity and hence undermine essentialist notions of selfhood, though it can also affirm these concepts" (101). One of the most radical ways for this type of displacement to occur is through time shifts. I explain in the following discussion how time-shifted historical fiction potentially helps young readers understand how history and context influence subject formation and that the construction of narrative actually parallels the fluidity of subject formation and history. To do so I study two texts that aptly demonstrate my argument: Jane Yolen's *The Devil's Arithmetic* and Avi's *Something Upstairs*. Both of these novels do what traditional historical fiction for young readers is supposed to do: they situate readers in what might be an unfamiliar time as a way to convey another dimension of history. Additionally, they personalize history in that readers will find similarities between themselves and the protagonists. However, because Yolen and Avi incorporate time shifts in different ways, they accomplish different goals. Yolen divides her protagonist, Hannah, by sending her back in time, where she participates in and becomes part of the past. Hannah is aware of her own fragmentation as she enters the past with memories of her present; because of this she has the opportunity to contemplate how history and context are crucial to her subject formation. She is both the same person and a different person as she engages with the past. On the other hand, Avi's protagonist, Kenny, slips back and forth between past and present without losing his sense of self; subject formation does not seem to be the emphasis. Rather, Avi pays particular attention to the construction and representation of history, for history actually changes due to Kenny's influences (as a parallel to history "changing" due to scholarly revisionism). Ultimately, both of these approaches potentially help young readers understand the construction of self and history in historical fiction.

The Divided Subject, the Amalgamated Subject

Hannah, the twelve-year old protagonist of *The Devil's Arithmetic*, begins her odyssey in the home of relatives in New Rochelle, New York, where the family meets for the first night's Passover seder.

In Jewish tradition this is a time for Jews to remember their history as a people. As part of the ritual a family member pours a glass of wine for the prophet Elijah, and a chosen individual—in this instance, Hannah—goes to the door to invite Elijah in as a reminder "of the time Jews were forced to keep their doors open to show the Christians [they] were not practicing blood rituals" (19–20). Hannah is chosen to open the door, but when she does she finds herself in unfamiliar surroundings and in the presence of two people she has never before met, Gitl and Shmuel. They refer to Hannah as "Chaya," Hannah's Hebrew name, and she discovers that they are her aunt and uncle. Hannah has entered some kind of portal that takes her to 1942 Poland, a place where she is orphaned and will experience the Holocaust and imprisonment in a concentration camp.

Hannah does eventually return to her present, but it takes the death of Chaya to do so. When one of the concentration camp guards chooses Rivka, Chaya's best friend, for the death chamber, or "Lilith's Cave, the cave of death's bride" (116), Chaya takes Rivka's place (159). As Chaya enters Lilith's Cave, she returns to her contemporary world. No time has elapsed. The dinner table is still laden with food, and everyone at the table looks expectantly at Hannah as she returns from the doorway. Later, as she speaks with her Aunt Eva, she discovers that Eva changed her name from Rivka when she came to the United States. Chaya's gesture permitted Rivka/Eva to live. Now Hannah can no longer dismiss or ignore the past, for she represents living proof of the past, as does her Aunt Eva.

As depicted in *The Devil's Arithmetic*, history can be viewed as a continuum—part of Hannah's present and future. Indeed, in this case the past and present are separated only by a door. But Hannah also experiences the duality of living in two worlds in that she maintains her memories of her contemporary world while in Poland and memories of 1942 Poland when she returns to her contemporary world. This particular narrative approach results in the depiction of a divided subject. That is, we can see Yolen's focalizer as Hannah/Chaya. In the process the focalizer experiences a fragmentation of the self. We see not a whole individual but a divided one. Rather than reflecting what Catherine Belsey describes as "the fixed identity of the individual," an "essence which cannot change" (49), Hannah/Chaya becomes an active construction of sociolinguistic factors. Additionally, this type of narrative device also emphasizes the nature of adolescence itself in that adolescence by definition is a period of fluctuation, experimentation, and transition and is anything but fixed. The process of creating or constructing a sense of self becomes quite evident when we examine how Hannah/Chaya attempts to define who she is through her contemporary world, 1942 Poland, and the stories that shape her as a subject in both places.

During Chaya's incarceration at the concentration camp, she tells Rivka that her memories are layered, "memory on memory, like a layer cake" (157). She remembers her life in New Rochelle (Hannah and the future), her life with Gitl and Shmuel (Chaya and the very recent past), and part of her life in Lublin before her mother and father died, although she tells Rivka that her memories of Lublin are "like a story [she's] been told." She explains, "I don't remember Lublin, but I remember being there" (156). She also has memories of the concentration camp. However, Hannah's descriptions of her memories do not so much suggest a fractured, fragmented self as they do an amalgamation of selves, whole but simultaneously partitioned and divided. Thus, the layer cake as a metaphor reveals how Hannah builds on her stories and memories of her past and present. Those stories and memories will eventually allow the self-absorbed twelve-year-old Hannah to develop into a sensitive girl who is aware of the many influences on her life. She has begun the maturation process, which is made visible by the time shift.

Chaya/Hannah is also an amalgamation of stories in that she consistently refers to the narratives with which she is familiar and which are parts of her. As the novel begins, Hannah tells her brother "a gruesome tale about the walking dead, borrowing most of the characters, plot, and sound effects from a movie she'd seen on television the night before" (6). This intertextual reference resurfaces when Rivka speaks of her brother Wolfe (Hannah's Grandpa Will) as "a *Sonderkommando*, one of the walking dead" (113). In Poland she is an expert on American popular culture and a consummate storyteller: "Stories seemed to tumble out of Hannah's mouth, reruns of all the movies and books she could think of. She told the girls about *Yentl* and then about *Conan the Barbarian* with equal vigor; about *Star Wars*, which confused them; and *Fiddler on the Roof*, which did not [. . .] . Hannah wondered at this strange power she held in her mouth" (51). She also tells them about *The Wizard of Oz* and "a muddled version of *Hansel and Gretel*" (52).

Additionally, and equally important (maybe more so), Chaya *is* or *becomes* the stories she tells. Perry Nodelman and Mavis Reimer speculate that children possibly "become what they read about. The story lines of the subject positions they know and choose do have a profound effect on them [. . .] . [The] narratives children see on TV or read in books play an important part in making them who they believe themselves to be. In offering subject positions, fictional texts for children work to construct their readers' subjectivity" (178). Their assertion is realized in *The Devil's Arithmetic*, for Chaya does in a sense become Gretel, the child kept as a prisoner and subjected to another's will and power. Indeed, Chaya sometimes experiences difficulty separating herself from the stories she tells as is indicated when Rivka tells her one morning that "anyone who cannot get out of bed today will be chosen" to die (128). Hannah replies, "Hansel, let out your finger, that I may see if you are fat or lean" (128). And later, as she and three others walk to their death through the doors of Lilith's Cave, she tells them a story "about a girl. An ordinary sort of girl named Hannah Stern who lives in New Rochelle" (159). The Hannah of New Rochelle is now only one more narrative in her collection. Even though Hannah is not necessarily ordinary, her story serves as a reminder to readers that what happened during the Holocaust happened to "ordinary" people.

One other indication that Hannah/Chaya represents an amalgamation is the number tattooed on her arm, J197241, which she receives in exchange for her name. Rather than simply accepting the number, Rivka asks Hannah/Chaya to construct a narrative concerning the number, one that gives significance to the impersonal numbers she now wears. Chaya draws from her life as Hannah and Chaya:

> *J* for Jew. And *1* for me, alone. I am very, very much alone. And *9* is for . . . well, in English it is pronounced "nine," which is like the German word for *no.* No, I will not die here. Not now. Not in my sleep like . . . little . . . little children. . . .
> J—1—9—7. *Seven* is for—for each and every day of the week I stay alive. One day at a time. Then *2* for Gitl and Shmuel, who are here in this place, too. . . .
> And *4* is for my family, I think. I almost remember them. If I close my eyes they are there, hovering within sight. But when I open my eyes, they are gone. (120)

The stories she constructs are a way of subverting the power that the Nazis have over her and a way of asserting her limited agency. But Hannah's story also suggests the way she actively constructs her sense of self, who she is, was, and will be in the world. As such she occupies numerous subject positions constructed from the remnants of her lives.

The novel itself is also an amalgamation. Yolen admits in the afterword, titled "What Is True about This Book," that "the characters are made up—Chaya, Gitl, Shmuel, Rivka, and the rest—though they are made up of the bits and pieces of true stories that got brought out by the pitiful handful of survivors" (168). She also explains that the concentration camp she describes "did not exist. Rather, it is an amalgam of the camps that did" including Auschwitz, Treblinka, Chelmno, Sobibor, Belzec, Majdanek, Dachau, Birkenau, Bergen-Belsen, Buchenwald, Mauthausen, and Ravensbruck (168). She does what storytellers do. They take "bits and pieces" from here and there, from fact and recollection, to construct an apparently seamless whole. The act of storytelling, of writing fiction, or of recording history is a matter of choosing what will be included or excluded and stacking the materials on top of one another, similar to the way Hannah describes her memories as being a layer cake.

This approach to historical fiction, then, allows for some interesting observations. Just as Yolen draws from stories and history to construct this particular narrative, Hannah also draws from stories and history to construct who she is. While in 1942 Poland, Hannah uses her contemporary understanding of the world as a way of making a place for herself in this unsettling past. When she returns to her present, she discovers that what happened in the past very clearly influences what happens in the present. If not for Chaya, Rivka would have died. Hannah and the stories she tells remind readers that they are in large part a result of historical circumstances.

Something Upstairs: *Constructing*
Narrative, Reconstructing History

Because subject formation is in part a result of historical circumstances, how history itself is represented should be a major concern. Although any number of instructional texts will detail what educators should look for in historical fiction written for young readers, including historical accuracy, they do not generally encourage readers to consider how various histories are constructed. For many readers history might seem concrete. It is identifiable by dates, places, and people, but representations of history are necessarily incomplete. Thus historical fiction that illustrates the arbitrary and constructed nature of history itself becomes useful in helping readers understand that how history is represented is subject to interpretation and agendas.

Yolen conveys a sense of verisimilitude in the way she reconstructs history—at least as much as time travel can be characterized as reflecting reality. Not all historical fiction, however, "re-presents" history in this manner. Avi's *Something Upstairs* makes the retelling or reconstruction of history more transparent through its narrative frame and approach to history in general. For unlike Yolen, who waits until the afterword to actively insert herself into the text, Avi becomes part of the narrative from the beginning. This is not necessarily preferable to Yolen's approach; it merely makes visible the author's role in creating the narrative.

The plot of *Something Upstairs* revolves around Kenny's discovery of the ghost of a murdered slave in the attic of his eighteenth-century home. Every night the ghost, Caleb, arises out of a bloodstain and searches for a way out of the room (61). Kenny witnesses this event and becomes acquainted with Caleb, who enlists Kenny's help to find his murderer. To solve the mystery and thus permit Caleb's soul to rest, Kenny travels between his contemporary world and the year 1800. The house itself serves as a portal and was the site of Caleb's death. Kenny, however, has done some research at the library and discovers that newspaper accounts report that Caleb, approximately sixteen years old, has committed suicide in a room locked from the inside. That it is a suicide is questionable—he has been shot in the back—but as Caleb explains, "They would say I took my own life. Far better to announce that a slave—some miserable black—killed himself than to confess their own crime. Who would care besides other blacks?" (65).

During the course of Kenny's research, he becomes acquainted with Pardon Willinghast, the present-day library historian. As it turns out, Willinghast, who presumably enters the past and the present through his own portal, is Caleb's murderer. He travels to the future—Kenny's present—in order to foil Caleb's attempts to find his murderer and resolve his past. If Willinghast is unsuccessful, he will die in the past and Caleb will live. Thus Willinghast guides Kenny in a particular direction in an attempt to maneuver Kenny into shooting Caleb. As a way of ensuring Kenny's complicity during one of his visits to 1800, Willinghast takes Kenny's key chain and tells him, "Alter yourself, hurt yourself, lose something you have carried with you, and you become something different. Become something different and you cut yourself off from your own time. You shall be a ghost, haunting *this* time!" (76, author's emphasis). Once Kenny shoots Caleb, Willinghast will return the key chain and he can return to the future, Kenny's present. Thus Avi (via Willinghast) establishes the rules for this particular excursion from reality. Kenny also discovers that this is not the first time Caleb has enlisted someone's help, nor the first time that Willinghast has engaged in the same type of manipulative behavior. The difference, of course, is that Kenny will succeed where others have failed.

Avi takes an explicitly metafictional approach to his novel. Avi's narrative technique to history reveals—and in the process, deconstructs—the sometimes fictional (or selective) nature of how history is represented: "the relationship between fiction and reality" (Waugh 2). Avi wastes no time in establishing that relationship, for he begins *Something Upstairs* with an "Author's Explanation," which serves to immediately situate readers, to place them in a particular subject position, to believe or not, to be receptive or not. Avi situates (manipulates?) readers to believe the ghost story he is about to convey. He admits from the beginning that "this is the strangest story I've ever heard" and continues by telling us how he came to write the story; he does this as a fictionalized real author—a characterized author (1). In his explanation he tells of Kenny, a young boy who comes to him with an unbelievable story, which Avi will commence telling in the remainder of the novel. All the while, Kenny plays with a chain, which is brought to our attention when Avi tells Kenny, "Why don't you put that chain away? It's distracting" (3). A few moments later Avi again asks Kenny to put the chain away. As I have indicated, Kenny's chain will play an important role in the remainder of the novel.

At first Avi is somewhat impatient with Kenny, but he nevertheless listens to his story. Avi ends his introduction with the following: "It was, as I said, the strangest story I've ever heard. Not only did I listen then, but I spent the afternoon after school listening. And the evening. What's more, I stayed over at a local hotel a second day to check out what he'd told me—at least those aspects that were possible to check. When I was done I offered to write it all down as a book. With what I took to be great relief, Kenny Huldorf agreed. This is it. His story. My writing. I think it's true" (4–5). Thus, even though Avi previously tells Kenny that he writes from the imagination, readers are encouraged to also look at what transpires as the truth. And what is history but one version of the "truth"?

In this instance Avi takes a very different approach to retelling history than Yolen in that he conflates the actual author (the award-winning, recognized author of young adult fiction), who provides the introduction to the novel, and the characterized author in the novel itself. Avi also conflates external narration and character narration, for Avi is not actually a character in the action, but he is part of the narrative, for he admits to telling Kenny's story: Kenny is the focalizer of the novel. Avi also plays a character role in the peritextual element of the introduction, which we don't think of as part of the fiction, so here Avi plays the peritext against the text and, by doing this, takes a traditionally nonfiction element and makes it fictional. As the reteller of the narrative, Avi also serves as a second mediator, Kenny being the first. As Avi indicates, this is Kenny's story but Avi's writing. Thus the story is at least once removed from the events. But Kenny also tells Avi what Caleb tells Kenny. Consequently, some parts are twice removed from the events.

The significance of this approach is that we observe the reconstruction of history through the narrative frame and Avi's narrative voice as narrator and as and with author(ity). As any storyteller does, Avi takes literary license by providing Kenny's observations, emotions, and a considerable amount of dialogue. Thus readers are to consider the narrative as something of an embellished transcript. Kenny reports to Avi, who then reports to readers. Although Kenny might have conveyed to Avi that he was "shocked and fascinated" upon his entrance into 1800, we do not know for certain that this is how Kenny described his surprise (43). And it is unlikely that Kenny would have said that his shock and fascination "gave way to a bursting desire to see more" (43). Additionally, Avi includes dialogue between Kenny and the people he encounters on his trips to the past, between Kenny and Caleb, and between Kenny and those living in his contemporary world. We see what might (or might not) be considered speech patterns appropriate for 1800 when he overhears a discussion between two men: "They were stout enough to fight thy battles in the late war," says one of the men, and moments later he tells Kenny, "I shall be much obliged to you if you would take this to number eighty-four Benefit" (44–45). The note reads, "W says he is Ready to act. He has His man. As Brown and his Faction Will not listen to Reason I believe he is right. Meet on the morrow, evening, nine, The Gaspee, to Plan" (46). The man's spoken syntax and word choice differ enough to permit us to believe that he is from the year 1800. In his written correspondence he also capitalizes words that twentieth-century writers would not ("Ready," "His," "Faction" "Will," "Reason") and includes the word "morrow" in place of "tomorrow." However, Avi does something unusual with Caleb's speech patterns. Observe the following excerpts of Caleb's conversations with Kenny:

> "'If I knew who murdered me,' Caleb continued, 'I might be able to prevent it from happening and thus be free to leave this place'" (54).
> "'Esek Ormsbee!' Caleb cried. 'A slave merchant. To whom did you deliver the note?'" (55).
> "'For whom?' said Caleb, making no attempt to hide the scorn in his voice, and forcing Kenny to turn away from his accusing eyes" (59).

Granted, this text was published in 1988, and Caleb is a young adult who has encountered twentieth-century people numerous times, but he uses neither the speech patterns of Mr. Ormsbee nor a dialect that might be associated with a slave. Rather, we read the narrator's (Avi's) speech patterns, who uses perfect Standard English, and no other characters use "thus" or "whom." These kinds of incidents offer readers opportunities to contemplate how contemporary authors represent history or, for that matter, how historians reconstruct history. For instance, Willinghast tells Kenny, "After all, I am a historian, a guardian of memory, memories which *I* choose and shape" (98, author's emphasis).

And Kenny already realizes that he is "caught between contending memories—Caleb's and Willinghast's—of August 17, 1800" (76). These contending memories will also become further complicated by a news account of Willinghast's death that Kenny will read. In this case Willinghast represents a traditional approach to history where the white male scholar tells the version he sees and desires to perpetuate, and Caleb represents the revisionist approach to history in the extreme. In short, if Caleb succeeds, which he does, Willinghast and his account will disappear, and Caleb and his account will persist. Indeed, at the end of the novel, Kenny takes Avi to a cemetery to see the following tombstone:

Pardon Willinghast
Born 1704
Died in Providence August 18, 1800
Aged 96
Taken in Violence by his own Hand
R.I.P. (115)

Additionally, the librarian tells Kenny that nobody by the name of Pardon Willinghast works at the library, and Kenny discovers that the account of Caleb's death no longer exists. Instead, there is a newspaper report of how Mr. Willinghast apparently committed suicide. Whether Willinghast did commit suicide is never disclosed. Indeed, it is very possible that Kenny is responsible for Willinghast's death, for this particular event ends with Kenny holding a gun and a shot being fired. Unlike other historical novels, which convey a sense that history is a fixed phenomenon, *Something Upstairs* does precisely the opposite and demonstrates history's arbitrariness depending on one's perspective. In this way we see some of the various and competing motives in the retelling of history, whether it be in history books or historical fiction.

In addition to Avi making the reconstruction of history visible, he also makes the writing of fiction visible. That is, he approaches the novel in a metafictive manner. We see this in the way Avi depicts Caleb's speech patterns. But it also calls into question the accuracy of dialogue in any narrative, something most readers ignore. For instance, in novels that consist of diary entries, there might be pages of description and dialogue. It is unlikely that many readers even consider how diarists can possibly recall the many details they describe or the specific conversations they include. It is something readers simply learn to accept as part of conventional narrative approaches. Additionally, we can assume that Kenny has not had time to express all the adjectival descriptions that Avi includes, for Avi spends only an afternoon and evening with Kenny. Nevertheless, Avi takes the liberty of including, presumably from what he infers, Kenny's, and to some degree Caleb's, emotional reactions. For instance, in the quotation cited earlier, we find out that Caleb has "scorn in his voice" and "accusing eyes" (59).

That this is metafiction becomes most obvious in the "Author's Explanation," when Avi tells readers that this is Kenny's story but Avi's writing. If one has read the introduction, one likely continues to hear Avi's voice as a storyteller in the beginning of chapter 1, although his storytelling voice diminishes. Initially, Avi provides mostly facts absent any type of commentary other than what Kenny might have provided in his narrative to Avi: "As far as Kenny Huldorf was concerned, Los Angeles, California was perfect" (6). The first portion consists mainly of facts. Kenny moves to Rhode Island, notices how different Rhode Island is, describes the house, and so on. All of this is told in past tense, and if one has not read the introduction, one could assume that this is a third-person account, either omniscient or limited omniscient. But the narrator/Avi consistently breaks with narrative convention in that he reasserts himself throughout the novel by reminding us that Kenny is the originator of the tale:

"The movers hadn't arrived so there was nothing in any of [the rooms]. And yet, he remembers having the distinct sensation that the house was *not* empty" (8, author's emphasis).

"Kenny remembers being bored. Restless. Edgy. He kept

trying hard to find a place for himself, but without much success" (11).

"What Kenny recalls is that a few nights after they moved in the heat had become so awful it was particularly hard for him to fall asleep" (12).

"The figure [Caleb's ghost] had no shoes. But Kenny recollects seeing trousers and a shirt, not tucked in, whose frayed sleeves reached midway between elbows and wrists" (15).

These serve as reminders that this is Kenny's story but that Avi has written it, though we can see how Avi also effaces his narrative voice, which is indicated by his use of past tense. One can almost visualize Avi glancing at the notes he has taken from the interviews: *The house was NOT empty. Can't get to sleep—too hot. Caleb dressed in shirt and pants, no shoes, frayed sleeves.* As the novel continues, these intrusions become less frequent, but they still occur. Thus we experience a tension among what constitutes the competing objectives: Caleb's desire to find freedom and peace, Kenny's desire to convince Avi that this really happened, and Avi's desire to tell a compelling story.

Avi also offers one other and final authorial interruption, which would usually be called an author's note, epilogue, or something similar. This inclusion is quite common in historical fiction and provides readers with the "facts." In *The Devil's Arithmetic* Yolen provides an afterword wherein she explains how she came to write the story. More significant, however, is what follows in that she tells readers what they can believe:

All the facts about the horrible routinization of evil in the camps is true: the nightmare journeys in cattle cars, the shaving of heads, the tattooing of numbers, the separation of families, the malnutrition, the *musselmen* and the *Kommandos*, the lack of proper clothing, the choosing of victims for incineration. Even the midden [garbage] pile comes from the camp experiences of one of my friends.

Only the characters are made up—Chaya, Gitl, Shmuel, Rivka, and the rest—though they are made up of the bits and pieces of true stories that got brought out by the pitiful handful of survivors.

The unnamed camp I have written did not exist. Rather, it is an amalgam of the camps that did. (168)

She ends the chapter by stating, "Fiction cannot recite the numbing numbers, but it can be that witness, that memory. A storyteller can attempt to tell the human tale, can make a galaxy out of the chaos, can point to the fact that some people survived even as most people died" (170). Readers can infer that we can also be "that witness, that memory" once we have read the novel.

Yolen's author's note establishes her ethos, but in the process she writes in a metafictive mode. Readers have completed the novel, so she can abandon the fiction's verisimilitude she has worked so diligently to construct. In effect authors employing this approach have the last word regarding the narratives: Here's what could've happened, here's what you need to know about the history I have just told you, and here's what you need to do or think. Avi also has the last word, but he continues the fiction with the description of Willinghast's gravestone. And we do not know what to think, for Kenny worries about Caleb: "Kenny's look had become imploring. 'Do you think he's free yet?'" he asks Avi. "'I mean really free?'" (116). And finally, the last words of the actual narrative are "May 1988" and "Providence, R.I.," which coincides with the publisher's blurb about the author, which states, "In 1987, Avi moved from Los Angeles to Providence, Rhode Island, the city whose history he presents so vividly in *Something Upstairs*" (n.p.)—another interesting conflation of reality and fiction. Avi does, incidentally, live in Providence.

One could argue that a difference between traditional historical fiction and time-shifted historical fiction is similar to what Mikhail Bakhtin suggests regarding the difference between the epic and the novel. The epic, Bakhtin argues, is "an absolutely completed and finished generic form, whose constitutive feature is the transferal of the world it describes to an absolute past of national beginnings and peak times" (15). He continues: "In ancient literature it is memory, and not knowledge, that serves as the source and power for the creative impulse. That is how it was, it is impossible to change it: the tradition of the past is sacred. There is as yet no consciousness of the possible relativity of any past. The novel, by contrast, is determined by experience, knowledge and practice (the future)" (15). Although I have never been entirely convinced by Bakhtin's either/or argument, his assertion that "the epic world is an utterly finished thing," that the past "is impossible to change, to re-think, to re-evaluate anything in it" in some ways coincides with traditional historical fiction (17). Authors construct a reality from the past and offer a version of that past. It is a genre whose foundations, according to John Stephens, "lie firmly within the tenets of the humanism" characterized by "an essential human nature which underlies all changing surface appearances; important human qualities, such as Reason, Love, Honour, Loyalty, Courage, etc." (203). He adds that in historical fiction, qualities are depicted as "transhistorical; human desires are reasonably constant, and what differs are the social mechanisms evolved to express or contain them; individual experiences thus reflect constant, unchanging truths; history imports 'lessons' because events, in a substantial sense, are repeatable and repeated" (203). In other words the history represented is nothing less than the present retold in the past.

Stephens also believes historical fiction to be one of the "most radically ideological" genres written for young readers (202). Unquestionably, authors can offer an alternative perspective that one might not expect, which is in itself ideological. That is certainly the case with historical fiction that describes the role of women in the Revolutionary War, the role of blacks during the Civil War, or the internment of the Japanese in the United States during World War II. However, in historical fiction that includes a time shift, the constructions of self, narrative, and history become more evident and transparent in that authors distort the notion of time and space. That historical fiction written for young readers generally offers insights about what it means to be human as well as a series of lessons regarding the past, present, and future becomes particularly evident when a time shift is part of the narrative.

Admittedly, historical novels that include time shifts represent only a small portion of the genre. They are also often problematic in that authors include contemporary voices in the midst of the historical milieu, which violates the standard that authors should maintain a "truthful" approach to history. Nevertheless, they are significant in the way they reveal the tension between the constructedness and the seamlessness of subjectivity, narrative, and history.

With *The Devil's Arithmetic* readers are encouraged to look through the eyes of a character who, through time-shift narrative strategies, achieves an amalgamated subject position. This approach produces metafictive qualities in the narrative that portray the historical period differently than in historical fiction that does not include time shifts. This is particularly significant in historical fiction written for young readers, for it offers an opportunity to view history from both the inside—through their relationship with the traveler—and the outside, as a reader. The method potentially leads to an understanding of how humans are subject to time and place, something that young readers might not normally contemplate.

The use of spatiotemporal displacement in historical fiction also offers a point of identification for readers in that they potentially see themselves in the time traveler. In this way they often see history in light of continuity—that everything is connected—for the traveler provides a link between past and present as the traveler serves as a guide to both. It is also a convenient way to displace focalizers, which justifies the inclusion of contemporary attitudes, for characters usually retain the memory of their present even as they enter history. Thus, they come equipped with opinions and experience formed by their cultural context, which enables them to critique offensive attitudes and institutions. If they have no recollection of their present when they enter the past, they will undoubtedly retain the memories of the past if they reenter the present, which similarly allows a critique. Regardless of their memory, however, their trip to the past generally results in their growth from solipsism to an acute awareness of the past, the present, and the world around them—a goal associated with adolescence and adolescent literature. Indeed, their encounters with the past provide the stimulus to identify their (or their culture's) present-day mistakes or shortcomings. Equally important, time-shifted historical fiction for children offers young readers a way to analyze the construction of subjectivity, history, and the structure of narrative as characters enter or exit a particular time period. They, or readers, then have the opportunity to explore how cultural or historical circumstances influence who they are in the world and how they came to be that way. In other words by seeing how history or culture or subjectivity shifts over time, that nothing is fixed, that everything is subject to change depending on interpretation, they will possibly become aware of the need to examine the nature of history, cultural imperatives, and their own subject formation. This is a crucial strategy for understanding a world that becomes smaller and simultaneously grows more expansive with each passing day and event.

Works Cited

Avi. *Something Upstairs: A Tale of Ghosts*. New York: Avon, 1990.

Bakhtin, M. M. *The Dialogic Imagination: Four Essays*. Trans. Caryl Emerson and Michael Holquist. Ed. Michael Holquist. Austin: University of Texas Press, 1981.

Belsey, Catherine. "Constructing the Subject: Deconstructing the Text." *Feminist Criticism and Social Change: Sex, Class and Race in Literature and Culture*. Ed. Judith Newton and Deborah Rosenfelt. New York: Methuen, 1985. 45–64.

Lieby, David. "The Jaws of the Intellect Grip the Flesh of Occurrence: Order in Time Travel." *Worlds Enough and Time: Explorations of Time in Science Fiction and Fantasy*. Ed. Gary Westfahl, George Slusser, and David Lieby. Westport CT: Greenwood, 2002. 36–47.

McCallum, Robyn. *Ideologies of Identity in Adolescent Fiction: The Dialogic Construction of Subjectivity*. New York: Garland, 1999.

Nodelman, Perry, and Mavis Reimer. *The Pleasures of Children's Literature*. 3rd ed. Boston: Pearson, 2003.

Stephens, John. *Language and Ideology in Children's Fiction*. London: Longman, 1992.

Waugh, Patricia. *Metafiction: The Theory and Practice of Self-Conscious Fiction*. London: Methuen, 1984.

Yolen, Jane. *The Devil's Arithmetic*. New York: Puffin, 1990.

13

"Whose Woods These Are I Think I Know"

Narrative Theory and Diana Wynne Jones's Hexwood

MARTHA HIXON

Young adults, and the books written for and about them, are keenly interested in growing up or in achieving autonomy through the development of an individual sense of self and how that self connects to the world in which the young adult is expected to function. In other words young adults are very much engaged in the writing of their own adult stories, and the literature produced for this audience provides vicarious experiences of doing so. In fantasy fiction for adolescents, the achievement of such agency typically occurs in connection with the fantasy element: the emergence of magical powers for the child protagonist, for example, or via magical events that the protagonist must navigate and learn to cope with. As fantasy critic Farah Mendlesohn observes, Diana Wynne Jones's works in particular demonstrate to her adolescent readers that self-realization is an ongoing process rather than a closed set of events (22). Jones's novel *Hexwood* does this through mimicking or enacting the process that a novelist himself or herself engages in while creating a fictional story, thus melding the purpose and the process of literature for children and young adults while providing, as

Jones says, "a blueprint for dealing with life" ("Profession of Science Fiction" 14).

In his essay "Nameless Things and Things Nameless," postmodern fantasy critic Lance Olsen suggests that contemporary fantasy "is a mode which interrogates all we take for granted about language and experience, giving these no more than shifting and provisional status" (3). Along these same lines, Brian Attebery argues in *Strategies of Fantasy* that "unlike realist texts, fantasies freely acknowledge their own disjunctions [. . .] but the result is not disorder and disillusionment. Rather than leaving us in a solipsistic void, fantasy invites us to recreate what it has denied" (67). We do so, he argues, by making the fantasy world "real"—as readers we instinctively impose rational order and believable details on the diegetic level of a text, in collusion with the storyteller, in order to produce a narrative that can sustain the willing suspension of disbelief so necessary to successful fantasy. While such an exercise is intuitive when reading a work of mimetic realism, a work of fantasy forces the reader to actively disregard obvious impossibilities in the story at the basic level of plot, character, and setting. In other words, by "forcing a recognition of the arbitrariness of [. . .] narrative conventions" (Attebery 67), fantasy, even more so than realist texts, invites the reader to participate in the creation of the story. As a fantasy writer and critic, Diana Wynne Jones is aware of this innate function of the fantasy genre, and she explores its ramifications in nearly all her novels, often provoking her readers to consider issues such as character, setting, and cause and effect in a new way. Specifically, in her 1993 novel *Hexwood* the paradigms regarding story structure are at the forefront of critical examination. As Farah Mendlesohn observes, *Hexwood* "is about writing as editing (or editing as a creative process)" (189). More than this, though, as I hope to illustrate, *Hexwood* is a metafictional commentary on the process of story making: through its nonlinear plot and the concomitant shifting of identities of the characters involved in that plot, the novel highlights the artificial conventions of narrative and the assumptions that readers bring to a text regarding story structure, the creation of character, identity, and self-determination. That such complexities are held within a book marketed for a young adult audience implies that Jones has respect for the acumen of her readers and that such open-endedness in narrative structure is compatible with the open-endedness of adolescence itself.

An Oxford graduate in English, Jones is deeply aware of how to construct a narrative, as comments she has made in various venues make clear. One such is her essay "The Shape of the Narrative in *The Lord of the Rings*," included in a 1983 collection of critical essays on J. R. R. Tolkien by various scholars. In this essay she theorizes that "the bare plot is to any writer no more than the main theme of a sort of symphony which requires other themes added to it and the whole orchestrated into a narrative. To shape a narrative, you have to phase the various incidents and so control their nature that you set up significances, correspondences, foretastes and expectations, until your finished story becomes something else again from its simple outline" (88).[1] Elsewhere she has discussed how influential the plot devices of medieval narratives have been on her work, such as *Piers Plowman*, which is "orchestrated in a tidelike advance and retreat, full of partial repetitions, where some things acquire a new meaning at each advance" ("Inventing the Middle Ages")—a description equally applicable to Jones's own *Hexwood*, *Fire and Hemlock*, and *Archer's Goon*. The Gawain Poet, she says, showed her how to use the medieval technique of "story-time," or setting magical events in the author's own time period ("Inventing the Middle Ages"), a technique characteristic of nearly all her novels. *Sir Orfeo* taught her that myths and folklore can be "translated" from one genre to another, a device used in several of her novels and which she herself points out appears in *Hexwood*: "I had real medievalizing fun translating chunks of Arthurian stories into a story about a super computer" ("Inventing the Middle Ages"); thus the nonlinear story structure of *Hexwood* is intentional and meaningful.[2]

The term "story," in its most basic sense, refers to the order of events in a narrative. The conventional ordering of such events is a straightforward one—or, as the King of Hearts tells Alice, "Begin at the beginning, and when you get to the end, stop." *Hexwood*, however, offers an alternative to this linear pattern: the novel seems rather to be a montage of mininarratives, disjointed pieces of story that occur out of sequence and are sometimes obvious rewrites of story bits already told, with abrupt shifts of focalizers and settings, whose characters seem to be in flux, fluid and undefined. The action of the novel takes place primarily in 1992 in the ostensibly innocuous Banners Wood, which encircles a housing estate called Hexwood Farm outside London. Such details in location and the dates of action in the novel, both of which are supplied to the reader at the opening of the story, lend it at the outset a misleading sense of straightforward and linear narration. The reader's experience, however, is not unlike that of the novel's Ann Stavely: entering Banners Wood means leaving the familiar world behind and entering a world where time lacks coherence, identities shift, and British folktales come to life. In short the plot of *Hexwood* is anything but straightforward and linear. Yet the novel is not a typical *non*linear narrative, either; unlike postmodern works such as those by Pynchon or Barthes, which seem unreadable by design—this incoherency being part of the author's point—*Hexwood* is an eminently readable novel, despite its seemingly willy-nilly plot.

In its discontinuous narrative structure, *Hexwood* exemplifies J. Hillis Miller's argument that "[narrative] always begins and ends still *in medias res*," that there is no true beginning or ending to a story (4). For example, Ann enters Banners Wood twice in chapter 3 seemingly for the first time, and she does so again in the fifth chapter of the book, chapter 1 of part 2. Each "new" story seems to be a rewrite of the one that preceded it, with changes in the plot that evoke new reactions from the characters or that illuminate their actions and motivations in new ways, and the reader is constantly presented with a "new" story to understand, a new way to order the plot or sequence of events that have been tangled together in this narrative. The novel ends at a point that implies a "new" story for the main characters as they assume their roles as the new group of Reigners: their story is not over. Also, as a novel *Hexwood* seems to begin at least three times, in three different locations and with three different focalizers and seemingly unconnected plot events. Chapter 1 is mimetic in style and linear in its presentation of events, with a discernible setting, realistically presented characters, and a forward movement to the beginning exposition of the story. The setting is another planet, not Earth, with references to "Homeworld" governed by a group of five people called the Reigners and a transportation system of wormholes and "gates" by which people can literally walk from world to world. Earth is considered a small outpost in this interplanetary system. Thus the genre with which the novel opens seems to be science fiction, a genre characterized by logic and reason.

Chapter 2, however, completely switches gears and undercuts this narrative beginning: it begins with the sentence "A boy was walking in a wood" and gives no clues as to the boy's relationship to the story just presented, his reasons for being in the woods, or even where the woods are in terms of the previous chapter or otherwise. The boy has almost no sense of self, no memories of his past or connection to the present—he has no narrative as yet. The mood of this chapter is dreamlike, even archetypal, moving the story "out of time, away from internal referents" (Mendlesohn 72), and placing it clearly within the realm of Jungian fantasy.[3] In this brief chapter the child encounters a reptilian creature, runs away, and meets what apparently is a robot of some sort, who seems to know the boy and, when told of the creature, says, "It was killed. But maybe we have yet to kill it, since I see you are quite small right now," and "if the reptile is alive, we have come to the wrong time and must try again" (15, 17). Clearly, time in this wood is fluid, and the sequence of events can be entered into at any point; the story in this chapter is anything but mimetic or conventional and seems completely unrelated to the events that the reader is presented with in chapter 1.[4]

Chapter 3 quickly shifts gears again, focusing on Ann Stavely, a teenager who decides to explore the nearby woods after recuperating from an illness. Ann enters and exits these woods repeatedly in this chapter and throughout the novel, and each time she seems to enter a story that is already in progress, a story about a boy named Hume, a man named Mordion who is attempting to raise the child, and a robot named Yam that helps them. Ann, and the reader, soon learn that the story that Hume, Mordion, and Yam are experiencing is being controlled by a machine called the Bannus, an artificial intelligence programmed to manipulate the "paratypical field" or "theta-space"—terms Jones uses that are equivalent to the "story-space" of Seymour Chatman's analysis of narrative structure (96–107) and Mikhail Bakhtin's "chronotope" in which "the knots of narrative are tied and untied" (250)—around Hexwood Farm in order to enact scenarios designed to test the will and character of those persons drawn into its field of influence. As the Bannus creates these scenarios, time in Banners Wood seems to run backward or forward, to repeat, and to skip rather than run continuously, and characters too shift identities and even species (four of the characters become dragons for a time), much as a storyteller manipulates time and character in drafting his or her narrative, trying to find the best way to present the characters and plot.

Character, like plot, is an artificial construct, composed of a "set of textual fragments scattered through a narrative" (Attebery 69): descriptive phrases, bits of dialogue, moments of action that forward the plot. The reader puts all these fragments together into a coherent "person" based on his or her perceptions and experiences of people in this real world, thus lending these fictional constructs solidity and meaning. We as readers sometimes forget the implied cooperation between author and reader in establishing this construct, and we also, since we are reading a "finished" work of fiction, tend to forget the process of development that the author went through in choosing these textual fragments with which the reader is to work in creating the identities within the story. *Hexwood*, however, refuses to let the reader forget this process; Jones takes the idea of "open-endedness" in characters—the idea that, as Chatman argues, "we come to anticipate, indeed to demand, the possibilities of discovering new and unsuspected traits" (132)—to the extreme: the characters in this novel are continually being constructed and deconstructed before the reader's eyes, so to speak.

Focalization in the novel shifts from Ann to Mordion to the various Reigners as well as occasionally to other, minor characters, and with these shifts the reader gets bits of Jones's overall story from different points of view and sometimes in different settings. Ann Stavely is the dominant focalizer of much of the novel, especially at the beginning. A seemingly typical teenager, she is the one with whom the reader most readily and consistently sympathizes as the novel progresses: in the "Ann" sections of the novel, which predominate, the reader experiences the events in the plot along with Ann and tends to accept her interpretation of those events, as well as her perceptions of the reality of her fictionalized world, such as where she lives, details of her daily life, where the wood begins and ends, and her assumption that the fantasy elements lie *inside* the wood, not outside it. Yet an awareness of dissonance in the story—and in the various narrative points of view—also occurs for the reader quite often apart from Ann's realizations, as, for example, when Reigner One neatly elides into a dragon persona as he is walking along outside the factory near the woods, an event of major significance in the story that Ann knows nothing about since she is not present at this point of the novel (Reigner One also seems not to notice his own shift in persona). Even when she is present, however, the reader is sometimes aware of narrative dissonance or unreliability, such as how often she actually enters and exits the wood in chapter 3; as much as the reader sympathizes with Ann, through the shifts in focalization and the moments of obvious dissonance, Jones never lets the reader completely accept her version of events for long. The artificiality of focalization is clear to the reader of *Hexwood*: the reader "sees" the events unfold through Ann's eyes or the eyes of other characters within the novel, yet context clues undercut the reliability of their versions of events, and the reader is asked to impose logic and meaning on the narrative from outside the various focalizers, to understand the story in ways that they as individuals within the story do not. Thus as the unity of the narrative seems to dissolve and the containment of the fantasy within the wood breaks apart, erupting into Ann's own village, along with the metamorphosing of identities at an increasingly rapid pace, the reader is able to follow the story: the narrative coalesces even as it dissolves, and the end of the novel is not a "solipsistic void," to use Attebery's term, but rather a satisfying and comprehensible culmination of events.

Identity is just as fluid as plot in this novel; the textual bits of character that the reader is given to work with sometimes do not add up into a coherent whole, or they add up in a kaleidoscopic sort of way, forcing the reader (and the characters themselves, on occasion) to go back and question the fictional personas that have been created in the reading of this story. During the course of the novel, Ann, Mordion, Hume, and others enact the hypothesis that Mark Currie presents in *Postmodern Narrative Theory*: "The only way to explain who we are is to tell our own story, to select key events which characterize us and organize them according to the formal principles of narrative" (17). The various characters define and redefine themselves as they write their own stories and explore their own identities through the aegis of the virtual reality provided by the Bannus, a process reflective of how adolescents also create and re-create themselves, "trying on" different personas in their quests to define themselves as independent adults. If, as Robyn McCallum argues, "focalization is instrumental in constructing a character as an ideologue" or fixed set of social constructs and assumptions (31), Jones's repeated undercutting of the focalization of the novel through the fluctuating identities and unreliability of the narrative points of view counter the construction of a static ideology connected with the characters: identity can be imposed from within as much as from without, and self definition is a recursive process. This aspect of *Hexwood*, perhaps, is the one most relevant to Jones's targeted audience of young adult readers, since adolescence is a period in which identity is indeed fluid and under construction by the individual as he or she moves from the familiar and socially imposed childhood self toward a new, adult sense of self.

In its emphasis on this fluidity of character identity, *Hexwood* exemplifies the narrative theory of performativity, that identity is a created concept built up by reenactment over time and experience. Since the creation and re-creation of character operate at the diegetic level of the novel as the reader moves through the narrative, the reader is confronted with the flimsiness of the identities, both self-imposed and imposed by other forces, of most of the characters; they are not who they say—or think—they are. For example, the primary focalizer, who is named by the external narrator and by herself through most of the novel as "Ann Stavely," a supposed adolescent whose parents run a greengrocers shop in the little village of Hexwood Estates, eventually realizes that she is actually twenty-one-year-old Vierran of Guaranty, daughter of one of the heads of the Great Houses on the Reigner home world; the Bannus's story line has caused her to see herself as someone else, a village teenager from Earth. Her "brother" Martin is eventually revealed as a character from early British legend, Fitela, and the boy she and Mordion have been calling "Hume" (and who they thought had been created within the wood primarily through their actions) actually has had several historical identities: in past lives he was Merlin, the ancient Viking hero Wolf, and Martellian Pender, the great foe of the current Reigners. Other characters shed and shift identities in this novel as well once they get inside the Bannus's theta-space and influence, becoming dragons, various Arthurian personas, and villagers or outlaws to round out the Bannus's cast of characters.[5]

Through participating in the Bannus's role-playing game, several of the main characters come to see themselves differently, to face flaws and to grow beyond them. Vierran realizes that in her old life she had been playing games herself; "like the high-class sheltered little deb she was, she had been fascinated by violence, murder, secret missions—all the things her life had shielded her from," and that she had had a crush on the Reigners' Servant (Mordion) because he embodied all the things she found foreign and therefore fascinating (311). Hume, who in his previous incarnations as Wolf and Merlin had avoided fighting his own dragons, in the Bannus's story has to face one on his own, to accept responsibility for his own fights. As the Bannus informs him pedantically, "Your rehabilitation was of some concern to me" (433).

That each of the characters accepts at least to some extent the constructed identity that the Bannus imposes on him or her enables the reader to consider the process of constructing one's own identity, as well as the process by which an author constructs the fictional personas within a text. Vierran, for example, realizes that she accepted her fictionalized persona of Ann Stavely as a way of avoiding the unpleasant reality she was currently experiencing at the hands of Reigners One and Three, and her parents accepted her "brother" Martin because they so badly wanted a son. Mordion realizes that he became a reptile upon entering the Bannus's theta-space because that epitomized what he had become through the control of the Reigners—this persona is his simulacrum, in Jean Baudrillard's terminology.[6] As these characters exert more and more control over the Bannus's story line—writing their own narratives rather than passively accepting the roles given to them by the Bannus, they achieve agency, power over their lives and self-identities, and eventually they shut down the Bannus's fictional work. Jones's characters in a literal sense take on a life of their own. In other words they "grow up" and write their own story rather than accepting the one presented to them by an authority figure that heretofore has been in control of their lives. As Mendlesohn observes, "Agency is about the ability to make conscious choices," and *Hexwood* is very much about achieving such agency (21).

Of all the characters in Jones's story, Mordion's fragmented identity is the most significant; he is the most emotionally damaged of the characters, having been raised by Reigner One to deny his heritage, kill on order, and in short, act counter to his innate feelings of compassion, justice, and respect for the rights of others. He is the one who most wants to, and even needs to, forget who he is and re-create himself. Mordion is in need of redemption and self-forgiveness, and he finds these through the Bannus's forced plots and staged events. When he first enters the wood, he loses his memory—and therefore his identity—and at first unconsciously takes the form of a reptile (the same reptile, it turns out, that the young boy, who is Hume, encounters in chapter 2). This self-definition changes when Ann enters the Wood and he returns to human form; he is literally "born again"—he seems to rise from the dead out of a coffin in front of Ann's eyes and change from a skeleton into a living person. Through most of the action of the novel, he tries to suppress the return of those memories; his final metamorphosis, into a dragon, forces him to face his past and move on from it. The Bannus dryly tells him, "You have been quite a problem to me. I have had to keep much of the action marking time while I induced you to remove the blocks that had been put upon you. It has taken so long that feeding everyone has become quite difficult" (378). Mordion's eventual acceptance of who he is and the reasons for being so allow him finally to take full control of his identity, and at this point he can shapeshift at will, from dragon to man, which is indicative of the fact that he now has power over how his memories shape his sense of self.[7]

Hexwood takes Genette's narrative levels of diegesis (the story being narrated) and metadiegesis (a story within the narrated story), to the extreme. As anyone who has read the novel will observe, the multivalent narratives of *Hexwood* have been simplified for this discussion. I have noted that the primary storyteller in the novel is the Bannus, who manipulates the theta-space around his container to create story scenarios intended to choose a new set of Reigners and exact his revenge on the current set, who imprisoned him in order to keep their positions. Also, there are the characters, mainly Mordion, Ann/Vierran, and Hume, who gradually begin to exert their will over the Bannus's story line and write their own stories, which run counter to or that bend the Bannus's intended story, and there are minor twists to the Bannus's story line when the five Reigners eventually enter the Bannus's theta-space field. There is also the fact that the novel actually begins with a letter, yet another level of narrative. I have not noted, however, the Wood itself, which is also manipulating theta-space, sometimes working with the Bannus but at other times, especially at the conclusion of the novel, establishing plot episodes that the Bannus does not want or intend, in order to achieve its own ends. In fact, by the end of the novel it is questionable to what extent the story has been a product of the Bannus's intentions and how much has happened because of the Wood's desires and force: the Wood refuses to let the players—or the Bannus—out until Mordion and the rest work their power to reify the Wood's theta-space so that it can last forever. If, as Mendlesohn argues, *Hexwood* "is precisely about control of the tale" (189), the question is, who *is* in control, precisely? There is a constant tension between the story line as the Bannus writes it and the assertion of the various characters' will over that story line. And although the Bannus appears to be controlling the story throughout much of the novel—and in fact has created 697 "plans of action" all designed, it says, to end in the death of Orm Pender, or Reigner One (*Hexwood* 427)—the Bannus can only do what the Wood allows it to do. As it tells Mordion, "The Wood has me in its field. To some extent, I have the Wood in mine also. I was placed in it, and over the centuries our two fields have mingled. [. . .] The fact remains that I am in its power" (385), and that "most of what has happened here [. . .] is according to the desires of the Wood" (386).

Then there is the minor yet important character Harrison Scudamore (who is also known as Henry Stott and later as Sir Harrisoun in the Bannus's Arthurian retelling—more shifting identities). A worker at Hexwood Farm, he sets events in motion by activating the Bannus, thinking it is simply an ultrasophisticated role-playing game, in order to create either a fantasy football team of legendary heroes (2) or else a game that involves "hobbits on a Grail quest" (398); these stories, too, are not consistent. Harrison is described by Sir John Bedford as a "confirmed liar" (179)—or to put it another way, an inveterate storyteller: as Mordion muses,

Harrison "seems to be one who liked to translate his dreams into reality" (182). But in one of the darker comic scenes, he is eaten by the dragon form of Reigner One—devoured by his own story, perhaps, or his deluded self-identity as the controller of the action. Then there is the ultimate author, Diana Wynne Jones herself, who we can imagine sitting at her computer creating the novel we are reading, consciously setting the action in her own time-space continuum: England in 1992. Yet even this is a fictionalized persona, one that is only perhaps close to the truth; we do not really know the conditions under which the book was written, and in fact Jones has commented that when she writes, she does not "feel in total control [. . .] . It is more as if I am moving the pieces of idea around until they reach a configuration from which I, personally, can learn" ("Profession of Science Fiction" 7), a position that both the Bannus in this story and Quentin in Jones's *Archer's Goon* find themselves. Clearly Jones's novel highlights Baudrillard's "fictive realities" to an extraordinary degree.

In her illuminating study of Jones, Farah Mendlesohn writes that in *Year of the Griffin* "repeatedly Jones shows us that learning (and criticism) are about questioning the premises. From there, students must begin the process of developing their own paradigms" (xxii). *Hexwood* too asks the reader to reconsider his or her assumptions, or premises: Ann (and consequently, the reader) assumes that her own actuality is the "real" one, an assumption that is quickly and repeatedly challenged and destabilized and is only one of many assumptions within the novel that are continually undercut by seemingly contradictory story bits, as are assumptions about plot, character identity, and even who is controlling the story being played out. The reader of *Hexwood* is alerted at the outset to examine closely the conventionality of the narrative premise. The challenge then posed is how to order the sequencing of events and identification of the characters in this novel. One of Mendelsohn's theses in her study of Jones's works is that Jones is a critical writer and all her work asks the reader to think carefully about what is going on in the story he or she is reading. In this particular novel the fragmentation of the plot forces us as readers to exercise our own powers of storytelling to create a coherent narrative of our own: we construct the story as we go, much in the same way as Ann/Vierran and the others do, yet that story is ever shifting. There is an order to the universe, Jones perhaps is saying, but finding it is not so easy sometimes.

Story is the way we as human beings give meaning to ourselves and our relationships with others and with the universe itself. Narrative is the basis of memory, the way in which we store these meanings within our consciousness as individuals and as a race. The story of the novel *Hexwood*—or rather, the various bits of story supplied by Jones and, inside that, the stories created by the Bannus and the individual characters—is not conventional in the Aristotelian sense of a story having a beginning, a middle, and an end, yet the story of *Hexwood* is actually more realistic than is an artificially linear plot: the disjointed stories mimic memory, which is nonlinear, fragmented, and recursive, leaving out clear transitions and connecting incidents, and even altering characters (the remembered persons, and the one remembering himself or herself) to suit the "story" that is being created by that memory. In chapter 2 Yam tells Hume, "This wood . . . is like human memory. It does not need to take events in their correct order" (17). This comment is the key to the meaning of the structure of this novel. In *Moon Tiger*, by Penelope Lively, Claudia muses about writing her story: "The question is, shall it or shall it not be a linear history? [. . .] There is no chronology inside my head. [. . .] The pack of cards I carry around is forever shuffled and re-shuffled, there is no sequence, everything happens at once" (2). The story elements in *Hexwood* are Jones's cards that she as the storyteller shuffles and reshuffles until the story reaches the end. The result is a very readable, coherent work, and once the end is actually reached, the reader has understood what has happened along the way to get to that point. Reading such a metafictional novel is a bit like putting a jigsaw puzzle together, yet there is far more to this work that just a mind game; Jones is making very serious commentary on the nature of identity, agency, power, redemption, and the construction of story itself—issues very relevant to adolescents, and adolescence, today. Through its discontinuous structure and fluid characterizations, *Hexwood* is a young adult novel that models growing up for its adolescent audiences in ways relevant for that audience.

Notes

1. This comparison of writing a story to creating a symphony Jones has used elsewhere, specifically in discussing how she constructed her novel *Fire and Hemlock*. See "Heroic Ideal."

2. Elsewhere I have discussed the innate significance of the narrative structure of another complex Jones novel, *Fire and Hemlock*. See "Importance of Being Nowhere."

3. That Jones mixes the genres of science fiction and fantasy in this story is not unusual; in fact it is one of the hallmarks of her writing style. See Karina Hill's "Dragons and Quantum Foam" for a discussion of how these two genres are connected in Jones's novels.

4. Farah Mendlesohn analyzes the various manipulations of time in *Hexwood* in terms of A-series relative and B-series absolute structures. See chapter 3 of her *Diana Wynne Jones*.

5. Ann's "voices" are a particularly intriguing layer of this multiplicity of identity. The reader is presented with this element very early in the novel: Ann Stavely converses in her mind with various persona that she half-laughingly refers to as her "voices," people who she tells herself are just imaginary anyway. The four personas are The Boy, The King, The Prisoner, and The Slave, and they each refer to her as The Girl-Child. One of the ways that Ann marks her comings and goings into the manipulated theta-space of Banners Wood is whether she can converse with her voices, and more than once the voices give her a corrected version of how much time has passed and whether she really has left the wood or not. Near the end of the novel, she realizes that the personas are not just her imagination but actual people whom she is able to talk to telepathically through space and time, and in several last-minute surprise twists she—and the reader—learn the real-life identities of the voices: they are people in the story, yet another incarnation of Mordion, Martin, Hume, and a minor character named Sir Artegal, who is best known in other narratives as King Arthur. That he is just a minor character in this story is yet another ironic commentary on identity as created through narratives, as is the premise that these folkloric characters are historical personages.

6. Other simulacra appear in the novel, too, most notably the forms

of the Bannus: it is supposed to be a machine, a "man-high box" that "weighs like solid lead" (*Hexwood* 436), but that form, Reigner Five learns, is "only a simulacrum of the bannus" (254). Other simulacra of the Bannus occur within the story: as a computer screen in the abandoned building on Hexwood Farm that pretends to direct Reigner Four to where the Bannus is (194), and as the Holy Grail (261). Eventually we learn that it has taken the form of Yam, the robot that has been helping Mordion and Hume, but to what extent the Bannus has been Yam all along is left unclear in the novel. Even the fact that the word "bannus" is not capitalized in the narrative when the speaker considers the Bannus an object but is capitalized when it signifies the sentient being controlling the story is indicative of the Bannus's fluid identity.

7. Though not overtly commented on in the novel, the fact that Mordion is a rather primitive reptile in his first incarnation in Banners Wood and a dragon at the end does not seem coincidental; Jones undoubtedly is tacitly commenting on Mordion's potential self: the reptile is a rough draft, so to speak, of the dragon.

Works Cited

Attebery, Brian. *Strategies of Fantasy*. Bloomington: Indiana University Press, 1992.

Bakhtin, M. M. *The Dialogic Imagination: Four Essays*. Trans. Caryl Emerson and Michael Holquist. Ed. Michael Holquist. Austin: University of Texas Press, 1981.

Chatman, Seymour. *Story and Discourse: Narrative Structure in Fiction and Film*. Ithaca NY: Cornell University Press, 1978.

Currie, Mark. *Postmodern Narrative Theory*. New York: St. Martin's, 1998.

Genette, Gérard. *Narrative Discourse: An Essay in Method*. Trans. Jane E. Lewin. Ithaca NY: Cornell University Press, 1980.

Hill, Karina. "Dragons and Quantum Foam: Mythic Archetypes and Modern Physics in Selected Works by Diana Wynne Jones." *Diana Wynne Jones: An Exciting and Exacting Wisdom*. Ed. Teya Rosenberg, Martha P. Hixon, Sharon M. Scapple, and Donna R. White. New York: Peter Lang, 2002. 40–52.

Hixon, Martha P. "The Importance of Being Nowhere: Narrative Dimensions and Their Interplay in *Fire and Hemlock*." *Diana Wynne Jones: An Exciting and Exacting Wisdom*. Ed. Teya Rosenberg, Martha P. Hixon, Sharon M. Scapple, and Donna R. White. New York: Peter Lang, 2002. 96–107.

Jones, Diana Wynne. "The Heroic Ideal—A Personal Odyssey." *The Lion and the Unicorn* 13 (1989): 129–40.

———. *Hexwood.* New York: Greenwillow, 1993.

———. "Inventing the Middle Ages." *The Diana Wynne Jones Fansite.* 6 July 2009. Meredith MacArdle and Helen Scott. 24 July 2009. http://www.leemac.freeserve.co.uk/medieval.htm.

———. "The Profession of Science Fiction: Answers to Some Questions." *Foundation* 70 (Summer 1997): 5–14.

———. "The Shape of the Narrative in *The Lord of the Rings.*" *J. R. R. Tolkien: This Far Land.* Ed. Robert Giddings. London: Vision; Totowa NJ: Barnes and Noble, 1983. 87–107.

Lively, Penelope. *Moon Tiger.* New York: Grove, 1988.

McCallum, Robyn. *Ideologies of Identity in Adolescent Fiction: The Dialogic Construction of Subjectivity.* New York: Garland, 1999.

Mendlesohn, Farah. *Diana Wynne Jones: Children's Literature and the Fantastic Tradition.* New York: Routledge, 2005.

Miller, J. Hillis. *Reading Narrative.* Norman: University of Oklahoma Press, 1998.

Olsen, Lance. "Prelude: Nameless Things and Things Nameless." *Ellipse of Uncertainty: An Introduction to Postmodern Fantasy.* New York: Greenwood, 1987. 1–23.

14

"Time No Longer"

The Context(s) of Time
in Tom's Midnight Garden

ANGELIKA ZIRKER

In *Tom's Midnight Garden* wishes magically come true: when Tom Long arrives at his aunt and uncle's flat, he longs for a garden (his "longing" is even expressed in his name), and then he finds one; in a manner familiar from fairy tales, the wish for something leads to its appearance. Yet he can only enter the garden at midnight; during daytime it is gone, and all that Tom finds in its place is a backyard with dustbins. In the garden he meets a girl whom he befriends, Hatty, who is slightly younger than Tom but who grows into a woman over the summer. Only toward the end of the story does he learn that Hatty is actually Mrs. Bartholomew, his aunt and uncle's elderly landlady. She remembers and dreams of the garden of her childhood throughout the summer, and Tom is able to enter those dreams.

In Philippa Pearce's novel the realms of past and present, dreams and memories, the fantastic and reality are linked through the friendship between Tom and Hatty, which eventually overcomes time: in the garden the two children become friends; her dreams and the memories embedded in these dreams enable an old woman to return to the past and play with a boy in the garden of her childhood; in the end this boy meets the old woman in his "present reality." Thus time is overcome not merely in the sense of a time journey but basically through memories.

Time is a prevalent topic and motif in *Tom's Midnight Garden*. The whole story is triggered by a grandfather clock that has magic qualities. It strikes thirteen times at one o'clock in the morning and thus opens the garden for Tom, which he can enter through a backyard door. In her study *Children's Literature Comes of Age*, Maria Nikolajeva observes that passages between worlds are "most tangible in time fantasy. The passage is often connected with patterns like the door, the magic object and the magic helper" (124). The magic object in Tom's case is the grandfather clock. In what Tom up to this point perceives as his real world, time stands still while he is in the garden.

Time is fantastical in this novel: dreams and memories become reality; laws that govern time and place are suspended in the midnight garden, the fantastical world that Tom enters is a part of reality, namely, of Hatty's past, and it is real to Tom, for he does not merely sleep and dream of the garden. Hatty's dreams and memories are no longer subjective, but they become shared experiences, and they go beyond temporal and spatial limits. Hence, in *Tom's Midnight Garden* different layers of time are interlinked. The fantastic lies in the coexistence of these layers; it magically joins together the boy Tom with both Hatty the girl and the old woman. Their friendship is represented as a relationship that comes about through magic and through magical wish-fulfillment but, at the same time, is real.

Magic: The Grandfather Clock

When Tom has to leave his family because his brother has fallen ill with measles, he is not very happy. He feels like a person in exile when he arrives at his Uncle Alan and Aunt Gwen's flat, which does not even have a garden. When he enters the house, he feels that its "heart [. . . is] empty—cold—dead" (9). But the house is not dead; there is a sound: "the tick, and then tick, and then tick, of a grandfather clock" (10).

The clock immediately stirs Tom's curiosity, even more so when he finds that although it keeps good time, it seldom chooses "to strike the right hour" (10), which he at first considers "senselessly wrong" (18). When at night he cannot sleep because he has been overfed by his aunt—who sees her vocation in spoiling him with food to make his stay more agreeable—he listens to the clock and counts, which has "become a habit with him at night" (19):

> "It's one o'clock," Tom whispered angrily over the edge of the bedclothes. "Why don't you strike one o'clock, then, as the clocks would do at home?" Instead: Five! Six! Even in his irritation, Tom could not stop counting [. . .] . Seven! Eight! After all, the clock was the only thing that would speak to him at all in these hours of darkness. Nine! Ten! "You are doing it," thought Tom, but yawning in the midst of his unwilling admiration. Yes, and it hadn't finished yet: Eleven! Twelve! "Fancy striking midnight twice in one night!" jeered Tom, sleepily. Thirteen! proclaimed the clock, and then stopped striking. (19)

The passage shows the fantastical workings of the clock: Tom thinks he must have imagined the thirteen strokes while dozing off, yet he does not feel comfortable with this explanation. The clock is not only personified but also animated: it not only "speaks" to Tom but goes on chiming, and finally "proclaim[s]" the thirteenth hour. The house at last "convinces" him to get up: when Tom is reluctant to check the time shown on the clock, the house more or less urges him to do so, "sigh[ing] impatiently" and telling him that while he is reflecting he is "missing [his] chance" (21) to explore and start his "expedition" (22) during which he finds the door to the garden. Hence Tom was right in his observation that the clock was situated at the "heart of the house" (10), with its regular sound of "ticking" resembling the heartbeat. The ticking of the clock later even encourages him to climb the stairs to Hatty's room: "Its ticking sounded to him like a human heart, alive and beating—and he thought of Hatty when he thought that" (133). In her later novel, *The Children of Charlecote*

(1989), Pearce would write: "It's the house that remembers" (qtd. in Hall 155). The continuance of both the house and the clock as a permanent part of it means that "time's passage does not matter, for despite it, things do continue in the same way" (Nodelman 8). Pearce refers at least to two earlier children's texts, namely, Alison Uttley's *A Traveller in Time*, which appeared in 1939, and Lucy M. Boston's *The Children of Green Knowe*, published in 1954 (Nodelman 7–9): in both the house that is entered by the strange child acts as a medium that enables contact with the past.[1] Nodelman states that what makes *Tom's Midnight Garden* different lies in the fact that "Pearce makes the Victorian Hatty an equal partner in the modern Tom's play, quite unlike the mysterious presences of Jacobean children that flit around the edges in Tolly's consciousness [in *The Children of Green Knowe*]" (9). The achievement of Pearce is to credibly link the past and the present through the existence of Hatty in Tom's reality; she is not a ghost from the past but a real person.

Hence Tom's discovery of the garden happens, more or less, by mere chance: he needs light to read the face of the clock, and as he cannot find a light switch, he opens the door at the end of the hall to let in a moonbeam from outside. Upon opening the door he is no longer interested in turning "to see what it showed him on the clock-face" (24) for he sees a beautiful garden. This has two effects on him: first, he believes that his aunt and uncle have deceived him because they had told him that there was only a backyard, "very poky, with rubbish bins" (24), and second, he starts to plan further explorations of the garden during the following day.

Upon retreating into the house he again forgets to check the clock; he sees a maid and, since he cannot find a hiding place, speaks to her. When she does not react, he notices that the hall has changed completely. It is richly decorated, but very soon the decoration fades, "furniture and rugs and pictures" begin "to fail to be there" (28). Yet he is still able to see the garden, and "after a long look" (28) Tom returns to bed.

After his first discovery Tom goes to the garden every night and soon realizes that during his explorations, time in his "real world" stops: during his first thorough exploration of the garden, he is "uneasily aware of the passage of time" (43), but, upon returning to the flat, finds that it is "only a few minutes past midnight" (47). This suggests that as soon as Tom enters the garden, he enters a different temporal realm; only those minutes he needs to walk downstairs and return to the flat are reflected on the clock in his world. What is more, time in his world is not the same as in the garden: "He had come down the stairs [. . .] at midnight; but when he opened that door and stepped out into the garden, the time was much later" (41). This also becomes evident with regard to the hyacinths he smells during his first visit to the garden and his aunt's reaction when he tells her about them: "Hyacinths don't flower even out of doors at this time of year—it's too late in the summer" (33). This shows that not only the hours are different but also months and the season, which becomes even more evident later when Tom enters the garden in winter and goes skating with Hatty.

Mrs. Bartholomew, that is, Hatty, does not dream in chronological order either. The night when Tom sees the storm and lightning in the garden illustrates this. This occurs at a rather early stage of his visit still, for he does not yet know Hatty, but it is actually the last time Hatty ever sees him (211–12). During the storm Tom hears a cry "of the terror he himself felt" (56) when he sees the fir tree fall; the experience makes him very uneasy. But it is during the next night that he has "the greatest shock of all" (57), for he then sees that the tree is actually there; "the ivy-grown fir tree still towered above" (57) the other trees. This puzzles him immensely, and he even asks his uncle whether it is possible that a tree could lie "fallen at one time, and then be standing up again as it was before it fell" (59). Uncle Alan, however, answers that something like this could not have happened, quoting the proverb "unless you put the clock back" (59). But this is exactly what happens: the proverb is to be understood literally, for Mrs. Bartholomew in her dreams actually does turn the clock back. This shows that time, as presented in the story, is not linear and continuous, and that Tom's "journeys into time are not continuous; they are not even in chronological order" (Aers 78). The supernatural events that seem to be possible only in fairy tales—as Aunt Gwen points out to Tom—become explicable:[2] what Tom experiences happens in Mrs. Bartholomew's dreams, that is, her memories. The dream thus serves as a means of explanation of those events that are fantastical; "prominent within a work of fantasy is some element of the *im*possible or *super*natural, the writer relying on our consensus as to the nature of the possible or natural within the world of non-literary experience" (Attebery 54). Tom thus not only exists in two times simultaneously, but he seems to move also in four different states and realms at the same time himself: he is someone else's memory, and to be this he has to literally have been there in the past. Further, he is part of someone else's dream and simultaneously exists in his own current waking reality.

Memories and the Past: "Time No Longer"

Mrs. Bartholomew's dreams are the key to understanding Tom's "multiple" existence: they are associative, not chronological.[3] One example may help clarify this: after the geese have entered the garden, Hatty is found to be responsible for it. She is scolded by her aunt and told that she was "a charity child, a thankless pauper that she had received into her home as a duty to her late husband" (95). Tom witnesses the scene and subsequently falls asleep in the garden. When he wakes, he is "aware of some difference in his surroundings—a difference in time" (96): he sees Hatty, dressed in mourning, "sobbing into her hands" (96), and suddenly he is conscious of her being younger. Because of her having been called "a charity child," Hatty is reminded of her status and subsequently dreams of her grief following her parents' death—a chain of associations is set loose by the memory of the geese incident that also helps Tom understand that she is an orphan.

When Hatty has hurt her head after falling from the branch of a tree, Tom visits her in the room that is now his. There he begins to think "about the Past, that Time made so far away. Time had taken this Present of Hatty's and turned it into his Past. Yet even so, here and now, for a little while, this was somehow made his Present too—his and Hatty's. Then he remembered the grandfather clock, that measured out both his time and Hatty's and he remembered the picture on the face [of the clock]" (143).[4] In fact it is here that he begins "to ponder the meaning of time and to question Hatty about the clock" (Wolf 145). The following day a letter arrives asking him to come home next Saturday, which leaves him only four nights to answer all his questions and to spend time in the garden. During his visit in Hatty's room, he asks her about the clock and wants to find out more about it. She promises to "unlock the pendulum case. [. . .] Then Tom [can] read the secret for himself" (144).

It is winter when he next meets her, and Hatty is outside, skating. She is rather reluctant to go inside the house, and Tom has to persuade her to unlock the clock and have him take a look. He is now able to read the inscription on the pendulum that says "Time No Longer": "'Time no longer?' said Tom in surprise. [. . .] 'But no longer than what?'" (157). He does not understand, and Hatty shows him the text below the picture, "Rev X. 1–6" (157). Yet, he is not able to decipher and understand the emblem.

"Time no longer," as Tom will find out shortly afterward, is a quotation from the book of Revelation, and since Tom does not understand what is meant by it, he and Hatty go to the heating house to check in the gardener Abel's Bible. They find the relevant passage about the "annihilation of time at the end of the world" (Wolf 145) and learn that the Book of Life will be opened on the Day of Judgment and that then "there should be time no longer" (159). Tom at first has a very literal understanding of this; he thinks "of all the clocks in the world stopping ticking, and their striking stopped too, drowned and stopped for ever by the sound of the great Trumpet" (160). This gives him so much to think about that he does not even want to stay in the garden with Hatty but returns to the house. Back in his bed, he cannot sleep: "But if Time is ever to end, that means that, here and now, Time itself is only a temporary thing. It can be dispensed with perhaps; or rather, it can be dodged. Tom himself might be able to dodge behind Time's back and have the Past—that is, Hatty's Present and the garden—here, now and for ever. To manage that, of course, he must understand the workings of Time" (162). In this, however, he is wrong, as he will later come to understand: he is not able to stay in the garden, that is, in the past, forever.

The next morning he enters a discussion with his uncle, who presents him with theories of time that Tom cannot follow. His uncle coincidentally mentions Rip van Winkle. Tom immediately starts thinking about Rip van Winkle "because he was the first person Uncle Alan had mentioned that Tom really knew anything about: indeed, Tom knew all about him" (165). Tom starts to see himself as a

> Rip van Winkle in reverse [. . .] . Instead of going forward for twenty years, Tom went back a hundred and more, to Hatty's lifetime. He did not always go back to exactly the same Time, every night; nor did he take Time in its usual order. [. . .] He had seen Hatty as a girl of his own age, then as a much younger one, and recently as a girl who—although Tom would not yet fully admit it—was outgrowing him altogether. In flashes, Tom had seen Hatty's Time—the garden's Time—covering what must be about ten years, while his own Time achieved the weeks of a summer holiday. (165)

This is a revelation and insight to Tom, whose efforts as a detective have finally brought him to a solution. He can now even be sure that "neither of [them are] ghosts" and has settled "things to his own satisfaction" (166).[5]

In the wake of his reflections on time, he has an idea when he next meets Hatty—in winter still. He notices that she is older and, what is more, that she has followed her cousin James's advice that she "should meet more people" (138) and make friends. Yet she sees Tom, who makes her promise that she will leave her skates underneath the secret floorboard of her bedroom cupboard: "I only want you to keep your skates, always when you're not using them, in that secret place you showed me in your bedroom cupboard, under the floorboards" (169). After she has made the promise, he returns to the house but can only open the cupboard floorboard in the morning: "He saw two brown-paper packages in the hole [. . .] : they were a pair of skates, with boots still screwed and strapped to them" (172). With them he finds a note referring to Hatty's promise; she left the skates when she left the house. While oiling the skates, he finds "the solution—rounded and perfect—of his problem of Time. [. . .] The hours after the twelfth do not exist in ordinary Time; they are not bound by the laws of ordinary Time; they are not over in sixty ordinary minutes; they are endless" (173–74). He concludes from this that he "could, after all, have both things—the garden and his family— because he could stay for ever in the garden, and yet for ever his family would be expecting him next Saturday afternoon" (174).

The following night he again goes to the garden and skates with Hatty to Ely—"two skaters on one pair of skates" (181); the skates "now exist, like Tom, in both past and present" (Krips 178). Thus the skates have the effect of making the story of Tom fully credible and also more plausible:[6] he does not simply imagine things, nor does he merely travel into the past, but the two layers of time, past and present, are interlinked by material objects. Like the house and the grandfather clock, the skates become a part of Tom's reality and are, at the same time, a part of Hatty's dreamworld and thus of her memories.

The idea of past and present existing simultaneously goes back to Augustine, who stated that "all this while in the eternal nothing is flitting, but all is at once present, whereas no time is all at once present" (*Confessions* 11.11). Hence all time is eternally present, that is, past, present and future are simultaneous. The borders between the different strands of time can thus be overcome, a thought that is also expressed in T. S. Eliot's *Four Quartets*, specifically in "Burnt Norton," a text that may very well have served as a direct source for Pearce, especially if one considers the parallels between *Tom's Midnight Garden* and the beginning of Eliot's poem:

Time present and time past
Are both perhaps present in time future,
And time future contained in time past.
If all time is eternally present
All time is unredeemable.
[. . . . .]
What might have been and what has been
Point to one end, which is always present.
Footfalls echo in the memory
Down the passage which we did not take
Towards the door we never opened
Into the rose-garden. (1.1–14)

Past, present, and future merge, "all time is eternally present," and the theme of time is ultimately linked to place, that is, "place and time-and-eternity" (Leimberg 65). In Eliot's poem the garden is a place revisited that is both present in memory and in experience; revisiting this place evokes memories, and "memory is the place where time past and time future are present" (Leimberg 72).[7] In Pearce's novel the garden is the place where time future is contained in the past insofar as Tom already lives in Hatty's memories of the past; interestingly the passage about the door that leads to a rose garden in Eliot's poem has been associated with another classic of children's literature, *Alice's Adventures in Wonderland*, and with Alice's wish to enter the garden she can only see through the little door after her fall through the rabbit hole. In Eliot's poem the speaker is called into the garden, and the entering of the garden becomes the entrance to "our first world" (1.21–22), which implies paradisiacal notions that also emerge in Pearce's text.[8] Moreover, Eliot stresses the notion of memory, that is, "the realm of possibility and loss through time that is unique to individual memory" (Klein 26), which is also an affective memory. In *Tom's Midnight Garden* memory likewise works as the means to unite different strands of time. "Only in time" can things "be remembered" (Eliot, "Burnt Norton" 2.85, 88), and "only through time time is conquered" (2.89).

When Tom sees someone's epitaph in the cathedral of Ely—he reads that the person "had exchanged Time for Eternity" (184)—he plans "to exchange ordinary Time, that would otherwise move on towards Saturday, for an endless Time—an Eternity—in the garden" (184). But his plan fails; as a matter of fact, it must, for only "through time time is conquered," and Tom cannot close "the gap between time and eternity" (Malkoff 251). He cannot escape time, which becomes evident to him when, after visiting the cathedral they meet young Barty, who gives them, that is, Hatty, a ride home. During their journey Hatty seems to forget about Tom, and Tom starts to think "of Time: how he had been sure of mastering it, and of exchanging his own Time for an Eternity of Hatty's and so of living pleasurably in the garden forever. The garden was still there, but meanwhile Hatty's Time had stolen a march on him, and had turned Hatty herself from his playmate into a grown-up woman"(196).[9] By the end of the journey, Hatty does not even any longer see Tom; and the following night the garden is "no longer."

The End of Eternity

When Tom, expecting to run into the garden that night, actually runs into dustbins, he cries for Hatty. He suffers from a shock at his discovery that he cannot enter the garden anymore. The next morning he is expected to apologize for making so much noise and goes upstairs to Mrs. Bartholomew. This is when Tom finds that Mrs. Bartholomew *is* Hatty and that he was able to enter her dreams of the past, her memories, and thus also her past.[10]

During their conversation Tom learns that he cannot stop the course of time and that he cannot exchange "Time for Eternity," although he is able to experience things past: both to the young and the old only a shadow of eternity is granted. The most revealing sentence by the old Hatty is that "nothing stands still, except in our memory" (212); Hatty knows that from experience: on the last night before her wedding, during the storm, and before the fir tree fell, she thought that the garden would never change, but she then saw that it did, and this is why Tom heard a "cry of horror." That the fir tree falls in the night before Hatty's married life begins has a symbolic quality: it marks the end of her childhood, the end of her stay at her aunt's—and thus also the end to her playing in the garden. She has to leave the paradise of her childhood.

Her cry was caused not only by the shock and alarm at the moment of falling but also by her realization that even her garden, like everything, is subject to change and to time. This constant change even results in the garden's full disappearance in Tom's present, where it has been replaced with houses. However, Tom at first does not understand and thinks that all that happens in the garden is somehow reversible because, when he enters the garden the following night (in his present), he sees the tree towering above the garden as it had before the storm.

He furthermore realizes that what for him is only a few hours each night and, eventually, the time span of a school holiday is for Hatty more or less her whole childhood and youth and thus covers years: "'I shall see you tomorrow,' said Tom. Hatty smiled. 'You always say that, and then it's often months and months before you come again.' 'I come every night,' said Tom" (146). Because this, from Hatty's experience and point of view, is not the case, during each of Tom's visits "her secrets and stories [pour] from her with haste and eagerness as though she were afraid that Tom's company would not be hers for long" (81); to her Tom's company actually never does last long, and she yearns for company since her cousins would not play with or listen to her. Time, thus, has a very personal quality; "Time travels in divers paces with divers persons," as Rosalind puts it in *As You Like It* (3.2.299–300). And she goes on: "I'll tell you who Time ambles withal, who Time trots withal, who Time gallops withal and who he stands still withal" (300–02).

In the course of the story, Tom comes to regard time both as his friend and as his enemy: "It [the grandfather clock] would tick on to bedtime, and in that way Time was Tom's friend; but, after that, it would tick on to Saturday, and in that way Time was Tom's enemy" (153). This image of time implies a strong ambivalence in

Tom's perception of Time: it brings him nearer the moment he has to leave the garden, and he "hated the clock for that" (151). At the same time he wants the clock's secret to be revealed and longs "for the minutes and hours to pass quickly" (151): "Time was so long from now until then; so short from now until Saturday" (151). Hence there is a stark contrast between time in the garden and in the Kitsons' flat. While Tom knows that he need not worry or care about time in the garden, he is all the more conscious of it during daytime.

Pearce presents us with a subjective and magical, not linear, movement of time; it is through dreams and memories that one can overcome time.[11] However, this magical quality is not restricted to time but is also linked to place.[12] The garden appears to Tom—and turns out to be—a magical place, yet it is, simultaneously, a place that is real: "The garden was the thing. That was real" (29).

Tom's midnight garden is thus represented as "a world unto itself: [. . .] everything one could possibly imagine or desire in a garden is there" (Wolf 143), and it is Hatty's company that makes "this garden a kind of kingdom" (83). Tom and Hatty show a fascination with the garden that, particularly in the form of the walled garden, has a long tradition in children's literature: Alice wants to enter a walled garden, and all her adventures in Wonderland start with this longing; Mary in *The Secret Garden* has a similar desire. The place is hence shaped not only by the wall, trees, flowers, but also by human company and the friendship between two children. Hatty and Tom are somehow destined for each other, though not in the sense of Hatty and her future husband, Barty.[13] They need each other, and it is this need that makes the transition of time limits possible: theirs is a relationship that transcends time but is also determined by time. Tom's desire to have a garden "creates" one for him, and Mrs. Bartholomew notices that during the summer she felt a "longing for someone to play with and for somewhere to play" (214).[14] Their longing for friendship makes them find each other, and in the end this friendship even overcomes the age gap between Hatty and Tom when they finally meet outside the garden. As Aunt Gwen observes: "He hugged her good-bye as if she were a little girl" (217).

Through her dreams of her childhood, Hatty has attained a second childhood based on memories, while Tom even forgets to be a detective when he is in the garden. The reliving of her childhood and youth very much resembles Scrooge, who likewise "re-live[s] certain key moments in his former life" when he is visited by the Ghost of Christmas Past (Prickett 60).

The garden is a world of play; its "favourite time [is] summer, with perfect weather" (49).[15] It is a place of mutual giving and taking: Tom teaches Hatty to climb trees, and Hatty shows him her secret places in return. And it is also a mysterious place: Tom is weightless and invisible to almost all humans, except Abel and Hatty, yet he can be seen by all animals: "If he were invisible to the people in the garden, he was not completely so at least to some of the other creatures. [. . .] Birds cocked their heads at him, and flew away when he approached" (51). All things are immaterial to him, "without substance" (52); he can even walk through doors and leaves no footsteps on the grass. Nevertheless, he can wear the skates because they also exist in his time, and he takes them with him from the present into the past, namely, into the garden.

That there is a magical or even supernatural quality to the garden is particularly perceived by Hatty, to whom it is also a sort of retreat from her aunt's household. She actually plays with the notion of the garden's magic: in the glass-paneled door of the greenhouse is an engraved pane of glass through which one cannot see anything. Hatty thinks this "best of all [. . .] . You look and see nothing, and you might think there wasn't a garden for you; but, all the time, of course, it is there, waiting for you" (80). Tom and Hatty "see through a glass, darkly" (1 Cor. 13:12), but they do know that their garden, that is, their paradise, exists. This proves to be true, for after all those years and the disappearance of the garden in the real world, it is still there, in Hatty's memory.

Credible Fantasy: Narrative
Voice and Focalization

Most of the story is told through Tom's eyes, including his perceptions and feelings, as when he notes, "The stillness had become an expectant one" (19), as well as his reasoning and disbelief: "Thirteen? Tom's mind gave a jerk: had it really struck thirteen? Even mad old clocks never struck that. He must have imagined it. Had he not been falling asleep, or already sleeping? But no, awake or dozing, he had counted up to thirteen. He was sure of it" (19). Thus the reader is able to follow Tom's thoughts one by one while he weighs all the pros and cons.[16] The effect of following his argumentation is that the reader understands him and thinks like him; he or she may hence find it likewise a curious idea that a day should suddenly have "twice thirteen" hours (20). The reader's belief in Tom is enhanced by his own skeptical reaction to the supernatural events. There are no hints in the story that he invents his experiences and the nightly events in the garden: this makes him and his experiences credible; the fantasy earns our belief, and if it did not, it would fail.[17]

Yet not only is Tom's disbelief described but also his pondering about time and all the questions he asks in this context. He so very much wants to understand, and by following the story so does the reader. Shortly before Tom has to leave the Kitsons, he asks his aunt: "'What is the time, please?' 'Nearly four o'clock.' Was that all?" (153). Tom expects secrets and mysteries to be linked with time, yet in the real world the answer to "what is the time?" is not the revelation of a secret but the down-to-earth statement "nearly four o'clock." "Was that all?" expresses Tom's disappointment that there apparently is nothing more to time. Yet to him, more and more understandably, there is.

The meaning of time and its passing becomes clear to him when after his last night at his aunt and uncle's he wakes up and realizes that he will not be able to reenter the garden:

> Sometimes before in his life, Tom had gone to sleep in disappointment or sadness, but always he had woken up to a new

day and new hope. This time he found that the morning was only a continuation of the night and the day before: even as his mind stirred awake, the horror and grief of yesterday were already there. This was Saturday; he had lost his last chance; he had lost the garden. Today he went home. The tears fell from his eyes, and he could not stop them falling. Aunt Gwen came to him early [. . .] . Now, at last he wanted to tell her—to share and perhaps thereby lessen his grief. But now it was too late [. . .] . He gazed at her in silence, and wept. (205–06)

He feels "horror and grief," he realizes that he has "lost his chance," and he weeps: the intensity is conveyed both through the choice of words and the conveyance of feelings through Tom as focalizer. Through him the reader participates in the discovery of the garden, Tom's adventures with Hatty, and eventually in the loss of the garden. Time has simply gone on passing, although he wanted to stop his own time by spending it in the garden: "The passage of time means that everything must change, so that everything must die; [. . .] if the past can still be entered by people in the present, then it is not yet over. That represents a triumph over death" (Nodelman 8). This triumph, however, is not possible. Tom loses the garden and cannot eternally overcome time with its help but has "to accept the inevitability of time's passage" (Nodelman 10).

There are only a few instances when Tom's viewpoint is interrupted by the voice of the narrator, which, whenever it intrudes into the story, proves to be omniscient. In one of the first instances, he tells us that "Mrs. Bartholomew was asleep and dreaming" (23), which belongs to a knowledge that goes beyond Tom's. Thus there are instances when important information is given that cannot, however, be Tom's and goes beyond his immediate experience. When one reads the book a second time, this simple statement gains deeper meaning and can be seen as a first hint that Mrs. Bartholomew's dreams are essential to what Tom experiences during the night.

The second comment of this kind occurs when Tom starts his second exploration: "She [Mrs. Bartholomew] was lying tranquilly in bed: her false teeth, in a glass of water by the bedside, grinned unpleasantly in the moonlight, but her indrawn mouth was curved in a smile of easy, sweet-dreaming sleep. She was dreaming of scenes of her childhood" (38). Thus the narrator hints at what is happening already very early in the course of the story and furthermore directs the reader's attention to particular events, as when Tom is standing at Hatty's window, looking over the garden, he does "not linger over this view, but later he had cause to remember it" (134).

Although Tom himself finds that "his story was too long and too fantastic for belief" (206), fantasy as such is not introduced "until Chapter III when Tom gets out of bed at midnight"; until then Pearce's presentation stays within the realm of a "recognizably ordinary world of England in the mid-twentieth century" (Wolf 143).

Tom enters Hatty's dreams, which can bridge a time gap of more than sixty years. After a few nights in the garden, Tom comes to the following conclusion: "The garden and its surroundings, then, were not, in themselves, outside the natural order of things; nor was Tom alarmed by his own unnatural abilities. Yet to some things his mind came back again and again, troubled: the constant fine weather, the rapid coming and going of the seasons and the times of day, the feeling of being watched" (55). In its being fantastic Pearce's novel is credible, and the world Tom enters is not an alternative world to reality but an extension of it; it lies somewhere between the fantastic and psychological realism. Thus fantasies, dreams, and memories do not merely reflect reality, but their contents become reality.

Hatty remembers her childhood and especially her time in the garden with Tom as an ideal state of being. Because of this, her memories become affective, which leads to their being so lively and vivid. The affective quality of Hatty's memories also explains the fact that there is almost always fine weather in the garden. The garden as a place to be remembered is thus determined by emotions, which usually results in a loss of factuality. This, however, is not the case in Pearce's novel: the events are real because they are experiences shared and remembered by two persons; the garden is thus a place both of experience and of memory.

Tom can move between past and present, and Mrs. Bartholomew also can, at least in her dreams. At the same time, there is movement toward the future: Mrs. Bartholomew's dreams are memories in which Tom appears from the future. Through sharing the experience of the garden with Tom, she makes it available to him and hence to *his* memories. Thus the garden is brought back to life, both in Hatty's memory but also in Tom's reality: "That which hath been is now; and that which is to be hath already been" (Eccles. 3:15).

Hatty's memories in her dreams are both a nostalgic return to her childhood and a foundation of her friendship with Tom, which, paradoxically, becomes part of her future. It should in this context be remembered that the clock moves only because of Mrs. Bartholomew, who winds it. Tom once watches her winding the clock (36). As long as she lives, the clock is ticking, and hence the heart of the house beating. She can therefore be regarded as "a sort of Father Time figure" (Rees 43) who is responsible for the ongoing ticking of the clock. Thus the clock is the means both to overcome time and to indicate its progression; it links the past and the present just as Hatty's dreams and memories do, and it is the magical contact between the girl Hatty and the boy Tom, as much as between the old woman and the young boy, that makes the garden eternal. This magic enables them to overcome temporal boundaries.

Tom's Midnight Garden *and the Time-Slip Novel*

Although by sending her protagonist back in time Pearce follows the earlier example of Edith Nesbit's *The House of Arden* (1908) and its sequel *Harding's Luck* (1909), and also her contemporary Lucy M. Boston's *The Children of Green Knowe* (1954), she then varies this idea in that she neither has a character from the past enter Tom's present nor does Tom merely travel into the past. In *The House of Arden*, for instance, the latter is the case; and in Lucy M. Boston's narrative, characters from the past actually enter Tolly's, the protagonist's, present world. Pearce, however, links the existence of Tom and Hatty through her memories of a past that is simultaneously a part of Tom's present life.

What happens in the novel is neither rationally explicable nor logically possible. Their friendship is brought about through magic, based on their shared longing for company. Tom does not look for a treasure, like Edred and Elfrida in Nesbit's *The House of Arden*; it is basically his psychological makeup that enables him to travel back in time (cf. Lehnert-Rodiek 63)—and, one might argue, also Hatty's (in her case it is even double for it concerns both the girl in the past and the old woman in the present). They are able to meet in the Victorian garden because of their solitude and wish for a playmate.[18] Time travel is caused not by an external factor but by Tom's (and Hatty's) wish to play in a garden. Because of the concurrent "reality" of the past and the present and their coexistence through Hatty's dreams, "there is more preoccupation with the notion and nature of Time in *Tom's Midnight Garden* than in most so-called time-shift fantasies" (Nikolajeva, *From Mythic to Linear* 105).

Critics have noted that the "time-slip novel," such as *Tom's Midnight Garden*, became hugely popular in the 1950s and explain this mainly in the context of the aftermath of the Second World War and the destruction of many historical sites in its course (cf. Hall; Lucas xix). Time-slip novels are supposed to guarantee "personal and cultural continuity" (Hall 154).[19] Through Tom's eventual memory of his summer in the garden with Hatty, her memories of the garden will live on.

The novel leaves all questions open as to how such a travel back in time is possible at all (cf. Lehnert-Rodiek 63). In *Tom's Midnight Garden* "an ostensibly realist past is introduced in a realist present" (Gavin 159). Nevertheless, time travel in Pearce's novel is not historiographical (cf. Kullmann) but "owes more to Victorian novels than to 'strict' Victorian history" (Gavin 162). It is rather a story about two people who befriend each other and find their paradise in a garden that no longer exists in the present. Thus the "fantasy and the fantastic have an end in themselves. The fascination with the past; the belief in the power of the imagination, wishes and dreams; the joy of making up stories" (Lehnert-Rodiek 64). This "end in itself" of the time-slip story of *Tom's Midnight Garden* is what makes it so different from the other novels of that genre: everything that happens serves not some higher aim but rather the well-being and contentment of a girl, an old woman, and a boy who long for company.

Notes

I wish to express my thanks to Prof. Matthias Bauer for discussing with me the manuscript of this essay and also to Mike Cadden for his helpful comments.

1. Hall likewise refers to both Boston's and Pearce's texts in her essay on the house and the garden in "time-slip" stories.

2. "'It was a fairy tree!' said Aunt Gwen, returning with desperate playfulness to her first suggestion. 'Goblin woodcutters laid it low, didn't they, Tom?'" (60). Tom's insistence on the reality of the fallen tree shows that unlike C. S. Lewis's *The Lion, the Witch and the Wardrobe*, where the fantastical world the children enter is a world of fairy tales, in *Tom's Midnight Garden* the garden is part of reality because it is a part of a real and historical past.

3. Aers calls this "dream time" (78).

4. "In the semicircular arch above the dial stood a creature like a man but with enormous, sweeping wings. His body was wound about with something white. His face was a round of gold, and his feet were of the same colour and were planted on either side of the clock-dial. One foot seemed to stand on a piece of grassy land: the other went into the sea— Tom saw painted fishes that swam round the creature's foot, and seaweed. In one hand he held a book, opened towards himself" (37).

5. Tom and Hatty have this discussion quite early in their friendship when she asks him what it is like to be a ghost (105), and they start to argue because they both think that the other is a ghost.

6. Tom's leaving his slippers in the door when he goes downstairs has a similar function. It becomes clear that he does not dream his nightly wanderings in the garden, for he sometimes finds himself in his room but has not entered the flat through the door: "He was about to climb into his cold bed, when he remembered the bedroom slipper that wedged the flat

door open. [. . .] He got the slipper, shut the front door and went back to bed" (148).

7. Leimberg continues: "The places to be revisited are select ones, charged with the presence of past and future, connected with the elements of personal existence, felt to be meeting places, places of accepting and being accepted, visiting and being visited, points of intersection where 'the unseen eyebeam crossed' and experience is full of meaning, in other words, places of recognition" (75).

8. The image of paradise and the garden as Eden is evoked both through the tree itself and its fall; Tom comments that the garden for him is "a kind of kingdom" (83).

9. Jones states that Tom does not notice Hatty's change: "Hatty, whom he has failed to recognize as getting older" (216), yet there are several instances in the text when Tom sees for himself that Hatty grows: "She seemed to have been growing up a good deal too much recently" (105); "She had certainly grown a great deal since those early days in the garden" (158). However, it is Peter who recognizes how old she *really* is.

10. This link between dreams and memories is likewise expressed in the introductory poem to *Alice's Adventures in Wonderland*: "A childish story take, [. . .] / Lay it where Childhood's dreams are twined / in Memory's mystic band" (Carroll 4 [ll.37–40]).

11. In the context of *Tom's Midnight Garden* as a fantasy novel, Hatty's dreams "are as important as the clock in opening the door to the past for Tom [. . .] . The leap across the abyss of time is thus more often associated, in serious fantasy, with the power of the mind and the strength of the memory than with superficial devices" (Swinfen 51).

12. In Nikolajeva's (and Bakhtin's) terminology, the garden is a chronotope; there is an "*indivisible* unity of time and space" (*Children's Literature Comes of Age* 121). Time stops in the real world but goes on in a past period that is indivisibly linked to the garden. Nikolajeva would most probably even call it "secondary chronotope," for it is "a magical world with its own specific time which contrasts with our primary world and time" (123), comparable to, for example, the passage of time in C. S. Lewis's *The Lion, the Witch and the Wardrobe*. She also states in her study *From Mythic to Linear* that "in the garden, both protagonists step out of their chronos into kairos: Mrs. Bartholomew by returning to her childhood and becoming a little girl again, Tom by going into the past" (105).

13. Pearce's novel in this respect differs from Kipling's story "The Brushwood Boy." There, two children also meet in their dreams and experience many adventures together, and when they finally meet in reality they are both adults and decide to get married because of their feel-

ing that they are destined for each other. My attention to this story was drawn by Prickett (204).

14. This desire has been described as a central feature of the fantasy genre: "the fantasy of desire [. . .] for another world [or a lost world]" (Manlove 91). The fantasy genre has been defined as the "recovery of a religious dimension permeating everyday work, an edenic return to innocence, or the recovery [. . .] of a sense of the wonder of creation" (Jasper xii). Swinfen likewise states that it is the need and desire for company that triggers the meeting of Tom and Hatty: "Unhappy and neglected, Hatty reaches out for love and companionship across the gulf of years, and Tom, who is unaware that he is responding to her need for him as much as to his own curiosity [. . .] steps in and out of the past" (59). Dunne in his *Experiment* states that desire is an important and "powerful [. . .] stimulant" when it comes to "tracks leading [. . .] to the future and [. . .] to the past" (219).

15. According to Carpenter, the "garden is childhood itself" (219). Swinfen links "the memories of Hatty's times of happiness" with the "memory of ideal seasons" (51).

16. For a detailed study of narrative voice in children's literature, see Wall.

17. Wolf states that Pearce's story is one of the few fantasies "set in the here and now" that do not "use some rational explanations to achieve credibility as does, for example, Lewis Carroll's *Alice's Adventures in Wonderland*, Mary Norton's *The Borrowers*, and E. B. White's *Charlotte's Web*" (142).

18. The solitary child must be "lonely and longing for company" in order to get "in touch with [. . . the] past" (Hall 155).

19. Linda Hall explains that "there was a real threat to the past" because many houses had been destroyed during the Second World War and the "past was often obliterated by anonymous modern blocks" (154) in the 1950s. This concept is at the heart of the 1998 movie version of *Tom's Midnight Garden*, in which the story of Tom and Hatty is framed by an adult Tom going to Hatty's house for the last time and witnessing it being demolished. For further characteristics of the time-slip novel and its relation to heritage in particular, see Cosslett 244.

Works Cited

Aers, Lesley. "The Treatment of Time in Children's Books." *Children's Literature in Education* 2 (1970): 69–81.

Attebery, Brian. *Strategies of Fantasy*. Bloomington: Indiana University Press, 1992.

Augustinus, Aurelius. *St. Augustine's Confessions*. 1631. Trans. William Watts. 2 vols. Cambridge MA: Harvard University Press, 1995.

The Bible: Authorized King James' Version with Apocrypha. Ed. Robert Carroll and Stephen Prickett. Oxford: Oxford University Press, 1997.

Boston, Lucy. *The Children of Green Knowe*. London: Faber, 2000.

Burnett, Frances Hodgson. *The Secret Garden*. 1911. London: Penguin, 1995.

Carpenter, Humphrey. *Secret Gardens: A Study of the Golden Age of Children's Literature*. Boston: Houghton, 1985.

Carroll, Lewis. *Alice's Adventures in Wonderland*. 1865. *Alice's Adventures in Wonderland and Through the Looking-Glass*. Ed. Roger Lancelyn Green. Oxford: Oxford University Press, 1998.

Cosslett, Tess. "'History from Below': Time-Slip Narratives and National Identity." *The Lion and the Unicorn* 26.2 (2002): 243–53.

Dunne, J. W. *An Experiment with Time*. 3rd ed. London: Faber, 1934.

Eliot, T. S. *Four Quartets: The Complete Poems and Plays of T. S. Eliot*. London: Faber, 1969. 171–98.

Gavin, Adrienne. "The Past Reimagined: History and Literary Creation in British Children's Novels after World War Two." *The Presence of the Past in Children's Literature*. Ed. Ann Lawson Lucas. Westport CT: Praeger, 2003. 159–66.

Hall, Linda. "'House and Garden': The Time-Slip Story in the Aftermath of the Second World War." *The Presence of the Past in Children's Literature*. Ed. Ann Lawson Lucas. Westport CT: Praeger, 2003. 153–58.

Jasper, David. "Making Words Mean a Great Deal." Foreword. *The Victorian Fantasists: Essays on Culture, Society and Belief in the Mythopoeic Fiction of the Victorian Age*. Ed. Kath Filmer. Basingstoke, England: Macmillan, 1991. ix–xiii.

Jones, Raymond S. "Philippa Pearce's *Tom's Midnight Garden*: Finding and Losing Eden." *Touchstones: Reflections on the Best in Children's Literature*. Ed. Perry Nodelman. 3 vols. West Lafayette IN: Children's Literature Assn., 1985. 1:212–21.

Kipling, Rudyard. "The Brushwood Boy." *The Day's Work*. London: Macmillan, 1923. 360–406.

Klein, William H. "Aspects of Time in Eliot's *Four Quartets*." *Yeats Eliot Review* 13.1–2 (1994): 26–36.

Krips, Valerie. "Presencing the Past." *Signal: Approaches to Children's Books* 90 (Sept. 1999): 176–86.

Kullmann, Thomas. "Constructions of History in Victorian and Edwardian Children's Books." *The Presence of the Past in Children's Literature.* Ed. Ann Lawson Lucas. Westport CT: Praeger, 2003. 73–79.

Lehnert-Rodiek, Gertrud. "Fantastic Children's Literature and Travel in Time." Trans. Caroline Höyng. *Phaedrus: An International Annual for the History of Children's and Youth Literature* 13 (1988): 61–72.

Leimberg, Inge. "The Place Revisited in T. S. Eliot's *Four Quartets.*" *Connotations* 8.1 (1998/99): 63–92.

Lewis, C. S. *The Lion, the Witch and the Wardrobe.* 1950. New York: Harper Trophy, 1978.

Lucas, Ann Lawson. "Introduction: The Past in the Present of Children's Literature." *The Presence of the Past in Children's Literature.* Ed. Ann Lawson Lucas. Westport CT: Praeger, 2003. xiii–xxi.

Malkoff, Karl. "Eliot and Elytis: Poet of Time, Poet of Space." *Comparative Literature* 36.3 (Summer 1984): 238–57.

Manlove, Colin. *The Fantasy Literature of England.* Houndmills, England: Macmillan, 1999.

Nesbit, Edith. *Harding's Luck.* London: Benn, 1949.

——. *The House of Arden.* New York: Dutton, 1909.

Nikolajeva, Maria. *Children's Literature Comes of Age: Towards a New Aesthetic.* New York: Garland, 1996.

——. *From Mythic to Linear: Time in Children's Literature.* Boston: Scarecrow, 2000.

Nodelman, Perry. "Interpretation and the Apparent Sameness of Children's Novels." *Studies in the Literary Imagination* 18.2 (1985): 5–20.

Pearce, Philippa. *The Children of Charlecote.* London: Gollancz, 1989. Originally published as *The Children of the House* (1968).

——. *Tom's Midnight Garden.* 1958. London: Puffin, 1976.

Prickett, Stephen. *Victorian Fantasy.* Hassocks: Harvester, 1979.

Rees, David. "Achieving One's Heart's Desire: Philippa Pearce." *The Marble in the Water: Essays on Contemporary Writers of Fiction for Children and Young Adults.* Boston: Horn Book, 1980. 37–55.

Shakespeare, William. *As You Like It.* 1599. Ed. Juliet Dusinberre. The Arden Shakespeare. London: Thomson, 2006.

Swinfen, Ann. *In Defence of Fantasy: A Study of the Genre in English and American Literature since 1945.* London: Routledge, 1984.

Tom's Midnight Garden. Dir. Gavin Finney. Perf. Greta Scacchi, James Wilby, and Joan Plowright. MGM, 1998.

Wall, Barbara. *The Narrator's Voice: The Dilemma of Children's Fiction.* Basingstoke, England: Macmillan, 1991.

Wolf, Virginia L. "Belief in *Tom's Midnight Garden*." *The Child and the Story: An Exploration of Narrative Forms*. Proc. of the Ninth Annual Conf. of the Children's Literature Assn., University of Florida, March 1982. Ed. Priscilla A. Ord. Boston: Children's Literature Assn., 1983. 142–46.

Further Reading

Titles cited in the introduction or in the volume's chapters are not reprinted here. For instance, see the introduction for critical readings on the peritextual in children's and young adult literature.

Anthropomorphism

Blount, Margaret. *Animal Land: The Creatures of Children's Fiction.* London: Hutchinson, 1974.

Gubar, Marah. "Species Trouble: The Abjection of Adolescence in E. B. White's *Stuart Little.*" *The Lion and the Unicorn* 27.1 (Jan. 2003): 98–119.

Magee, William H. "The Animal Story: A Challenge in Technique." *Only Connect: Readings on Children's Literature.* Ed. Sheila G. Egoff, T. Stubbs, and L. F. Ashley. 2nd ed. Toronto: Oxford University Press, 1980. 221–32.

Morgenstern, John. "Children and Other Talking Animals." *The Lion and the Unicorn* 24.1 (Jan. 2000): 110–27.

Nelles, William. "Beyond the Bird's Eye: Animal Focalization." *Narrative* 9.2 (May 2001): 188–94.

Parris, Brandy. "Difficult Sympathy in the Reconstruction-Era Animal Stories of *Our Young Folks.*" *Children's Literature* 31 (2003): 25–49.

Rahn, Suzanne. "Cat-Quest: A Symbolic Animal in Margaret Wise Brown." *Children's Literature* 22 (1994): 149–61.

Crossover Writing

Beckett, Sandra L. *Crossover Fiction: Global and Historical Perspectives.* New York: Routledge, 2008.

———. "Crosswriting Child and Adult in France: Children's Fiction for Adults? Adult Fiction for Children? Fiction for All Ages?" Beckett, *Transcending Boundaries* 31–62.

————, ed. *Transcending Boundaries: Writing for a Dual Audience of Children and Adults*. Ed. Sandra Beckett. New York: Garland, 1999.

Falconer, Rachel. "Crossover Literature and Abjection: Geraldine McCaughrean's *The White Darkness*." *Children's Literature in Education* 38.1 (Mar. 2007): 35–44.

————. *The Crossover Novel: Contemporary Children's Fiction and Its Adult Readership*. New York: Routledge, 2008.

Galef, David. "Crossing Over: Authors Who Write Both Children's and Adults' Fiction." *Children's Literature Association Quarterly* 20.1 (1995): 29–35.

Knoepflmacher, U. C., and Mitzi Myers. "'Cross-Writing' and the Reconceptualizing of Children's Literary Studies." *Children's Literature* 25 (1997): vii–xvii.

Shavit, Zohar. "The Double Attribution of Texts for Children and How It Affects Writing for Children." Beckett, *Transcending Boundaries* 83–98.

Thum, Maureen. "Misreading the Cross-Writer: The Case of Wilhelm Hauff's *Dwarf Long Nose*." *Children's Literature* 25 (1997): 1–23.

Ethics

Cadden, Mike. "Speaking to the Needs of Genre: Le Guin's Ethics of Audience." *The Lion and the Unicorn* 24.1 (2000): 128–42.

Collins, Louise. "The Virtue of 'Stubborn Curiosity': Moral Literacy in *Black and White*." *The Lion and the Unicorn* 26.1 (Jan. 2002): 31–49.

Gooderham, David. "Still Catching Them Young? The Moral Dimensions in Young Children's Books." *Children's Literature in Education* 24.2 (June 1993): 115–22.

Mills, Claudia. "The Ethics of the Author/Audience Relationship in Children's Fiction." *Children's Literature Association Quarterly* 22.4 (1998): 181–87.

————. "The Structure of the Moral Dilemma in *Shiloh*." *Children's Literature* 27 (1999): 185–97.

Neff, Heather. "Strange Faces in the Mirror: The Ethics of Diversity in Children's Films." *The Lion and the Unicorn* 20.1 (June 1996): 50–65.

Phelan, James. *Living to Tell about It: A Rhetoric and Ethics of Character Narration*. Ithaca NY: Cornell University Press, 2005.

Reinstein, P. Gila. "Aesop and Grimm: Contrast in Ethical Codes and Contemporary Values." *Children's Literature in Education* 14.1 (Mar. 1983): 44–53.

Ringrose, Christopher. "Lying in Children's Fiction: Morality and Imagination." *Children's Literature in Education* 37.3 (Sept. 2006): 229–36.

Tal, Eve. "'From Both Sides Now': Power and Powerlessness in Two Contemporary Novels of the Middle East." *International Research in Children's Literature* 1.1 (July 2008): 16–26.

Tarr, Anita. "The Absence of Moral Agency in Robert Cormier's *The Chocolate War.*" *Children's Literature* 30 (2002): 96–124.

Walsh, Jill Paton. "The Writers in the Writer: A Reply to Hugh Crago." *Signal* 40 (1983): 3–11.

———. "The Writer's Responsibility." *Children's Literature in Education* 10 (1973): 30–36.

Genre

Alexander, Joy. "The Verse-Novel: A New Genre." *Children's Literature in Education* 36.3 (Sept. 2005): 269–83.

Esmonde, Margaret P. "Narrative Methods in Penelope Farmer's *A Castle of Bone.*" *Children's Literature in Education* 14.3 (Sept. 1983): 171–79.

Hunt, Peter, Millicent Lenz, and Cardiff Lenz. *Alternative Worlds in Fantasy Fiction.* Continuum, 2001.

Le Guin, Ursula K. *The Language of the Night: Essays on Fantasy and Science Fiction.* New York: HarperPerennial, 1989.

Lewis, C. S. "On Three Ways of Writing for Children." *Of Other Worlds: Essays and Stories.* Ed. Walter Hooper. New York: Harcourt, 1966. 23–27.

Mendlesohn, Farah. "Is There Any Such Thing as Children's Science Fiction? A Position Piece." *The Lion and the Unicorn* 28.2 (Apr. 2004): 284–313.

Nodelman, Perry. "Pleasure and Genre: Speculations on the Characteristics of Children's Fiction." *Children's Literature* 28 (2000): 1–14.

Pickering, Samuel. "The Evolution of a Genre: Fictional Biographies for Children in the Eighteenth Century." *Journal of Narrative Theory* 7.1 (Winter 1977): 1–23.

Ruwe, Donelle. "Dramatic Monologues and the Novel-in-Verse: Adelaide O'Keeffe and the Development of the Theatrical Children's Poetry in the Long Eighteenth Century." *The Lion and the Unicorn* 33.2 (Apr. 2009): 219–34.

Sale, Roger. *Fairy Tales and After: From Snow White to E. B. White.* Cambridge MA: Harvard University Press, 1978.

Small, Robert. "The Literary Value of the Young Adult Novel." *Journal of Youth Services in Libraries* (Spring 1992): 277–85.

Sommers, Joseph Michael. "'Are You There, Reader? It's Me, Margaret': A Reconsideration of Judy Blume's Prose as Sororal Dialogism." *Children's Literature Association Quarterly* 33.3 (Fall 2008): 258–79.

Metafiction

Attebery, Brian, "*The Beginning Place*: Le Guin's Metafantasy." *Children's Literature* 10 (1982): 113–23.

Bullen, Elizabeth. "Power of Darkness: Narrative and Biographical Reflexivity in *A Series of Unfortunate Events*." *International Research in Children's Literature* 1.2 (Dec. 2008): 200–12.

Didicher, Nicole E. "The Children in the Story: Metafiction in *Mary Poppins in the Park*." *Children's Literature in Education* 28.3 (Sept. 1997): 137–49.

Gates, Geoffrey. "'Always the Outlaw': The Potential for Subversion of the Metanarrative in Retellings of Robin Hood." *Children's Literature in Education* 37.1 (Mar. 2006): 69–79.

Jones, Dudley. "Only Make-Believe? Lies, Fictions, and Metafictions in Geraldine McCaughrean's *A Pack of Lies* and Philip Pullman's *Clockwork*." *The Lion and the Unicorn* 23.1 (Jan. 1999): 86–96.

Mackey, Margaret. "Metafiction for Beginners: Allan Ahlberg's *Ten in a Bed*." *Children's Literature in Education* 21.3 (Sept. 1990): 179–87.

Moss, Anita. "Varieties of Children's Metafiction." *Studies in the Literary Imagination* 18.2 (1985): 79–92.

Philpot, Don K. "Children's Metafiction, Readers, and Reading: Building Thematic Models of Narrative Comprehension." *Children's Literature in Education* 36.2 (June 2005): 141–59.

Sanders, Joseph Sutliff. "The Critical Reader in Children's Metafiction." *The Lion and the Unicorn* 33.3 (Sept. 2009): 349–61.

Stephens, John. "Metafiction and Interpretation: William Mayne's *Salt River Times*, *Winter Quarters*, and *Drift*." *Children's Literature* 21 (1993): 101–17.

Narration and Voice

Beavin, Kristi. "Audiobooks: Four Styles of Narration." *Horn Book Magazine* 72.5 (Sept./Oct. 1996): 566–73.

Blackburn, William. "'A New Kind of Rule': The Subversive Narrator in *Alice's Adventures in Wonderland* and 'The Pied Piper of Hamelin.'" *Children's Literature in Education* 17.3 (Sept. 1986): 181–90.

Cadden, Mike. *Ursula K. Le Guin Beyond Genre: Fiction for Children and Adults*. New York: Routledge, 2005.

Dean, Sharon. "The Dangers of Being Relaxed in a Fictional World: A Study of Subject Positioning, Focalisation and Point of View in Two Novels." *Papers: Explorations into Children's Literature* 6.2 (Aug. 1996): 31–36.

Fincke, Kate. "Lunch at the Idea Café: The Narration of Metaphor in Children's Lives." *The Lion and the Unicorn* 25.2 (Apr. 2001): 260–76.

Fisher, Leona. "'I'm thinking how nothing is as simple as you guess': Narration in Phyllis Reynolds Naylor's *Shiloh*." *Children's Literature Association Quarterly* 28.1 (Spring 2003): 17–25.

Golden, Joanne M. *The Narrative Symbol in Childhood Literature: Explorations in the Construction of Text*. New York: Mouton de Gruyter, 1990.

Heberle, Mark A., Elizabeth Goodenough, and Naomi B. Sokoloff, eds. *Infant Tongues: The Voice of the Child in Literature*. Detroit: Wayne State University Press, 1994.

Kawabata, Ariko. "Sense of Loss, Belonging, and Storytelling: An Anglo-Indian Narrator in *The Borrowers*." *Children's Literature in Education* 37.2 (June 2006): 125–31.

Koss, Melanie D. "Young Adult Novels with Multiple Narrative Perspectives." *ALAN Review* 36.3 (Summer 2009): 73–80.

McGillis, Rod. "The Embrace: Narrative Voice and Children's Books." *Canadian Children's Literature* 63 (1991): 24–40.

Mynott, Glen. "The Didactic Narrator in C. S. Lewis's *The Lion, the Witch and the Wardrobe*." *Papers: Explorations into Children's Literature* 12.1 (Apr. 2002): 40–46.

Olson, Greta. "Reconsidering Unreliability: Fallible and Untrustworthy Narrators." *Narrative* 11.1 (Jan. 2003): 93–109.

Phillips, Anne K. "'Yours most loquaciously': Voice in Jean Webster's *Daddy-Long-Legs*." *Children's Literature* 27 (1999): 64–86.

Schuhmann, Elizabeth C. "Shift Out of First: Third-Person Narration Has Advantages." *ALAN Review* 9.2 (Winter 1982): 40–42, 48.

Sircar, Sanjay. "The Victorian Auntly Narrative Voice and Mrs. Molesworth's *Cuckoo Clock*." *Children's Literature* 17 (1989): 1–24.

Stephens, John. "Maintaining Distinctions: Realism, Voice, and Subject Position in Australian Young Adult Fiction." *Transcending Boundaries: Writing for a Dual Audience of Children and Adults*. Ed. Sandra Becket. New York: Garland, 1999. 183–200.

Wasserman, Emily. "Epistolary in Young Adult Literature." *ALAN Review* 30.3 (Spring 2003): 48–51.

Westman, Karin E. "Perspective, Memory, and Moral Authority: The Legacy of Jane Austen in J. K. Rowling's *Harry Potter*." *Children's Literature* 35 (2007): 145–65.

Whyte, Padraic. "Validating the Veracity: Narrative Voice and the Construction of Authentic Histories in Joan O'Neill's *Daisy Chain War*."

New Review of Children's Literature and Librarianship 10.1 (Apr. 2004): 71–78.

Wyile, Andrea Schwenke. "First-Person Engaging Narration in the Picture Book: Verbal and Pictorial Variations." *Children's Literature in Education* 32.3 (2001): 191–202.

———. "The Value of Singularity in First- and Restricted Third-Person Engaging Narration." *Children's Literature* 31 (2003): 116–41.

The Picture Book

Bradford, Clare. "Schmalz Is as Schmalz Does: Sentimentality and Picture Books." *Papers: Explorations into Children's Literature* 7.3 (Dec. 1997): 17–32.

Desai, Christina M. "Weaving Words and Pictures: Allen Say and the Art of Illustration." *The Lion and the Unicorn* 28.3 (Sept. 2004): 408–28.

Kaplan, Deborah. "Read All Over: Postmodern Resolution in Macaulay's *Black and White*." *Children's Literature Association Quarterly* 28.1 (Spring 2003): 37–41.

Kummerling-Meibauer, Bettina. "Metalinguistic Awareness and the Child's Developing Concept of Irony: The Relationship between Pictures and Text in Ironic Picture Books." *The Lion and the Unicorn* 23.2 (Apr. 1999): 157–83.

McClay, Jill Kedersha. "'Wait a Second . . .': Negotiating Complex Narratives in *Black and White*." *Children's Literature in Education* 31.2 (June 2000): 91–106.

Pantaleo, Sylvia J. "'Everything Comes from Seeing Things': Narrative and Illustrative Play in *Black and White*." *Children's Literature in Education* 38.1 (Mar. 2007): 45–58.

Stewart, Michelle Pagni. "Emerging Literacy of (An)Other Kind: Speakerly Children's Picture Books." *Children's Literature Association Quarterly* 28.1 (Spring 2003): 42–51.

Wesseling, Elisabeth. "Visual Narrativity in the Picture Book: Heinrich Hoffman's *Der Struwwelpeter*." *Children's Literature in Education* 35.4 (Dec. 2004): 319–45.

Plot

Altmann, Anna E. "Welding Brass Tits on the Armor: An Examination of the Quest Metaphor in Robin McKinley's *The Hero and the Crown*." *Children's Literature in Education* 23.3 (Sept. 1992): 143–56.

Bixler, Phyllis, and Lucien Agosta. "Formula Fiction and Children's Lit-

erature: Thornton Waldo Burgess and Frances Hodgson Burnett."
Children's Literature in Education 15.2 (June 1984): 63–71.

Cadden, Mike. "Simultaneous Emotions: Entwining Modes in Children's
Books." *Children's Literature in Education*. 36.3 (Sept. 2005): 285–98.

Clausen, Christopher. "Home and Away in Children's Fiction." *Children's
Literature* 10 (1982): 141–52.

Ellis, Sarah. "A View Down the Microscope." *The Lion and the Unicorn*
32.2 (Apr. 2008): 155–68.

Higonnet, Margaret R. "Narrative Fractures and Fragments." *Children's
Literature* 15 (1987): 37–54.

Hirsch, Marianne. "Ideology, Form, and 'Allerleirauh': Reflections on
Reading for the Plot." *Children's Literature* 14 (1986): 163–68.

Homans, Margaret. "Adoption Narratives, Trauma, and Origins." *Narrative* 14.1 (Jan. 2006): 4–26.

McGillis, Rod. "'Secrets' and 'Sequence' in Children's Stories." *Studies in
the Literary Imagination*. 17.2 (Fall 1985): 35–46.

Nikolajeva, Maria. "Two National Heroes: Jacob Two-Two and Pippi
Longstocking." *Canadian Children's Literature* 23.2 (1997): 7–16.

Pantaleo, Sylvia. "The Long, Long Way: Young Children Explore the
Fabula and the Syuzhet of *Shortcut.*" *Children's Literature in Education*
35.1 (Mar. 2004): 1–20.

Russell, David L. "Pinocchio and the Child-Hero's Quest." *Children's Literature in Education* 20.4 (Dec. 1989): 203–13.

Stott, Jon C. "Running Away to Home—A Story Pattern in Children's Literature." *Language Arts* 55.4 (1978): 473–77.

Stott, Jon C., and Christine Doyle Francis. "'Home' and 'Not Home' in
Children's Stories: Getting There—and Being Worth It." *Children's Literature in Education* 24.3 (1993): 223–33.

Waddey, Lucy E. "Homes in Children's Fiction: Three Patterns." *Children's
Literature Association Quarterly* 8.1 (1983): 13–15.

Readers, Implied and Real

Chambers, Aidan. "The Reader in the Book." *Booktalk: Occasional Writing on Literature and Children*. New York: Harper, 1985.

Henderson, Laretta. "The Black Arts Movement and African American
Young Adult Literature: An Evaluation of Narrative Style." *Children's
Literature in Education* 36.4 (Dec. 2005): 299–323.

Lowe, Virginia. "'Stop! You Didn't Read Who Wrote It!': The Concept of
the Author." *Children's Literature in Education* 22.2 (June 1991): 79–88.

Mackey, Margaret. "Did Elena Die? Narrative Practices of an Online

Community of Interpreters." *Children's Literature Association Quarterly* 28.1 (Spring 2003): 52–62.

———. "Ramona the Chronotope: The Young Reader and Social Theories of Narrative." *Children's Literature in Education* 22.2 (June 1991): 97–109.

McCallum, Robyn. "The Present Reshaping the Past Reshaping the Present: Film Versions of *Little Women.*" *The Lion and the Unicorn* 24.1 (Jan. 2000): 81–96.

Richardson, Brian. "Singular Text, Multiple Implied Readers." *Style* 41.3 (Fall 2007): 259–74.

Saxby, Maurice. "Changing Perspectives: The Implied Reader in Australian Children's Literature, 1841–1994." *Children's Literature in Education* 26.1 (Mar. 1995): 25–38.

Stott, Jon C. "Narrative Expectations and Textual Misreadings: Jamake Highwater's Anpao Analyzed and Reanalyzed." *Studies in the Literary Imagination* 17.2 (Fall 1985): 93–106.

———. "'Will the Real Dragon Please Stand Up?' Convention and Parody in Children's Stories." *Children's Literature in Education* 21.4 (Dec. 1990): 219–28.

Travers, P. L. "On Not Writing for Children." *Reflections on Literature for Children.* Ed. Francelia Butler and Richard Rotert. Hamden CT: Library Professional, 1984. 58–65.

Walsh, Sue. "'Irony?—But Children Don't Get It, Do They?' The Idea of Appropriate Language in Narratives for Children." *Children's Literature Association Quarterly* 28.1 (Spring 2003): 26–36.

Series Books

Behr, Kate. "'Same-as-Difference': Narrative Transformations and Intersecting Cultures in Harry Potter." *Journal of Narrative Theory* 35.1 (Winter 2005): 112–32.

Black, Barbara. "Using Series as Bait in the Public Library." *Rediscovering Nancy Drew.* Ed. Carolyn Stewart Dyer and Nancy Tillman Romalov. Iowa City: University of Iowa Press, 1995. 121–23.

Butt, Bruce. "'He's Behind You!': Reflections on Repetition and Predictability in Lemony Snicket's *A Series of Unfortunate Events.*" *Children's Literature in Education* 34.4 (Dec. 2003): 277–86.

Davenport, Julia. "The Narrative Framework of *The Borrowers*: Mary Norton and Emily Brontë." *Children's Literature in Education* 14.2 (June 1983): 75–79.

Deane, Paul. *Mirrors of American Culture: Children's Fiction Series in the Twentieth Century*. Rowman, 1991.

Doyle, Christine. "Orson Scott Card's Ender and Bean: The Exceptional Child as Hero." *Children's Literature in Education* 35.4 (Dec. 2004): 301–18.

Gannon, Susan R. "Repetition and Meaning in Stevenson's David Balfour Novels." *Studies in the Literary Imagination* 17.2 (Fall 1985): 21–34.

Hutcheon, Linda. "Harry Potter and the Novice's Confession." *The Lion and the Unicorn* 32.2 (Apr. 2008): 169–79.

Inness, Sherrie A., ed. *Nancy Drew and Company: Culture, Gender, and Girls' Series*. Bowling Green OH: Bowling Green State University Press, 1996.

Jenkins, Ruth Y. "'I am spinning this for you, my child': Voice and Identity Formation in George MacDonald's Princess Books." *The Lion and the Unicorn* 28.3 (Sept. 2004): 325–44.

Jones, Caroline. "For Adults Only? Searching for Subjectivity in Phyllis Reynolds Naylor's *Alice* Series." *Children's Literature Association Quarterly* 30.1 (Spring 2005): 16–31.

Kensinger, Faye R. *Children of the Series and How They Grew or A Century of Heroines and Heroes, Romantic, Comic, Moral*. Madison: University of Wisconsin Press, 1987.

Kuznets, Lois R. "Permutations of Frame in Mary Norton's 'Borrowers' Series." *Studies in the Literary Imagination* 17.2 (Fall 1985): 65–92.

MacLeod, Anne Scott. "Secret In the Trash Bin: On the Perennial Popularity of Juvenile Series Books." *Children's Literature in Education* 15.3 (1984): 127–40.

Salstad, Louise. "Narratee and Implied Readers in the Manolito Gafotas Series: A Case of Triple Address." *Children's Literature Association Quarterly* 28.4 (Winter 2003–04): 219–29.

Schmidt, Gary D. "See How They Grow: Character Development in Children's Series Books." *Children's Literature in Education* 18.1 (Mar. 1987): 34–44.

Special Journal Issues on Narrative Theory and Children's Literature

Children's Literature 25 (1997). Ed. U. C. Knoepflmacher and Mitzi Myers.

Children's Literature Association Quarterly 15.2 (1990). Ed. Peter Hunt.

Children's Literature Association Quarterly 28.1 (Spring 2003). Ed. Mike Cadden and Andrea Schwenke Wyile.

The Lion and the Unicorn 32.2 (Apr. 2008). Ed. Deidre Baker.

Studies in the Literary Imagination 18.2 (1985). Ed. Hugh Keenan.

Anderson, Susan. "Time, Subjectivity, and Modernism in E. Nesbit's Children's Fiction." *Children's Literature Association Quarterly* 32.4 (Winter 2007): 308–22.

Hall, Linda. "Ancestral Voices—'Since Time Everlasting Beyond': Kipling and the Invention of the Time-Slip Story." *Children's Literature in Education* 34.4 (Dec. 2003): 305–21.

Nuzum, K. A. "The Monster's Sacrifice—Historic Time: The Uses of Mythic and Liminal Time in Monster Literature." *Children's Literature Association Quarterly* 29.3 (Fall 2004): 207–27.

Petersen, Robert C. "Snapshots from the Past: Time and Memory in Kyoko Mori's *Shizuko's Daughter*." *Canadian Children's Literature* 111–12 (2004): 68–77.

Scott, Carole. "A Century of Dislocated Time: Time Travel, Magic and the Search for Self." *Papers: Explorations into Children's Literature* 6.2 (Aug. 1996): 14–20.

Shaheen, Aaron. "Endless Frontiers and Emancipation from History: Horatio Alger's Reconstruction of Place and Time in *Ragged Dick*." *Children's Literature* 33 (2005): 20–40.

Contributors

HOLLY BLACKFORD (PhD University of California, Berkeley) is an associate professor of English at Rutgers University–Camden. She teaches and publishes literary criticism on American, children's, and adolescent literature. She is the author of *Out of This World: Why Literature Matters to Girls* (Teachers College Press, 2004), editor of *100 Years of Anne with an "e": The Centennial Study of Anne of Green Gables* (University of Calgary Press, 2009), and chair of the Children's Literature Association article award committee.

MIKE CADDEN is a professor of English, the director of childhood studies, and chair of the Department of English, Foreign Languages and Journalism at Missouri Western State University. He is the author of *Ursula K. Le Guin Beyond Genre: Fiction for Children and Adults* (Routledge, 2005) and was guest editor with Andrea Schwenke Wyile of a special issue of *Children's Literature Association Quarterly* on narrative theory and children's literature. He currently serves as president of the Children's Literature Association.

ELISABETH ROSE GRUNER is an associate professor of English and women, gender, and sexuality studies at the University of Richmond. Her research on children's literature has appeared in *The Lion and the Unicorn* and *Children's Literature*, and she writes a monthly column for LiteraryMama.com, "Children's Lit Book Group." She is currently working on a book on contemporary fantasy literature for children.

MARTHA HIXON is an associate professor of English at Middle Tennessee State University, where she teaches courses in children's literature, folktales, and British literature. She is coeditor of *Diana Wynne Jones: An Exciting and Exacting Wisdom* (Peter Lang, 2002), which includes her essay on Jones's novel *Fire and Hemlock*. Her publications have appeared in *Marvels and Tales*, *Journal of the Fantastic in the Arts*, *Children's Literature*, and *Children's Literature Association Quarterly*.

DANA KEREN-YAAR holds a PhD from Bar-Ilan University, Israel, in Hebrew literature. Her dissertation is a study of historiographical stages in Hebrew children's literature from 1880 to 1980. She is a frequent contributor of children's book reviews for Haaretz Books. She is the author of *Authoresses Write for Children: Postcolonial and Feminist Readings in Hebrew Children's Literature* (Resling, 2007, in Hebrew).

ALEXANDRA LEWIS has completed her PhD at the Faculty of English, Trinity College, University of Cambridge. Her doctoral dissertation uncovers an emergent discourse of mental trauma in nineteenth-century literature, culture, and psychology. She has published articles and reviews in *Women: A Cultural Review*, *Journal of African Literature and Culture*, *British Association for Victorian Studies Newsletter*, *eSharp*, and *antiTHESIS*, and has contributed chapters to two forthcoming volumes: *Acts of Memory: The Victorians and Beyond* (Cambridge Scholars Publishing) and *The Brontës in Context* (Cambridge University Press). She has taught post-1930 English literature for Churchill, Gonville and Caius, Robinson, Sidney Sussex, St. Edmund's, and Trinity Colleges, Cambridge, and is currently a visiting research fellow at the Institute of English Studies, School of Advanced Study, University of London.

CHRIS MCGEE teaches children's and young adult literature at Longwood University in Virginia. His interests are children's mysteries, series fiction, film, horror, and pedagogy. He is an avid Hardy Boys fan and collector. This essay was originally part of his doctoral dissertation on children's mysteries.

MARIA NIKOLAJEVA is a professor of education at the University of Cambridge, where she teaches children's literature. She is the author and editor of many books on children's literature, among them *Children's Literature Comes of Age: Toward the New Aesthetic* (Garland, 1996), *From Mythic to Linear: Time in Children's Literature* (Scarecrow, 2000), *The Rhetoric of Character in Children's Literature* (Scarecrow, 2002), *Aesthetic Approaches to Children's Literature* (Scarecrow, 2005), *Power, Voice and Subjectivity in Literature for Young Readers* (Routledge, 2009), and in collaboration with Carole Scott, *How Picturebooks Work* (Garland, 2001). She is the 2005 recipient of the International Brothers Grimm Award for lifetime achievement in children's literature scholarship, presented by the International Institute for Children's Literature, Osaka and the Kinran-kai Foundation.

NATHALIE OP DE BEECK is an associate professor in the Department of English at Pacific Lutheran University. Her projects include *Suspended Animation: American Picture Books and the Fairy Tale of Modernity* (University of Minnesota Press, forthcoming) and a critical facsimile edition of Mary Liddell's 1926 picture book, *Little Machinery* (Wayne State University Press, 2009).

DANIELLE RUSSELL is an instructor in the English department at Glendon College. She has also taught in both the English and the humanities departments at York University. Her recent publications include "Homeward Bound: Transformative Spaces in Alice Walker's *The Color Purple*," in *Alice Walker's The Color Purple* (Rodopi, 2009) and *Between the Angle and the Curve: Mapping Gender, Race, Space, and Identity in Cather and Morrison* (Routledge, 2006). Current areas of research include non-Western and eighteenth-century children's literature and models of motherhood in the Twilight series.

MAGDALENA SIKORSKA teaches Introduction to Literature and Children's Literature to undergraduate and graduate students at Kazimierz Wielki University in Bydgoszcz, Poland. In 2007 she completed her PhD dissertation on hybridity of meaning in children's literature. Her recent publications include articles about narrative techniques in picture books and translated children's literature. She lives with her husband and three children in Bydgoszcz.

SUSAN STEWART is an associate professor in the Department of Literature and Languages at Texas A&M–Commerce. She teaches undergraduate and graduate courses in children's and adolescent literature. Her research is informed by the ideological intersections among cultural studies, narrative theory, feminism, and Marxism in children's and adolescent literature.

ANDREA SCHWENKE WYILE is an associate professor of English at Acadia University in Wolfville, Nova Scotia. She is coeditor with Teya Rosenberg of *Considering Children's Literature: A Reader* (Broadview, 2008). Her work on narrative theory and children's literature has appeared in *Children's Literature* and *Children's Literature in Education*.

ANGELA YANNICOPOULOU is an assistant professor at Athens University. Among her research interests are children's literature (especially the picture book) and literacy. Her books include *Aesopic Fables and*

Children: Form and Function (Manutius, 1993), *Towards Reading* (Kastaniotis, 2005), *Playing with Phonemes* (Aegean University, 2006), *Literacy in Preschool Education* (Kastaniotis, 2005), and *In the Colourland: The Contemporary Picturebook* (Papadopoulos, 2008).

ANGELIKA ZIRKER teaches undergraduate courses at Tuebingen University in Germany. Her research interests include Shakespeare and Victorian literature as well as children's literature throughout all periods and the relation between literature and ethics. She is the assistant editor of *Connotations: A Journal for Critical Debate*. Her PhD dissertation deals with the aspects of language, salvation, and play in Lewis Carroll's Alice books. Her current research project explores the relations of early modern poetry and the stage.

Index

empathy, 78, 169, 189, 190, 196, 204, 216

endings, iv, xi, 4, 6, 7, 10, 19n15, 29, 45, 48, 49, 51, 57, 60, 129, 144, 175, 199, 200, 202, 254, 258, 264, 278; closed, xx, 14, 35, 44, 54, 113, 135, 223, 240, 243; open, xx, 15, 16, 35, 54, 122, 125, 133, 231, 253, 256; unconventional, 35, 72, 73, 79, 106, 107, 112, 262, 287

Engdahl, Sylvia, x

epilogue, 55, 198, 245

epitext, xxiiin2

ethics, xxi, 2, 18n12, 27, 40n16, 78, 166, 178, 200

"The Eye and the I" (Nodelman), 66, 74

fairy tales, ix, xii, 1, 3–17, 29, 30, 72, 100, 103, 107, 110, 141, 196, 199, 268, 273, 283, 287

fantasy, xvii, 1, 4, 6, 7, 30, 59, 86, 131, 137, 153, 159n9, 197, 198, 216, 225n3, 251, 252, 255, 257, 262, 265n3, 269, 273, 282, 284, 287, 288n11, 289n14, 289n17

"father's tongue," 210–15, 222

Faulkner, William, 180

fear, 26, 28, 31, 39, 96, 97, 109, 112, 133, 141, 145, 188, 194, 204, 212, 218–24

Feed (Anderson), 199

Feiner, Shmuel, 224n1

Felluga, Dino, 90

feminism, xviii, 3, 7, 14, 19n19, 100, 209

Fine, Laura, 172

Fisher, Leona W., xx, 77

flashback, 168, 177, 179. *See also* narrative

Fludernik, Monica, 66

focalization, xxi, xxii, 18n7, 63, 65–80, 184, 203, 248, 258, 282; alternating, 204, 254, 257; child, 78, 167, 168, 171, 173, 180, 182, 234, 241, 248, 283; collective, 66; external, 72, 73, 79; fixed, 68–70, 77; hypothetical, 66; internal, 4, 8, 32, 67–72, 77, 203, 257, 259; multiple, 71, 72, 79, 203, 204, 255; nonfocalization, 67, 76; variable, 70, 71; verbal, 73–75; visual, 73–75

folktale, ix, 4, 18, 86, 112, 113, 141, 178, 196, 253, 254, 265

Foner, Sara, 210, 224n1

foreshadowing, 87, 128, 168, 180

Friedlander, Yehuda, 225n4

"The Frog King," 11

From Mythic to Linear (Nikolajeva), 187, 286

Gannon, Susan, xvii

Gaudreault, André, 145, 152, 158n7

Gavin, Adrienne E., 38n8, 286

Gawain Poet, 253

Genette, Gérard, ix, xxiiin2, 18n7, 65–67, 81n2, 116, 203, 261

genre, xiii, xiv–xxii, 1, 2, 4, 26, 36, 37, 40n37, 48, 52, 57, 59, 63, 66, 80, 100, 111, 138, 175, 191, 199, 203, 205n3, 247, 248, 252, 253, 255, 265n3, 287, 289n14

The Giver (Lowry), 199, 200

Going, William T., 184n1

Goldberg, Leah, 213, 215, 225n3

"Goldilocks," 100, 110

gothic, 1, 26, 27, 38n7, 49

The Great Train Robbery, 145

Grimm brothers, 18n6

Gruner, Elisabeth Rose, 1

Gunning, Tom, 157n6; "Animated Pictures," 142; "The Cinema of Attraction," 145; "Now You See It, Now You Don't," 155, 156

Gupta, Suman, 54

Haase, Donald, 3, 19n16

Hale, Dorothy J., xxi

Hall, Linda, 271, 286, 287n1, 289n19

Merkin, Daphne, 26, 31

metafiction, vii, xii, xxi, xxii, 3, 40n17, 51–60, 63, 64, 72, 100–04, 108–16, 229, 231, 232, 240, 242–49, 252, 264

metaphor, 17n2, 59, 64, 87, 90, 92–98, 109, 121–25, 130–37, 140, 149, 235

Miller, J. Hillis, 254

Milne, A. A.: *The House at Pooh Corner*, vii, xxii; *Winnie-the-Pooh*, 187, 188, 193, 197

mimesis, 153, 252, 255

Moebius, William, 77, 144

monologue, 8, 79, 80, 88, 93, 95, 97, 115, 189, 218, 220, 224

morals, xii, 1, 2, 23–33, 39, 50, 75, 76, 103, 114, 123, 125, 137, 146, 191, 196, 200, 204

Morgado, Margarida, 110

Moss, Anita, 110

Moss, Howard, 148

"mother's tongue," 210–15

multivocality. *See* narration

Musser, Charles, 158

My Dad (Browne), 69

The Mysteries of Harris Burdick (Van Allsburg), x, xii

Nagel, Joane, 217

"The Narrating and the Focalizing" (Bal), 80n1

narration: address, xi, 8, 89, 143, 198, 220; character (first-person), ix, x, 8, 18n7, 32, 33, 57, 218–23; double, 99n5, 103, 198, 215; "drawing close," 213–16, 221, 223, 224; dual (alienated), 103; external, 8, 18nn6–7, 67–69, 76, 78, 127, 241, 259; filter, 66, 68, 168, 180, 181; framing, 36, 45, 46, 87, 104, 145, 166, 197, 238, 241, 289n19; heterodiegetic, 69, 81n3, 81n5; impersonal, 18n6, 203; multiple, 166, 175, 183, 193, 203; narratee,

103, 121, 184n1, 190, 218, 220; omniscient, 76, 79, 107, 166, 244, 283; perceptible, 32, 81n3, 164, 168, 192; reliability, 52, 78, 201, 257, 258; second-person (direct), 8, 30, 40nn17–18, 122, 127; single, 103, 198, 215, 218; slant, 66, 81n3, 168; stream-of-consciousness, 167, 180. *See also* focalization; voice

narrative: collective, 28, 36; conventions, xii, 22, 31, 46, 111, 115, 146, 252; fairy tale, 11; giganticism, 55, 56; linearity, 155, 232, 254, 255–57, 261, 264; master, 123–26, 130, 137; movie, 142–44, 149–52; multistranded, 35, 79, 86, 88, 91, 198, 203, 261; plot, 17, 26, 45, 46, 49, 51, 58, 59, 101, 106, 107, 138, 151, 155, 170, 194, 205, 216, 231, 253, 256, 263; puzzle, 71, 94, 254; shift, 73, 168, 202; space, 17n1, 29, 31, 32, 40n15, 63–66, 73, 105, 149–54, 172, 173, 182, 200, 248, 256, 259–63, 265n5, 288n12; time, xxii, 17n1, 19n17, 44, 60, 63, 64, 87, 92, 101, 106, 108, 111, 115, 121, 128, 136, 150, 156, 200–02, 231–87; timelessness, 4, 5, 14, 25, 30, 107, 200; twists, 31, 79; verbal and visual, 11, 31, 66, 68–78, 87–95, 121, 127, 134, 145, 149, 150, 156, 157n6. *See also* endings

Narratology (Bal), 18n7, 32, 40n18, 76, 81n2

Natov, Roni, 96, 97

Nelson, Hilde Lindemann, 121–25, 137

Nesbit, Edith, 285, 286

Neumeyer, Peter, xvii

Newbery Medal, vii, xxiiin1

Nicholson, William, 141, 157n3

Nikolajeva, Maria, 163; *Aesthetic Approaches*, xvi, xx; *Children's Literature Comes of Age*, xvi, 103, 269, 288n12; "The Dynamics of

vii, 4, 52, 112, 115, 129, 132, 133, 167, 190, 193–95; resistant, 41n20, 77, 78, 123, 132, 188, 191, 192, 194, 258, 263; young, 1, 18, 23, 31, 34–36, 38n9, 49, 64, 100, 110, 116, 143, 163, 165, 166, 179, 189, 190, 195, 214, 222, 229, 231, 251, 258, 265. *See also* reception theory

readerly text, 2, 53–59

Reading Contemporary Picturebooks (Lewis), 98n2, 104, 109, 113

realism, 1, 30, 97, 98, 110, 252, 284

reception theory, 39, 130, 157n6, 183, 188

The Red Tree (Tan), 120–38

Rees, David, 285

Reimer, Mavis: *The Pleasures of Children's Literature*, 117n4, 236

resolution. *See* endings

Retelling Stories, Framing Culture (Stephens and McCallum), 3, 4

The Rhetoric of Character (Nikolajeva), 193, 205n1

Rimmon-Kenan, Shlomith, 68, 76, 81n2

Robson, Jenny: *The Denials of Kow-Ten*, 199, 200

Rolton, Gloria, 114

Romalov, Nancy Tillman, 23

Ronen, Ruth, 81

Rose, Jacqueline, xviii, xix

Routledge, Christopher, 38n8, 48, 50

Rowe, Karen, 3

Rowling, J. K., 39n13, 46–48, 51, 54, 55, 58. *See also* Potter, Harry

Salinger, J. D.: *The Catcher in the Rye*, 19n21, 201

Saney, Isaac, 171

Sartin, Hank, 159n12

Schlitz, Laura Amy, vii

Schmidt, Gary, 115

Scholes, Robert, 134

Schwarcz, Joseph H., 196

science fiction, x, xvii, 249, 252, 255, 263, 265n3

Scieszka, Jon: *The Stinky Cheese Man and Other Fairly Stupid Tales*, ix, 116n3; *The True Story of the Three Little Pigs*, 78

Scott, Carole, 66, 75, 81n7, 98n2, 150

The Secret Garden (Burnett), 192, 280

secrets, 44–60, 279, 282

Sendak, Maurice, 157n2

sequels, 4, 5, 10, 19n17, 24, 285

series fiction, xxi, 1, 4, 22–60, 204

Sewall, Laura, 120–22, 130, 133, 134, 137, 138

Shakespeare, William: *As You Like It*, 279

"The Shape of the Narrative in *The Lord of the Rings*" (Jones), 253

Shavit, Zohar, xx; "Hebrew Children's Literature," 209, 213, 223; *Poetics of Children's Literature*, 75

Shaw, Harry, vii

Shields, Charles J., 169, 184, 184n1

Shilo, Margalit, 224n1

Shingler, Martin, 170

Signs of Childness in Children's Books (Hollindale), 113

Sipe, Lawrence, xxiiin2

Sir Orfeo, 253

Slaughter, Judith Pollard, 108

Smith, Lane: *The Stinky Cheese Man and Other Fairly Stupid Tales*, ix, 116n3; *The True Story of the Three Little Pigs*, 78

Snicket, Lemony, 22–60

"Snow White," 5–7, 12, 13, 16, 18n13, 19n18, 72

Soderbergh, Peter A., 22–24, 34, 37n2

Spanos, William V., 56

Speak (Anderson), 3–6, 11, 12, 15, 16

Spells of Enchantment (Zipes), 5, 14

Spyri, Johanna: *Heidi*, 191

Stahl, John Daniel, 47

Breinigsville, PA USA
25 October 2010
248032BV00002B/2/P